THE SOUTH AFRICAN CAMPAIGN.

THE

SOUTH AFRICAN CAMPAIGN,

1879,

COMPILED BY

J. P. MACKINNON,

LATE 25TH KING'S OWN BORDERERS, FORMERLY 72ND HIGHLANDERS,

AND

SYDNEY SHADBOLT,

OF THE INNER TEMPLE, BARRISTER-AT-LAW;

And Dedicated, by permission, to

FIELD-MARSHAL H.R.H. THE DUKE OF CAMBRIDGE, COMMANDING-IN-CHIEF.

A MEMORIAL VOLUME, CONTAINING SIXTY PERMANENT CABINET PHOTOGRAPHS OF THE OFFICERS OF THE BRITISH ARMY AND NAVY WHO LOST THEIR LIVES IN THE ZULU WAR, BIOGRAPHICAL NOTICES, DETAILED ACCOUNTS OF THE VARIOUS ENGAGEMENTS, MAPS OF THE COUNTRY SHOWING THE MOVEMENTS OF THE ARMY, SUMMARIES OF THE MOVEMENTS OF THE VARIOUS REGIMENTS IN THE FIELD, AND SEPARATE RECORDS OF THE SERVICES OF EVERY BRITISH OFFICER WHO WAS ENGAGED.

J. B. HAYWARD & SON

17, PICCADILLY ARCADE, PICCADILLY, LONDON SW1Y 6NL

ORIGINALLY PRINTED AND PUBLISHED IN 1882
REPRINTED IN 1973 BY EYRE & SPOTTISWOODE LIMITED AT GROSVENOR PRESS PORTSMOUTH

PREFACE.

IN placing this work before the public, its compilers leave it to be judged merely on its own merits; they are happy to be able to state that the wide and influential support which it has already met with more than justifies its publication.

They take this opportunity of acknowledging the ample use they have made, both direct and indirect, of the late Lieutenant-General Hart's valuable "Army List" (now ably edited by his son), and of the "Royal Navy List." They are also indebted to the "Royal Engineers' Journal" for most of the leading incidents detailed in the memoirs of Col. Durnford, Major Wynne, and Lieut. McDowel.

To the relations and comrades of those who lost their lives in South Africa in the service of their country; to the London Stereoscopic Company, for the unstinted labour which they have bestowed in producing artistic results from photographs in many instances small in size and faded in colour; and to the many officers of all ranks who have materially assisted them in their enterprise, they beg to return their most sincere thanks.

In extenuation of the delay which has arisen in the publication of "The South African Campaign," they would merely draw attention to the difficulties inherent to collecting records of the individual services of more than eleven hundred officers, scattered over all quarters of the globe, and to the time necessarily consumed in the enlargement and reproduction, under the conditions above alluded to, of the photographs which appear in the work.

Swart
Rensburg
WESSE

CONTENTS.

	PAGE
MAP OF ZULULAND, SHOWING THE MOVEMENTS OF THE COLUMNS AND DIVISIONS IN THE FIELD . . . . *facing*	1
SKETCH OF THE WAR, CONTAINING DETAILED ACCOUNTS OF THE VARIOUS ENGAGEMENTS .	1-32
MAP OF ISANDHLWANA . . . . *facing*	11
PORTRAITS AND BIOGRAPHICAL NOTICES OF THE OFFICERS OF THE BRITISH ARMY WHO LOST THEIR LIVES IN THE WAR	35-296
RECORDS OF THE SERVICES OF EVERY OFFICER OF THE BRITISH ARMY WHO WAS ENGAGED .	297-375

INTRODUCTION.

IN proroguing the Parliament of the Cape Colony on August the 2nd, 1878, his Excellency the Governor, Sir Bartle Frere, congratulated the House on the protracted war with the Galekas having been brought to a successful conclusion; and, in alluding to the existence of disquietude in the Transvaal, and disturbances among the native tribes in Griqualand West, expressed a hope that the reinforcements of Her Majesty's troops, then on their way out, would have the effect of restoring public tranquillity.

In Natal, however, a considerable feeling of uneasiness prevailed at this time from the proximity of the Zulus, a large and powerful race kept constantly on a war footing. Originally insignificant, it had been raised by the military talent of one of its chiefs to become, in times past, the greatest power in Africa south of the Zambesi River, and its pre-eminence among the native tribes had not been subsequently questioned.

From the date of the establishment of the British Government in Natal, the Zulus had acknowledged its suzerainty. In 1861, when the succession to their kingdom was in dispute, their headmen had petitioned the authorities to nominate a chief for them; and in 1873 they had further petitioned them to assist at his installation. The Government, laying down conditions, had complied with the request. In return for the countenance and support afforded him, Cetchwayo, the chief selected, had entered into specific obligations to conduct his rule in a more humane and peaceable manner than had heretofore obtained. These obligations had been but imperfectly fulfilled. A rigorous military organization, the leading feature of which was the enforced celibacy of every male subject until he should have acquitted himself in warfare or attained forty years of age, had been perfected; and a hostile bearing towards the Government—probably in consequence of its openly expressed distrust—had been assumed. Rumours, long current, concerning the threatening attitude of the tribe culminated, at the end of July, 1878, in official reports of two serious violations of British territory being sent in by the Natal border agents. Armed bands had crossed the Buffalo River in pursuit of women who had fled for protection to the huts of the Government Native Guards, and, having carried them back into Zululand, had there put them to death. Immediately upon receipt of these reports, Sir Henry Bulwer, the Lieutenant-Governor of Natal, despatched a message to Cetchwayo informing him of the offences which had been committed, and requesting him to deliver up the offenders to be tried under the laws of the Colony. A reply to this request was received at the latter end of August: in it the violations complained of were characterized as the rash acts of boys; and fifty pounds was offered to the British Government by way of *solatium*.

On September the 26th, 1878, Sir Bartle Frere arrived at Pietermaritzburg, and at once formed an opinion that the position of affairs in Natal was critical. Zulu regiments were reported to be moving about on unusual and special errands, organizing royal hunts on a great scale in parts of the country where little game was to be expected; and the hunters were reported to have received orders to follow across the border any game they might rouse—a recognized mode, according to Zulu custom, of provoking or declaring war. Unusual bodies of armed men were stated to be watching all drifts and roads leading into Zululand, and these guards were reported to be warning off Natal natives from entering the Zulu territory, accompanying their warning with contemptuous intimation that orders had been given to kill all Natalians who might trespass across the border. Zulu subjects were hastening into Natal to reclaim cattle which had been sent there to graze, and were stating, as their reason, that in consequence of Zululand being so disturbed they knew not what was going to happen. From this time forward, Sir Bartle Frere, in a series of despatches, expressed his conviction, in opposition to that of the Home Government, that war could not long be averted.

Previously to the happening of these events, the British Government had undertaken to define the boundary line between Zululand and the recently annexed Transvaal, concerning which there had long been dispute. A report had been drawn up on the 20th of June by commissioners appointed to collect evidence on which to base a decision, but it was not till November the 11th that Sir Henry Bulwer intimated to Cetchwayo that the High Commissioner was prepared to pronounce his award. The Zulus, without waiting for such arbitration, now took the matter into their own hands, and gave the inhabitants of the undefined territory summary notice to quit. Later, their attitude became still more menacing: the inhabitants of Lüneberg, a town in the Transvaal situated beyond the territory in dispute, received orders from one of the Zulu headmen to decamp; two officers of the Colonial Engineers' Department, who had descended into the bed of the Tugela River whilst engaged in inspecting roads, were taken prisoners, and, though they were eventually allowed to depart, were roughly handled; Natal natives, who had ventured across the border to buy cattle, were obliged to abandon their property and fly for their lives from large armed parties who were hurrying on to what they termed the "Great Place," with the avowed object of "fighting the English."

It now appearing probable that the immediate safety of the Colony would be imperilled by further inaction, Sir Bartle Frere took upon himself to issue to the King of the Zulus an ultimatum, in which were embodied what purported to be the demands of the Government. This was delivered to certain Zulu representatives, who assembled at the Lower Tugela Drift on December the 11th to receive an award favourable to the Zulu claims on the question of disputed boundary. Its requisitions were, that the King should send in to the Natal Government for trial those of his subjects who had committed the violations of territory, and pay a fine for the threatening and detention of the officers of the Engineers' Department, and a further fine for his delay in complying with the Government requests; also that he should disband the Zulu army as then constituted. It further informed him that a British officer would be appointed as resident in Zululand, to see that the reforms promised by him at his coronation should be carried out. "Let the King and the chief men of the nation," it ended, "consider these conditions, and give their answer regarding them within thirty days."

Rumours of Cetchwayo's willingness to comply with these demands at first reached the Natal Government, and a reply asking for an extension of time was received; on December the 30th, however, Mr. John Dunn, a British subject residing in Zululand, and in the confidence of the King, wrote to the Secretary of State for Native Affairs saying that he had received a message from Cetchwayo to the effect that the latter was "determined to fight, as, from what he had heard of the forces that were to be sent against him, he could easily dispose of them, one after the other." On January the 4th, 1879, Sir Bartle Frere placed the enforcement of the demands of the Government in the hands of Lord Chelmsford, the general commanding the forces in South Africa; but at the same time intimated that the latter would be willing to receive, until January the 11th, the unqualified acceptance by the King of the Zulus of all the terms offered him.

In the meantime Lord Chelmsford had made active preparations for the prosecution of the campaign which appeared imminent, and by the end of December such forces as he had available lay massed on the Natal and Transvaal frontiers ready to advance. Admiral Sullivan, commanding on the station, had placed at his disposal a Naval Brigade, which, later, was to do gallant service. The army of invasion was disposed in four columns, its distribution being in the form of a crescent, facing eastward, and circumscribing Zululand; and the General's purpose was to move these simultaneously along the rough tracks which converge from the principal fords of the rivers towards Ulundi, Cetchwayo's stronghold. The 1st (southernmost) Column, under Colonel C. K. Pearson, 3rd Foot, was encamped in the neighbourhood of Fort Pearson, in a position directly overlooking the Lower Tugela Drift. It had Durban for its base, with Stanger about fifty miles forward, and possessing telegraphic communication, as an advanced depôt. This column was to make its way by the coast road, after crossing the Tugela, to Etshowe, a deserted mission-station lying some thirty-five miles distant from the ford. The 2nd (right-centre) Column, under Lieutenant-Colonel A. W. Durnford, R.E., was stationed at Krantz Kop, one of the most commanding heights in the country, in the locality of Fort Buckingham, distant some sixty miles from the Lower Fort, and covering Pietermaritzburg, the capital of the colony. It was to act on the defensive until an advance should have been made and a footing established in Zululand, and two of its regiments were to be moved towards Helpmakaar, to prevent raiding into Natal. The 3rd (left-centre) Column, under Colonel Glyn, C.B., 24th Foot, with which were the General and his Staff, had its head-quarters at Helpmakaar, about seventy miles north-west of Fort Buckingham, with camps extending down to Rorke's Drift. It was expected that this column would be attacked whilst crossing the Buffalo River by Sirayo, a chief who had been concerned in the recent violations of territory, and who dwelt opposite to Rorke's Drift; and it was the General's intention to reduce his stronghold before making a further advance into the interior. The 4th (northernmost) Column, under Colonel Evelyn Wood,

V.C., C.B., 90th Foot, was stationed about twenty-five miles distant from the Head-quarters Camp, on the Blood River—the recently declared boundary between Zululand and the Transvaal—and had Utrecht for its base. Directions had been given that it should co-operate, as far as possible, with the movements of Colonel Glyn's column. A 5th Column, under Colonel Hugh Rowlands, V.C., C.B., composed of troops who had taken part in the Sekukuni Campaign of 1878, was concentrated at Derby, a group of deserted houses situated on the border of the Amaswazi country, with a view to inducing the already wavering King of the Amaswazies to throw in his lot with the English. Directions had been given that this column should, if joined by the Swazies, march south and cross the Pongolo River at the Dumbe Mountain, in the vicinity of which it would meet No. 4 Column, and that both columns, mutually supporting each other, should advance down the Black Umvolosi River on Ulundi, towards which the three other columns were to converge from the south. The following was the officially reported distribution of forces in the field :—

NATAL AND TRANSVAAL.

Lieutenant-General commanding the Forces.—F. A. Lord Chelmsford, K.C.B.

Personal Staff.—Assistant Military Secretary, Brevet-Lieutenant-Colonel Crealock, 95th Foot; Aides-de-Camp, Brevet-Major Gosset, 54th Foot; Captain Buller, R.B.; and Lieutenant Milne, R.N.

Head-quarters Staff.—Deputy Adjutant and Quartermaster General, Brevet-Colonel Bellairs, C.B. (unattached); Deputy Assistant Adjutant and Quartermaster Generals, Brevet-Major Spalding, 104th Foot, and Brevet-Major Grenfell, 60th Foot; Officer commanding Royal Artillery, Lieutenant-Colonel Law, R.A.; commanding Royal Engineers, Colonel Hassard, C.B., R.E.; commanding Natal Mounted Police and Volunteers, Major Dartnell, N.M.P.; District Commissary-General Strickland, C.B.; Commissary-General (Ordnance), Deputy Commissary-General Wright; District Paymaster, Staff Paymaster Ball; Principal Medical Officer, Deputy Surgeon-General Woodfryes, C.B., M.D.

No. 1 Column.—Colonel Commanding, Colonel Pearson, 3rd Foot; Staff—Orderly Officer, Lieutenant Knight, 3rd Foot; Principal Staff Officer, Brevet-Colonel Walker, C.B., Scots Guards; general Staff duties, Captain M'Gregor, 29th Foot; transport duties, Captain Pelly Clarke, 103rd Foot; Senior Commissariat Officer, Assistant Commissary Heygate; Sub-District Paymaster, Paymaster Gorges; Senior Medical Officer, Surgeon-Major Tarrant. Corps—Royal Artillery, two 7-pounders (mule), Lieutenant Lloyd; Royal Engineers, No. 2 Company, Captain Wynne, R.E.; 2nd Battalion 3rd Foot, Brevet-Lieutenant-Colonel Parnell, 3rd Foot; 99th Foot (six companies), Lieutenant-Colonel Welman; Naval Brigade, Commander Campbell, R.N.; No. 2 Squad, Mounted Infantry, Captain Barrow, 19th Hussars; Natal Hussars, Captain Norton; Durban Mounted Rifles, Captain Shepstone; Alexandra Mounted Rifles, Captain Arbuthnot; Stanger Mounted Rifles, Captain Addison; Victoria Mounted Rifles, Captain Saner; 2nd Regiment Native Contingent—Major Graves, 3rd Foot; Staff Officer, Captain Hart, 31st Foot; 1st Battalion, Major Graves, 3rd Foot; 2nd Battalion, Commandant Nettleton; No. 2 Company, Natal Native Pioneer Corps, Captain Beddoes.

No. 2 Column.—Commanding, Lieutenant-Colonel Durnford, R.E. Staff—For general Staff duties, Captain Barton, 7th Foot; for transport duties, Lieutenant

Cochrane, 32nd Foot; Senior Medical Officer, Civil Surgeon Cartwright Reed. Corps—Rocket Battery (mules), Brevet-Major Russell, R.A.; 1st Battalion 1st Regiment Natal Native Contingent, Commandant Montgomery; 2nd Battalion 1st Regiment Natal Native Contingent, Major Bengough, 77th Foot; 3rd Battalion 1st Regiment Natal Native Contingent, Captain Cherry, 32nd Foot; five troops Natal Native Horse; No. 3 Company Natal Native Pioneers, Captain Allen.

No. 3 Column.—Commanding, Brevet-Colonel Glyn, C.B., 24th Foot. Staff—Orderly Officer, Lieutenant Coghill, 24th Foot; Principal Staff Officer, Major Clery; for general Staff duties, Captain Gardner, 14th Hussars; for transport duties, Captain Essex, 75th Foot; Senior Commissariat Officer, Assistant-Commissary Dunne; Sub-District Paymaster, Paymaster Elliot (hon. captain); Senior Medical Officer, Surgeon-Major Shepherd. Corps—N Battery 5th Brigade Royal Artillery, Brevet-Lieutenant-Colonel Harness; Royal Engineers, No. 5 Company, Captain Jones, R.E.; 1st Battalion 24th Foot, Brevet-Lieutenant-Colonel Pulleine, 24th Foot; 2nd Battalion, 24th Foot, Lieutenant-Colonel Degacher, C.B, 24th Foot; No. 1 Squad, Mounted Infantry, Lieutenant-Colonel (loc. r.) Russell, 12th Lancers; Natal Mounted Police, Major Dartnell; Natal Carbineers, Captain Shepstone; Newcastle Mounted Rifles, Captain Bradstreet; Buffalo Border Guard, Captain Smith; 3rd Regiment Natal Native Contingent, Commandant Lonsdale; Staff Officer, Lieutenant Hartford, 99th Foot; 1st Battalion, Commandant Lonsdale; 2nd Battalion, Commandant Cooper; No. 1 Company Natal Native Pioneer Corps, Captain Nolan.

No. 4 Column.—Commanding, Brevet-Colonel Evelyn Wood, V.C., C.B., 90th Foot. Staff—Orderly Officer, Lieutenant Lysons, 90th Foot; Principal Staff Officer, Captain Hon. R. Campbell, Coldstream Guards; for general Staff duties, Captain Woodgate, 4th Foot; for transport duties, Captain Vaughan, Royal Artillery; Senior Commissary Officer, Commissary Hughes; Commissary of Ordnance, Assistant Commissary Phillimore; Sub-District Paymaster, Paymaster MacDonald; Senior Medical Officer, Surgeon-Major Cuffe. Corps—Royal Artillery, six 7-pounders, Major Tremlett, R.A.; 1st Battalion 13th Foot, Lieutenant-Colonel Gilbert, 13th Foot; 90th Foot, Brevet-Lieutenant-Colonel Cherry, 90th Foot; Frontier Light Horse, Brevet-Lieutenant-Colonel Buller, C.B., 60th Foot; Wood's Irregulars, Commandant Henderson.

No. 5 Column.—Commanding, Colonel Rowlands, V.C., C.B. Staff—Principal Staff Officer, Captain Harvey, 71st Foot; District Adjutant, Lieutenant Potts, 80th Foot; Senior Commissariat Officer, Assistant Commissary-General Phillips; Commissary of Ordnance, Commissary Wyon; Sub-District Paymaster, Assistant Paymaster Burgers; Senior Medical Officer, Surgeon-Major Johnson. Corps—80th Foot, Major Tucker; Schutte's Corps, Captain Schutte; Eckersley's Contingent, Captain Eckersley; Raaff's Corps, Captain Raaff; Ferreira's Horse, Captain Ferreira; Border Lancers, Lieutenant-Colonel Weatherley; Transvaal Rangers, Cape Mounted Rifles, one Krupp gun, two six-pounders, Armstrong.

LINE OF COMMUNICATIONS.

Greytown.—Helpmakaar.—Commanding, Brevet-Lieutenant-Colonel Hopton, 88th Foot. Staff.—District Adjutant, Lieutenant Morehead, 24th Foot; Commissariat Officer, Commissary Furse; Commissariat (Ordnance), Commissary Moors; District Paymaster, Paymaster Bacon; Senior Medical Officer, Surgeon-Major

Ingham; Commanding General Depôt, Brevet-Major Chamberlin, 24th Foot. One company 88th Foot, Fort Napier.

Greytown and Middledrift.—Commanding, Brevet-Major Black, 2nd Battalion, 24th Foot. Greytown. One company 2nd Battalion 4th Foot.

Helpmakaar.—Rorke's Drift.—Commanding, Colonel Bray, C.B., 4th Foot. Four companies 2nd Battalion 4th Foot.

Base of Operations, Durban.—Commanding, Major Huskisson, 56th Foot. Staff.—For general duties—Captain Somerset, R.B. For transport duties, Captain Spratt, 29th Foot; Senior Commissariat Officer, Deputy Commissary Granville; Commissary of Ordnance, Assistant Commissary de Ricci; Senior Medical Officer, Surgeon Jennings. One company 99th Foot.

Stanger. — Lower Tugela Drift. — Stanger. — Commanding, Brevet-Major Walker, 99th Foot. One company 99th Foot. Fort Pearson.—Detachment Naval Brigade.

STRENGTH OF COLUMNS.

No. 1.—20 Staff and departments, 23 Royal Artillery, 4 seven-pounders, 1 Gatling gun, 2 rocket-tubes and 1 trough, 1,517 infantry, 312 cavalry, 2,256 native contingent, 622 conductors, drivers, and foreloopers, 3,128 oxen, 116 horses, 121 mules, 384 waggons, and 24 carts. Total, 4,750 officers and men.

No. 2.—5 Staff and departments, 3,488 native contingent, 315 mounted natives, 3 rocket troughs, 63 conductors, drivers, and foreloopers, 480 oxen, 498 horses, 350 mules, and 30 waggons. Total, 3,871 officers and men.

No. 3.—20 Staff and departments, 132 Royal Artillery, 6 seven-pounders, 2 rocket troughs, 1,275 infantry, 320 cavalry, 2,566 native contingent, 396 conductors, drivers, and foreloopers, 1,507 oxen, 49 horses, 67 mules, 220 waggons, and 82 carts. Total, 4,709 officers and men.

No. 4.—25 Staff and departments, 108 Royal Artillery, 6 seven-pounders, 2 rocket troughs, 1,502 infantry, 208 cavalry, 387 native contingent, 48 conductors, drivers, and foreloopers, 260 oxen, 20 horses, 123 mules, 41 waggons, and 5 carts. Total, 2,278 officers and men.

No. 5.—15 Staff and departments, 1 Krupp gun, 2 six-pound Armstrongs, 834 infantry, 553 cavalry, 338 native contingent, 25 conductors, drivers, and foreloopers, 150 oxen, 10 horses, 12 mules, 17 waggons, and two carts. Total, 1,565 officers and men.

Transport.—756 conductors, drivers, and foreloopers, 430 oxen, 110 horses, 40 mules, 285 waggons, and 10 carts.

Grand Total.—85 Staff and departments, 263 Royal Artillery, 20 guns, 2 rocket tubes, 8 rocket troughs, 5,128 infantry, 1,193 cavalry, 315 mounted natives, 9,035 native contingent, 1,910 conductors, drivers, and foreloopers, 10,023 oxen, 803 horses, 398 mules, 977 waggons, and 56 carts. Total, 17,929 officers and men.

The time allowed for the acceptance of the terms of the ultimatum having expired on January 11th, without any reply from Cetchwayo having been received, active hostilities were commenced. No. 1 Column was enabled, by the exertions of the Naval Brigade, to cross the Tugela, which by this time was at full flood, on January 12th and 13th. Small parties of armed Zulus showed within range of it, but no act of hostility was offered. No. 3 Column, which had descended into the valley of the Buffalo on the 9th, crossed the river at Rorke's Drift at daybreak on the 11th. A heavy mist shrouded the crossing, which was not an easy one. No. 4

Column, which had crossed the Blood River on the 6th, had halted at Bemba's Kop, a position some thirty-five miles distant from Rorke's Drift. On the 11th, Colonel Wood, striking south with his mounted men by pre-arrangement, effected a junction with Lord Chelmsford, who had advanced to meet him, and returned to his camp on the same day. Lieutenant-Colonel Durnford was awaiting the General on the return of the latter to the Head-quarters Camp. He was directed to move one of his three battalions to watch, and eventually to cross at, the Gates of Natal, between Rorke's Drift and the Umsinga Mountain, while he, with his mounted men and Rocket Battery, were to join No. 3 Column : the other two battalions were to cross at Middle Drift as soon as Colonel Pearson should reach Etshowe.

On the day following the crossing of No. 3 Column at Rorke's Drift, Colonel Glyn was directed to make a reconnaissance with the mounted men in the direction of the Izipesi Hill, while the valley of the Bashee was to be traversed by a portion of the infantry. The troops left camp at daybreak. On reaching the Bashee valley, the mounted scouts reported that Zulus were leaving their kraals and driving cattle up from under the precipices. Colonel Glyn directed three companies 1st Battalion 24th Regiment, and the 1st Battalion 3rd Regiment Natal Native Contingent to advance and capture the cattle; while Lieutenant-Colonel Russell, 12th Lancers, in command of the mounted portion of the force, was directed to continue along the waggon-track to the high ground above. At 8.30 a.m. the precipitous sides of the Ingqutu Mountain were occupied by the infantry, when fire was opened upon them by the Zulus, who were occupying very strong positions in the caves and rocks above. A fight ensued, which lasted for about half an hour. The mountain-side was cleared, and the cattle and horses were captured : the Zulus left behind in the neighbourhood of the kraals made, however, a stubborn resistance; ten dead bodies were counted amongst the rocks, and nine prisoners were taken. In the meantime, before the mounted men had quite reached the higher terrace of the mountain, they were fired on by a force concealed by the rocks. These were attacked and dispersed with the loss of fifteen found killed, among whom was a son of Sirayo.

Excepting that a detachment was pushed forward into the Bashee valley for the purpose of road-making, Colonel Glyn's column, for the next week, remained stationary: a month's supplies had to be stored on the right bank of the Buffalo, in addition to fifteen days' rations to be taken with the column itself, before a further advance could be made; and considerable difficulties in the way of transport had arisen. Rain had fallen heavily. Between the Head-quarters Camp and Greytown alone, a distance of some seventy miles, three rivers were unfordable; and the ferrying across of laden waggons required more skilled labour than was to be had. The tracks had become mere marshy swamps or boulder-strewn chasms, according to the character of the country. The cumbersome ox-waggons of the colony, inadequate in number, and totally unsuitable for transport service, were the only vehicles available; and as every road to be traversed by them had to be remade, progress was necessarily slow.

On January 19th, Colonel Glyn's column broke up from its camp on the left bank of the Buffalo River, marched about ten miles along the waggon-track which leads from Rorke's Drift to the Indeni Forest, and encamped with its back to an isolated, precipitous-sided hill of peculiar appearance, known as Isandhlwana. On the 20th Lord Chelmsford made a reconnaissance about ten miles farther along the same waggon-track, which skirts the Inhlazatye Mountain, Matyana's stronghold—a deep valley, full of caves, with three precipitous sides, over one of which a small river falls, and, flowing along its bottom, enters the Buffalo River at a distance of about twelve or fifteen miles.

Not having time to properly examine the country round this peculiar stronghold, into which he had been told the enemy would very probably retire, Lord Chelmsford ordered that two separate parties should move out from camp at an early hour the next day, and bring back a full description of it. One of these, under Major Dartnell, consisting of the Mounted Police and Volunteers of which he was commandant, took the same road followed on the previous day; whilst another, consisting of two battalions Native Contingent under Commandant Lonsdale, worked round a flat-topped mountain, known as Malakata, the southernmost elevation of the Inhlazatye range.

The orders given to the commanders of these two parties were, that they were to effect a communication along the open ground on the Inhlazatye range, and then return to camp with such information as they might have been able to obtain. At about 3 p.m. one of Lord Chelmsford's staff officers, who had accompanied Major Dartnell, returned to camp, and reported that the latter had been unable to effect a complete reconnaissance of the country beyond the small river alluded to, as he had found it occupied by the enemy in some force; that he had called up the two battalions Native Contingent, and that if three companies of British infantry were sent to him to give them confidence he would be able to attack. The General did not consider it advisable to comply with this request, as the day was far advanced and the distance great. Biscuit was sent out to the force, which bivouacked on the northern edge of the Inhlazatye range. At 2.30 a.m. on January the 22nd, Colonel Glyn, having received a despatch from Major Dartnell stating that the enemy was in great force in front of him, sent his senior staff officer to inquire what course the General might require to be taken.

Feeling that the position was somewhat critical, Lord Chelmsford ordered Colonel Glyn to move to Major Dartnell's assistance with all the available men of the 2nd Battalion 24th Regiment, consisting of six companies; and also to take four guns and the Mounted Infantry.

Lieutenant-Colonel Pulleine, 24th Regiment, was left in command of the camp, with written instructions to the following effect:—"You will be in command of the camp during the absence of Colonel Glyn: draw in your camp (or, your 'line of defence') while the force is out; also draw in the line of your infantry outposts accordingly, but keep your cavalry vedettes still far advanced."

Soon after 2 a.m. Lieutenant-Colonel Crealock, Acting Military Secretary, received instructions from the General to send a written order to Colonel Durnford, R.E., commanding No. 2 Column (who was at Rorke's Drift with 500 natives, half of whom were mounted and armed with breechloaders), to the following effect:—"Move up to Isandhlwana camp at once with all your mounted men and rocket battery; take command of it. I am accompanying Colonel Glyn, who is moving off at once to attack Matyana and a Zulu force said to be 12 or 14 miles off, and at present watched by Natal Police, Volunteers, and Natal Native Contingent. Colonel Glyn takes with him 2-24th Regiment, four guns R.A., and Mounted Infantry."

The reinforcements under Colonel Glyn moved off at daybreak, accompanied by Lord Chelmsford, who, with a small escort of the Mounted Infantry, pressed forward and reached Major Dartnell at about 6.30 a.m. That officer was at once ordered to send out his mounted men to gain intelligence of the enemy, whose whereabouts did not appear to be very certain. The enemy shortly afterwards showed in considerable strength on some heights opposite to the Inhlazatye range, but at some distance; and appeared to be advancing to take possession of a spur which projected into the plain beneath and completely commanded it. Commandant Lonsdale's two battalions Native Contingent were immediately ordered to move across and occupy the spur in question; and word was sent to Colonel Glyn to move the guns and 2nd Battalion 24th Regiment up the valley which lay to the left of the spur. The mounted infantry looked after the left flank, and the mounted police and volunteers guarded the right. A general advance was then made, and the enemy retired without firing: on the extreme right, however, the Natal Carabineers, under Captain Shepstone, managed to cut off about three hundred, who took refuge on a hill of difficult ascent. These were finally dislodged, with the assistance of some of the Native Contingent, and fifty were killed. The main force of the enemy retired, on their flanks being threatened by the advance of the mounted corps, to the Izipesi Hill, about six miles distant.

Whilst these operations were going on, Colonel Glyn received, about 9 a.m., a short note from Lieutenant-Colonel Pulleine, stating that a Zulu force had appeared on the heights on his left front. An officer was immediately sent to the top of a neighbouring hill with a telescope, but was unable to detect anything unusual. At this time the attention of the officers commanding was bent on the enemy's force retiring from the hills in front, and especially upon a detached portion of it which was being pursued by Lieutenant-Colonel Russell three miles off. Shortly afterwards the 1st Battalion Natal Native Contingent was sent back to the camp, with orders to skirmish through the ravines by the way in the event of any Zulus being met with.

About 11 a.m. Lieutenant-Colonel Harness, R.A., was ordered to march with his four guns, two companies 2nd Battalion 24th Regiment, and about fifty Natal Native Sappers to the Mangane Valley to join Colonel Glyn, who, unimpeded by artillery, was about to proceed by a shorter route to the same spot with the remainder of the column. To carry out this order, Lieutenant-Colonel Harness's force had to retrace its way over two miles of the route taken earlier in the morning. About 12 noon the party reached rising ground, and, not being certain of the whereabouts of the valley, halted. Almost immediately afterwards the fire of cannon was heard, shells were seen bursting against the hills to the left of the camp, which was visible in the distance, and a large body of natives, whom the sappers pronounced to be Zulus, appeared in the plain below. Captain Church, one of the party, at once rode forward to verify these observations: he was met by a European officer, who informed him that the camp was surrounded and would be taken unless immediately reinforced. He returned with all speed, and reported the message to Lieutenant-Colonel Harness, who was then conversing with Major Black, 24th Regiment, and Major Gosset, A.D.C., who had just arrived. Colonel Harness at once started with his force for the camp, and Major Gosset rode off: before the former had proceeded two miles on his way, however, Major Gosset again appeared, bearing orders to him to continue his march to the rendezvous. In accordance with these orders he retraced his steps.

The enemy having retreated out of range before the advance of the main body of the column, the General proceeded with Colonel Glyn to fix a new site for the camp. At this time no suspicion of danger to the force left at Isandhlwana was entertained. About 1.45 p.m., however, a native appeared, and reported that firing had been going on round the camp. A hill whence the tents could be seen some twelve miles distant was at once ascended, but all appeared to be quiet. The General ordered Colonel Glyn to bivouac for the night in the position then occupied; and, in order to make sure that nothing was wrong, proceeded, with an escort of some forty volunteers, towards Isandhlwana. When he had advanced to within six miles of the hill, he came upon the 1st Battalion Natal Native Contingent, which had halted. Shortly afterwards Commandant Lonsdale, who was mounted, made his way up, and reported that he had ridden into the camp and found it in the possession of the enemy. An express was instantly sent back to Colonel Glyn, and upon the arrival of his force at 6 p.m., Lord Chelmsford formed it into fighting order, advanced, and reached the camp, which was evacuated by the Zulus upon his approach, as darkness came on.

The following is an account compiled from evidence adduced by a Court of Inquiry of what happened subsequently to the departure of Lord Chelmsford's force from Isandhlwana :—

After the main body of the column had left, nothing unusual occurred in camp until about 8 a.m., when a report arrived from a picquet stationed at a point about 1,500 yards distant, on a hill to the north of the camp, that a body of the enemy's troops could be seen approaching from the north-east. Lieut.-Colonel Pulleine, 1st Battalion 24th Regiment, commanding in camp, thereupon caused the whole of the troops available to assemble near the eastern side of the camp, facing towards the reported direction of the enemy's approach. He also despatched a mounted man with a report to the column, presumed to be then about twelve or fifteen miles distant. Shortly after 9 a.m. a small body of the enemy showed itself just over the crest of the hill, in the direction in which they were expected; but retired a few minutes afterwards, and disappeared. Soon afterwards information arrived from the picquet before alluded to that the enemy was in three columns, two of which were retiring, but were still in view, and the third of which had disappeared in a north-westerly direction.

In the meantime Colonel Durnford, upon receipt of the General's order to move up to Isandhlwana, had marched from Rorke's Drift about 7.30. a.m. When within half a mile from the camp he was met by Lieutenant Chard, R.E., who reported the movements of the enemy which had been observed from it. This officer was directed to ride on and request Major Russell, who was about a mile behind, to press forward at once with his rocket battery and to detach a company of Sikali men to protect the baggage which was following. Colonel Durnford, with 250 mounted natives, followed by the rocket battery, reached the camp about 10.30 a.m., and assumed command of it. The news was, that a number of Zulus had been seen since an early hour on the top of the adjacent hills, and that an attack had been expected; in consequence, the following disposition of the troops had been made :

The natives of Lonsdale's Contingent were on outpost duty on the hills to the left; the guns were in position on the left of the camp; the infantry were turned out, and formed in column in the open space in front of the General's tent; the

S

waggons, &c., were inspanned. Constant reports came in from the scouts on the hills to the left: "The enemy are in force behind the hills on the left." "The enemy are in three columns." "The columns are separating, one moving to the left rear, and one towards the General." "The enemy are retiring in every direction."

On hearing these reports, Colonel Durnford sent one troop of mounted natives to reinforce his baggage-guard, and said that he would go out and prevent the one column joining the "impi," which was supposed at that time to be engaged with the troops under the General. He asked Colonel Pulleine to give him two companies of the 24th to go with the natives. Colonel Pulleine objected, stating that he did not think he would be justified in sending away any men, as his orders were "to defend the camp." Colonel Durnford said, "Very well, perhaps I had better not take them. I will go with my own men."

Colonel Durnford now sent two troops of mounted natives, under Captains Shepstone and Barton, on to the hills to the left, to ascertain the enemy's movements. One troop moved along the crest of the hills, the other in the valley beyond. Colonel Durnford took to the front the remaining two troops and Russell's Rocket Battery, with a company of the Natal Native Contingent, under Captain Nourse, as escort to the battery. A company of the 1st Battalion 24th Regiment, under command of Lieutenant Cavaye, was directed to take up a position as a picquet on the hill to the north of the camp, distant about 1,200 yards; the remainder of the troops were ordered to march to their private parades, when the men were to lie down in readiness.

Colonel Durnford and his men, going at a canter, soon left the rocket battery and escort behind. When they had proceeded five or six miles, a mounted man came down from the hills on the left, and reported that there was an immense "impi" behind them. He had scarcely made the report when the Zulus appeared in force in front and to the left: they were in skirmishing order, but ten or twelve deep, with supports close behind. They opened fire at about 800 yards, and advanced very rapidly. Colonel Durnford's force retired steadily in skirmishing order, keeping up a steady fire for about two miles: here they came upon the remains of the rocket battery, which had been cut off and broken up, and found a hand-to-hand engagement going on between the enemy and the survivors. The left wing, while retiring, was wheeled up to the right, and drove the Zulus back.

The force in charge of the rocket battery and the escort, having heard heavy firing on their left, had changed their course in that direction. Before nearly reaching the crest of the hills on the left of the camp, they had been attacked on all sides. They had only had time to send off one rocket before the enemy was upon them. The first volley dispersed the mules and the natives; Major Russell, R.A., was killed, and the remainder of the force retired on to the camp. The retreat was continued until a "donga" was reached, about half a mile in front of the camp. Here a few mounted men—carabineers, Natal mounted police, &c.—reinforced their right. A stand was made, but the force was eventually driven in.

During this time the following were the movements at the camp:—About noon Captain Shepstone galloped back from the hills to the left with the warning that the whole Zulu army, which had been seen about five miles off, was advancing to attack it; but his statement was not credited. Almost immediately afterwards firing was heard on the hill where the company of the 24th was stationed. This company was in extended order, a section being detached about 500 yards to the left. A company under Captain Mostyn moved up into the space, and extended. Some native infantry were on the right of the line. The enemy were distant about 800 yards, moving towards the left.. The mounted natives were retiring down the hill. Orders to retire were received almost immediately, and the line retired to the foot of the slope, the enemy rushing forward to the crest of the hill as the men disappeared. Captain Essex, 75th Regiment, went to camp for ammunition, and on his return found that the companies of the 24th Regiment had retired to within 300 yards of the portion of the camp occupied by the Native Contingent. On his way he noticed a number of native infantry retreating in haste towards the camp, their officer endeavouring to prevent them, but without effect.

Captain Alan Gardner, who had been sent back with an order from the General addressed to Lieutenant-Colonel Pulleine, to send on the camp equipage and supplies of the troops camping out, and to remain himself at his present camp and entrench it, now arrived. As the enemy were already on the hill in large numbers, Colonel Pulleine decided that it was impossible to carry out the General's order. Captain Gardner at once sent off a message directed to the Staff Officer of the 3rd Column, stating that the left was attacked by about 10,000 of the enemy; and a message was also sent by Colonel Pulleine.

The guns under Major Smith, R.A., came into action about 400 yards to the left front of the camp, when they were able to throw shells into a large mass of the enemy that remained almost stationary, about 3,400 yards off. This was shortly after twelve o'clock. The 1st Battalion 24th Regiment soon came up, and extended in skirmishing order on both flanks. In about a quarter of an hour Major Smith took away one gun to the right, as the enemy were appearing in large numbers in the direction of the drift, in the watercourse in front of the camp. When the enemy had advanced to within about 400 yards, Major Smith returned with his gun, and came into action beside the other, which had been left in charge of Lieutenant Curling, R.A.

The two guns and the whole of the 24th extended were now about 300 yards from the left front of the camp; the Natal natives took post on the right of the 24th; then came Durnford's Basutos; and the extreme right was formed by about forty mounted Europeans. The force held the only position that afforded any shelter—viz., broken ground and a watercourse in front of the camp. The infantry were in good position among the stones and boulders to the left and left centre of the camp, and stood their ground most gallantly. The enemy, who in front were some 10,000 strong, now began to appear in the rear, having worked round the hills. Captain Essex rode up to Colonel Durnford, who was near the right, and pointed out to him that the camp was being surrounded. Colonel Durnford requested him to take men to the rear, and endeavour to hold the enemy in check; but, while he was speaking, those men of the Native Contingent who had remained in action rushed past in the utmost disorder, thus laying open the right and rear of the companies of 1st Battalion 24th Regiment on the left; and the enemy, dashing forward in a most rapid manner, poured in at this part of the line. In a moment all was disorder, and few of the men of 1st Battalion 24th Regiment had time to fix bayonets before the enemy were among them, using their assegais with fearful effect. Officers were heard calling to their men to be steady, but the retreat became in a few seconds general, and in a direction towards the road to Rorke's Drift; before, however, the neck near the Isandhlwana Hill was gained, the enemy had arrived on that portion of the field also, and the large circle they had now formed closed in. Hard by the neck, a gallant and desperate stand was made, with a view to cover the retreat. Here were subsequently found the bodies of Colonel Durnford, Lieutenant Scott and fourteen of his Natal Carabineers, and a few Natal police—all mounted men who could have tried to escape—together with about thirty men of the 24th Regiment; close by were a hundred and thirty more dead of the 24th, with their officers, Captain Wardell, Lieutenant Dyer, and a captain and subaltern not recognizable; another group of sixty, with Captain Younghusband and two other officers, lay under Isandhlwana; and other groups lay where they had fought gallantly to the end. The only space which appeared open in the encircling line was down a deep gully running to the south of the road, into which the retreating force plunged in great confusion. The enemy followed closely, and kept up with them at first on both flanks, then on their right only, firing occasionally, but chiefly making use of their assegais. The ground passed over further on in the retreat would at any other time be looked upon as impracticable for horsemen to descend; and many losses occurred, owing to horses falling and the enemy coming up with the riders. About half a mile from the neck the retreat had to be carried on in nearly single file, and in this manner the Buffalo River was gained at a point about five miles below Rorke's Drift. In crossing this river many men and horses were carried away by the stream, and lost their lives. After the crossing was made, the fire of the enemy was discontinued: pursuit, however, was still kept up, but with little effect, and apparently with the view of cutting the retreating force off from Rorke's Drift. The number of white men who crossed the river at this point was about forty. In addition to these, there were a great number of natives on foot and on horseback. Captain Gardner, who, assisted by a few mounted Basutos, had made his way down a steep ravine and escaped, immediately sent messages to Helpmakaar and Rorke's Drift, urging that the camps should be fortified, and then rode off to Utrecht, some eighty miles distant, to warn Colonel Wood. About twenty-five or thirty white men arrived at Helpmakaar between five and six p.m., when, with the assistance of others, a laager was formed with waggons round the stores. The strength of the enemy has been variously estimated at from 20,000 to 25,000. The British loss is given at 51 officers, and 786 men (whites only).

Upon the arrival of Lord Chelmsford's force in camp, after upwards of eighteen hours' continuous marching, officers and men lay down in the scene of slaughter to pass the night as they best could. Many a comrade lay stretched in his last sleep around them, while oxen lying dead in their yokes, horses which had been shot, and the *débris* from plundered waggons strewed the ground. All night long an attack was momentarily expected. In the rear was the large force which had retired before the advance of the column on the previous morning; on the right flank there was presumed to be the army which had destroyed the camp; in front could be seen the watch-fires of another force situated between the camp and Rorke's Drift. At early dawn on the morning of the 23rd Lord Chelmsford ordered the troops to move on with all speed to the latter post, concerning the safety of which great anxiety was felt. The march was made without incident. Zulus were hovering about, but were seemingly afraid to attack; twice columns of them were passed debouching from the Buffalo, while burning kraals on the Natal side showed plainly whence they were returning. On sighting the post at Rorke's Drift, heavy smoke was seen to be issuing from the hospital, and Zulus were seen to be retiring from it. To the intense relief of Lord Chelmsford's force, however, on nearing the Buffalo River, the waving of hats from the interior of a hastily-erected intrenchment was seen; and shortly afterwards it was ascertained that the gallant garrison of the post, consisting of some sixty men of the 2nd Battalion 24th Regiment, under Lieutenant Bromhead, and a few volunteers and Departmental officers, the whole (a total of one hundred and thirty-eight) under Lieutenant Chard, R.E., had for twelve hours held at bay some three thousand Zulus, three hundred and seventy of whose dead bodies lay scattered around the post to testify to the desperate determination with which it had been attacked. Lord Chelmsford, in a despatch bearing date January 27th, characterized the resistance made as the most gallant he had ever heard of; and later stated it as his opinion that it had no doubt saved Natal from serious invasion. The following is Lieutenant Chard's official report of the defence:—

"On the 22nd instant I was left in command at Rorke's Drift by Major Spalding, who went to Helpmakaar to hurry in the company 24th Regiment ordered to protect the ponts.

"About 3.15 p.m. on that day, I was at the ponts when two men came riding from Zululand at a gallop, and shouted to be taken across the river.

"I was informed by one of them, Lieutenant Adenhdorff of Lonsdale's regiment (who remained to assist in the defence), of the disaster at Isandhlwana camp, and that the Zulus were advancing on Rorke's Drift. The other, a carabineer, rode off to take the news to Helpmakaar.

"Almost immediately I received a message from Lieutenant Bromhead, commanding the company 24th Regiment at the camp near the commissariat stores, asking me to come up at once.

"I gave the order to inspan, strike tents, put all stores, &c. into the waggon, and at once rode up to the commissariat store, and found that a note had been received from the 3rd Column to state that the enemy were advancing in force against our post, which we were to strengthen and hold at all costs.

"Lieutenant Bromhead was most actively engaged in loopholing and barricading the store building and hospital, and connecting the defence of the two buildings by walls of mealie-bags and two waggons that were on the ground.

"I held a hurried consultation with him and with Mr. Dalton, of the commissariat (who was actively superintending the work of defence, and whom I cannot sufficiently thank for his most valuable services), entirely approving of the arrangements made. I went round the position, and then went down to the ponts and brought up the guard of one sergeant and six men, waggon, &c. I desire here to mention the offer of the punt-man Daniels and Sergeant Milne, 3rd Buffs, to move the punts in the middle of the stream, and defend them from their decks with a few men. We arrived at the post about 3.30 p.m. Shortly after, an officer of Durnford's Horse arrived, and asked for orders. I requested him to send a detachment to observe the drifts and punts, and throw out outposts in the direction of the enemy and check his advance as much as possible, falling back upon the post when forced to retire, and assist in its defence.

"I requested Lieutenant Bromhead to post his men, and having seen his and every man at his post, the work once more went on.

"About 4.20 p.m. the sound of firing was heard behind the hill to our south. The officer of Durnford's returned, reporting the enemy close upon us, and that his men would not obey his orders, but were going off to Helpmakaar; and I saw them, apparently about 100 in number, going off in that direction.

"About the same time Captain Stephenson's detachment of Natal Native Contingent left us, as did that officer himself.

"I saw that our line of defence was too extended for the small number of men now left us, and at once commenced a retrenchment of biscuit-boxes.

"We had not completed a wall two boxes high when, about 4.30 p.m., 500 or 600 of the enemy came in sight around the hill to our south, and advanced at a run against the south wall. They were met by a well-sustained fire, but, notwithstanding their heavy loss, continued the advance to within fifty yards of the wall, when they were met with such a heavy fire from the wall and cross-fire from the store that they were checked, but, taking advantage of the cover afforded by the cookhouse, ovens, &c., kept up a heavy fire. The greater number, however, without stopping, moved to the left, around the hospital, and made a rush at our N.W. wall of mealie-bags, but after a short but desperate struggle were driven back with heavy loss into the bush around the work.

"The main body of the enemy were close behind, and had lined the ledge of rock and caves overlooking us about 400 yards to our south, from whence they kept up a constant fire, and, advancing somewhat more to their left than the first attack, occupied the garden, hollow road, and bush in great force.

"Taking advantage of the bush, which we had not time to cut down, the enemy were able to advance under cover close to our wall, and in this part soon held one side of the wall, while we held the other. A series of desperate assaults were made, extending from the hospital, along the wall, as far as the bush reached; but each was most splendidly met and repulsed by our men with the bayonet, Corporal Schiess, N.N.C., greatly distinguishing himself by his conspicuous gallantry.

"The fire from the rocks behind us, though badly directed, took us completely in reverse, and was so heavy that we suffered very severely, and about 6 p.m. were forced to retire behind the retrenchment of biscuit-boxes.

"All this time the enemy had been attempting to force the hospital, and shortly after set fire to its roof.

"The garrison of the hospital defended it room by room, bringing out all the sick who could be moved before they retired—Privates Williams, Hook, R. Jones, and W. Jones, 24th Regiment, being the last men to leave, holding the doorway with the bayonet, their own ammunition being expended. From the want of interior communication and the burning of the house, it was impossible to save all. With most heartfelt sorrow I regret we could not save these poor fellows from their terrible fate.

"Seeing the hospital burning and the desperate attempts of the enemy to fire the roof of the stores, we converted two mealie-bag heaps into a sort of redoubt, which gave a second line of fire all round; Assistant Commissary Dunne working hard at this, though much exposed, and rendering valuable assistance.

"As darkness came on we were completely surrounded, and, after several attempts had been gallantly repulsed, were eventually forced to retire to the middle, and then inner wall of the kraal on our east. The position we then had we retained throughout.

"A desultory fire was kept up all night, and several assaults were attempted and repulsed; the vigour of the attack continuing until after midnight, and men firing with the greatest coolness did not waste a single shot; the light afforded by the burning hospital being of great help to us.

"About 4 a.m. 23rd instant, the firing ceased, and at daybreak the enemy were out of sight over the hill to the south-west.

"We patrolled the grounds, collecting the arms of the dead Zulus, and strengthened our defences as much as possible.

"We were removing the thatch from the roof of the stores when, about 7 a.m., a large body of the enemy appeared on the hills to the south-west.

"I sent a friendly Kaffir, who had come in shortly before, with a note to the officer commanding at Helpmakaar, asking for help.

"About 8 a.m. the third column appeared in sight, the enemy, who had been gradually advancing, falling back as they approached.

"I consider the enemy who attacked us to have numbered about 3,000 (three thousand).

"We killed about 350 (three hundred and fifty).

"Of the steadiness and gallant behaviour of the whole garrison I cannot speak too highly."

By this time, the No. 1 Column, under Colonel Pearson, which had been impeded in its advance by difficulties in the way of transport, was at length nearing Etshowe. Though it had been marching in constant expectation of being attacked, it was not until the morning of the 22nd—the date of what proved to be a preconcerted attack by the enemy along the whole line of invasion—that its expectation was fulfilled. On that day the march was resumed at 5 a.m. After the column, preceded by the mounted troops under Major Barrow, had advanced about four miles, the Inyezane River was reached, and it was decided to outspan for a couple of hours in order to feed and rest the oxen and to enable the men to breakfast. Colonel Pearson was in the act of giving directions about the picquets and scouts required for the protection of the column, and the waggons had already begun to park, when the leading company of the Native Contingent, which was scouting in front, discovered the enemy advancing rapidly in extended order over the ridges in front, and making for the clumps of bush around. It was then just 8 o'clock.

The Zulus at once opened a heavy fire upon the men of the company who had shown themselves in the open, and killed one officer, four non-commissioned officers, and three men, almost immediately after the firing began.

Colonel Pearson now directed the Naval Brigade, under Commander Campbell, Lieutenant Lloyd's division of guns, and Captain Jackson's and Lieutenant Martin's companies of the Buffs, to take up a position on a knoll close by the road, from whence the whole of the Zulu advances could be seen and dealt with.

Meanwhile, the waggons continued to park. As soon as the length of the column had thereby sufficiently decreased, two companies of the Buffs, which were guarding the waggons about half-way down the column, were directed to clear the enemy out of the bush, which had been already shelled and fired into with rockets and musketry by the troops on the knoll. These companies, led by Captains Harrison and Wyld, and guided by Captain Macgregor, D.A.Q.M.G., moved out in excellent order: quickly getting into position for skirmishing, they brought their right shoulders gradually forward, and drove the Zulus before them back into the open, where they were exposed to the rockets, shells, and musketry from the knoll. This movement released the main body of the Mounted Infantry and Volunteers, who, with the company of Royal Engineers, had remained near the Inyezane, to protect a portion of the convoy of waggons. When thus released, both the Engineers and mounted troops, under Majors Wynne and Barrow, respectively moved forward with the infantry. Skirmishers were thrown out on the left, and the whole force was supported by a half-company of the Buffs and a half-company of the 99th Regiment, sent out by Lieutenant-Colonel Welman, who, with the rear of the column, was now coming up.

About this time the enemy was observed by Commander Campbell to be trying to outflank the left of the column: he immediately proceeded with a portion of the Naval Brigade to attack a body of them which had got possession of a kraal about 400 yards from the knoll, and which was helping the turning movement. The Naval Brigade was supported by a party of the officers and non-commissioned officers of the Native Contingent, under Captain Hart, who were posted on high ground on the left of the Etshowe Road, and succeeded in effectually checking the Zulus from making any further attempt on the left.

Shortly afterwards, when the kraal was evacuated, Commander Campbell made a suggestion that the enemy should be driven off still farther, to which Colonel Pearson at once assented. Colonel Parnell was directed to take Captain Forster's company of the Buffs, which up to this time had remained at the foot of the knoll, and assist the Naval Brigade in attacking some heights beyond the kraal, upon which a considerable body of Zulus were still posted. The action was completely successful, and the Zulus fled in all directions, both from the front and left, and from before the skirmishers on the right. The last shot was fired about 9 a.m., the engagement having lasted one hour and a half. The estimated number of the enemy was 4,000, of whom 300 were killed. The loss of the British was 8 killed and 16 wounded.

On the following day the column marched into Etshowe, an abandoned Norwegian mission station, composed of a church and three thatched buildings, and lying a mile and a half off the main road from the Tugela Drift to Ulundi. It being Lord Chelmsford's intention that the station should eventually become an important commissariat depôt, Colonel Pearson at once took measures for equipping it as speedily as possible, and assigned to Major Wynne, R.E., the senior engineer officer, the duty of the defence. Orders were sent to Colonel Ely, who had started from the Lower Tugela on the 22nd for Etshowe with a large convoy of stores, to hurry on with all speed; and forty-eight empty waggons were sent back, under an escort, for further supplies. Work was commenced on the 25th, and by the 27th—the day on which news of the disaster at Isandhlwana first reached the column—the intrenchments had made considerable progress. On the morning of January the 28th, a messenger arrived with a telegram from Lord Chelmsford, confirming the news of the disaster, and desiring Colonel Pearson to consider all previous instructions as cancelled, and to act as he might think best in the interest of his column. Upon receipt of this message, Colonel Pearson assembled his commanding officers, and, after consulting them, decided to hold his ground. In order to reduce the consumption of the food supply, and to add to the defensive power of the Colony, the whole of the mounted troops attached to the column, together with two battalions of the Native Contingent, were sent back to the Tugela, leaving Etshowe at 2 p.m. on the 28th. The garrison now consisted of fifty-seven officers and 1,281 non-commissioned officers and men of the regulars, and twenty-nine Europeans and 121 natives of the colonial troops and native levies: in addition to these there were 164 conductors and drivers.

The work of defence was from the first rapidly pushed on: thick parapets were formed, and ditches dug to a depth of from seven to ten feet; the waggons were laagered along the parapets in such a manner as to protect the men from the fire to which they would be exposed in the event of an attack being made, and shelter was provided for them with the waggons themselves, and with tarpaulins stretched between them; the church was loopholed, and a gallery formed for the defenders, in such a manner as to interfere as little as possible with the use of the floor space, which was set apart for the use of hospital patients; platforms were made for four 7-pounders and one Gatling, and the batteries were masked with sand-bags. Only a few days had passed since the column had marched into Etshowe, and the construction of the fort was yet in its inception, when all communication with the outside world became cut off. Situated in the heart of the enemy's country, and unsupported from without, the besieged garrison was destined to hold the Zulu army at bay for a period of upwards of ten weeks.

In the meantime, Wood's Column had reached the Umvolosi River. On January the 20th, the date of its arrival, the chieftain Tinta tendered his submission and was conducted into camp, together with his people and his herds, under a strong escort. On the same day a party under Colonel Buller started to reconnoitre the Zunguin range, and by the 22nd effectually cleared it, dispersing a force of about 1,000 Zulus who opposed them, and capturing a large number of their cattle. The column halted on the 23rd, and on the 24th moved forward between the Zunguin and Ityentika ranges, skirmishing with the enemy as it advanced.

Immediately after the relief of the garrison at Rorke's Drift, Lord Chelmsford took measures to protect the Colony, and to prevent panic from spreading. The invasion of the enemy's country was temporarily suspended, pending the arrival of reinforcements from England, and a general retrograde movement was carried out. Colonel Wood, to whom news of the events of the 22nd had been promptly conveyed by Captain Alan Gardner, fell back from the Umvolosi to the slopes of the Kambula Mountain, thirty miles north-east of, and covering, Utrecht. In this position he confined his attention to harrying the enemy in a series of brilliantly executed reconnaissances, carried out under Colonel Buller. Such troops as could be spared from Capetown and King William's Town were ordered up to the front, and the opportune arrival at Natal of three companies of the 88th Regiment enabled two companies stationed between Durban and the Lower Tugela to be moved forward. Durban, Stanger, Pietermaritzburg, and Greytown, were placed in a position of defence, while the camps of the No. 3 Column at Helpmakaar and Rorke's Drift were strongly intrenched.

On February the 1st, a force from Wood's column, under Colonel Buller, attacked and destroyed the Amaqulisini kraal, a rallying-point of the enemy, situated about thirty miles east of the camp, and hitherto regarded as impregnable. Shortly afterwards Umbellini and Manyanyoba, two chiefs of the Intombi Valley district, led marauding parties of Zulus into the neighbourhood of Lüneberg, and perpetrated a series of barbarous outrages on the friendly natives. On February the 13th, Colonel Wood despatched a force under Colonel Buller to take retaliatory measures.

Upon reaching Manyanyoba's stronghold, Colonel Buller divided his force, sending a portion of it along a number of krantzes, among which were the hiding-places of the enemy, and with the remainder attacking them in detail from below. Five of the fastnesses were successfully stormed, thirty-four Zulus being slain, and a large number of their cattle captured. Colonel Buller returned to Lüneberg the same evening, with the intention of making a second attack on the following day; being informed, however, that Colonel Rowlands was moving a strong force in the same direction with a similar object, he abandoned his intention.

Colonel Rowlands, after having vainly endeavoured to induce the Swazies to co-operate with him, had marched with a portion of his column from Derby on the 13th: with this force he reached the Tolaka mountain on the 15th, and, after dispersing a body of the enemy who held it, arrived at Lüneberg on the same day. He was followed by the remainder of his column, under Major Tucker, which reached its destination on the 19th. On the following day, Captain Harvey, his staff officer, marched across the Pongolo River into Zululand, and, after a brisk engagement, succeeded in dislodging a force of the enemy who had interrupted communications between Lüneberg and the Kambula camp, from their stronghold in the Eloya mountain. A few days later the No. 5 Column was broken up: the mounted men joined Colonel Wood to assist in reconnoitering; Colonel Rowlands, with Captain Harvey and the remainder of his Staff, was ordered to proceed with all speed to Prætoria, the capital of the Transvaal, to strengthen its garrison, which was at that time threatened by 5,000 Boers, who were encamped within fifteen miles of the city; and five companies of the 80th remained at Lüneberg. About the same time the mounted infantry of the No. 3 Column, under Colonel Russell, 12th Lancers, joined Colonel Wood at Kambula.

As it had been found impossible, on the departure of the No. 5 Column from Derby, to carry away the large quantity of stores which had accumulated there, convoys of waggons were despatched in succession for them from Lüneberg. These convoys were at first escorted by two companies of the 80th, with a proportion of mounted men and natives, over that portion of the road which passes through the mountain fastnesses then occupied by Manyanyoba on the one side and Umbellini on the other. After the withdrawal of all the mounted men and the natives, only the two companies were available for this duty. This escort, consisting of 104 men of all ranks, under Captain D. B. Moriarty, 80th Regiment, was sent on March the 7th by Major Tucker, the officer commanding at Lüneberg, to accompany a convoy of eighteen waggons then on its way from Derby. Captain Moriarty's orders were to bring these waggons (some of which were reported to be broken down near the Intombi River), or their loads, into Lüneberg; but if this were impossible in consequence of the flooded state of the country, to laager his waggons at the river-side, and wait until he might be able to cross. During the 8th, 9th, and 10th, the river was too high to permit of anything being done; on the 11th it lowered somewhat, and an attempt was made: the stream, however, was rapid; night came on before all the waggons could be got across the drift, and the force became divided. On the morning of March the 12th, it was attacked by the enemy in overwhelming numbers, with disastrous effect. Lieutenant Harward, who had crossed the river, and was encamped with thirty-five men on the Lüneberg side, heard, at about 4 a.m., a shot fired in the distance. He got up and ordered the sentry to rouse the detachment on the side of the Intombi Drift nearest Lüneberg, and to apprise

Captain Moriarty of the fact, and ask for his orders. These were, that the escort should remain under arms. He returned to his tent close by, where he waited, dressed, and, about an hour afterwards, heard the words, 'Guard, turn out!' He instantly turned out, and saw, as the fog lifted, a dense mass of Zulus about 200 yards from the waggon laager, extending across the valley, with a front of two or three miles. Lieutenant Harward's men, under cover of a waggon near their tents, directed their fire on the flanks of the enemy, who were endeavouring to surround the waggon-laager on the other side of the river. It was next observed that the enemy had gained full possession of the camp, and were driving off the cattle, and that Captain Moriarty's men were retiring on the river, which was full of human beings. On seeing this, Lieutenant Harward's party directed its fire entirely with a view to cover the retreat. This fire was well sustained, and enabled many to get over the river alive. The enemy were now assegaing the men in the water, and were also ascending the banks of the river on the Lüneberg side. A hand-to-hand fight ensued. Lieutenant Harward, who reported, in a despatch bearing date March the 13th, that he endeavoured to rally his men, mounted his horse, and galloped into Lüneberg at utmost speed, with the news of what had occurred.

In this disastrous attack, Captain Moriarty, who, having emerged from his tent, rallied his men with desperate courage, fell pierced to the heart with an assegai, forty-three of his men met with a like fate, and several more were drowned whilst endeavouring to cross the river.

On the arrival of Lieutenant Harward at Lüneberg, at about 6.30 a.m., Major Tucker ordered all the horses belonging to the officers to be saddled, and, leaving directions that 150 men of the 80th Regiment should follow, proceeded to the scene of the disaster. Shortly after starting, a long, deep line of Zulus, estimated to consist of more than 4,000, was observed making its way slowly eastward. At the Intombi River, the laager was found completely wrecked, the cattle having been taken, and the contents of the waggons strewn about: the bodies of Captain Moriarty's men, which could be seen on the opposite side of the river, were collected and interred on the arrival of the men of the 80th from Lüneberg.

Colonel Wood, who, on March the 4th, had secured the submission of Oham, Cetchwayo's brother, left the Kambula Hill, with 390 men, on the morning of the 14th, for the purpose of escorting into camp such of the followers of that chief as had not already arrived. From the slopes of the Zlobane Mountain, under which the escort had to pass, the Zulus opened a desultory fire, but made no regular attack; the members of the tribe were safely conducted into camp, and were subsequently attached to Wood's Irregulars, a corps which, under Major W. K. Leet, had already done good service with the Mounted Volunteers. A week after Colonel Wood returned, he despatched, on March the 23rd, a force of 800 men to destroy the tribal power of the chiefs responsible for the massacre on the Intombi, and to restore order upon the Transvaal frontier.

By this time the reinforcements, which had been despatched by the Home Government on the news of the disaster at Isandhlwana reaching England, were arriving at Natal in quick succession, and arrangements for the relief of the beleaguered force at Etshowe were being pushed on. On March the 23rd, Lord Chelmsford took personal command of the column destined for this purpose, which was in course of formation on the Lower Tugela; and by the 28th, the whole force, organized in two brigades, was assembled on the left bank of the river ready to start.

Previously to advancing, the General, leaving the commanding officers unfettered as to the details of such action as they might take, gave instructions along the whole line to make demonstrations against the enemy. Colonel Wood decided to storm the rocky fastnesses on the heights of the Zlobane, and thus fulfil a project he had for some time had in view. The mountain, which is most difficult of access, is situated some ten miles to the eastward of the position then occupied by the camp at Kambula. It consists of two plateaux of unequal elevation, the higher of which, some three miles by one and a half in extent, surmounts an almost perpendicular ascent from the eastward, while the lower, about a mile by a mile and a half in extent, forms a step to the higher, and is joined to it by a narrow neck and an almost inaccessible ascent of some two hundred feet in height: from the latter elevation, the mountain side, irregular and boulder-strewn, slopes westward at a steep gradient.

Colonel Wood divided his force into two columns—one under Colonel Buller, consisting of 400 mounted men; the other, under Colonel Russell, 12th Lancers, consisting of 250 mounted men; and each including a Royal Artillery rocket party. Colonel Buller was directed to attack and clear the eastern plateau of the mountain; Colonel Russell to make a feigned attack on the western side. Both columns left camp on March the 27th, and bivouacked for the night within ten miles of each other, Colonel Buller's force having been joined at the Zunguin Neck by the 2nd Battalion Wood's Irregulars, under the Corps Commandant, Major Leet; and Colonel Russell's having been joined by the 1st Battalion, under Lieutenant Williams, 58th Regiment, on its arrival at the same place shortly afterwards.

Colonel Wood, accompanied by Captain Campbell, Coldstream Guards, Mr. Lloyd, Political Assistant, Lieutenant Lysons, 90th Light Infantry, and a mounted escort of fourteen men, joined Colonel Russell's column at dusk on the 27th, at his bivouac, about five miles west of the Zlobane Mountain; and at daybreak on the 28th followed on Colonel Buller's track. Shortly after starting, the party was met by Colonel Weatherley, who, with fifty-three men of his Border Horse, had been told off to join Colonel Buller's column, but who had lost his way on the previous night. Colonel Wood directed this force to move on to the north-east face of the mountain, where the rear of Colonel Buller's column could be now seen near the summit, from whence firing had become audible; and, together with his escort, commenced the ascent of the mountain immediately in the rear. The path followed passed through jagged masses of rock and immense boulders. Killed and wounded horses met with on the track gave evidence of Colonel Buller's advance having been opposed.

Ascending more rapidly than most of the Border Horse, Colonel Wood, with his staff and escort, passed to the front. When within a hundred feet of the summit of the mountain, they found themselves suddenly confronted by the enemy, who poured in a heavy fire upon them from behind the rocks and boulders. Mr. Lloyd fell mortally wounded, and Colonel Wood's horse was killed, falling on him. Colonel Wetherley, having now arrived with some of his men, was directed by Colonel Wood to dislodge the few Zulus who were causing most of the loss; his troopers, however, did not advance with such celerity as might have been desired, seeing which, Captain Campbell, Lieutenant Lysons, and three men of the 90th, jumped over a low wall, ran forward, and charged into a cave. Captain Campbell, leading in the most gallant and determined manner, was shot dead. Lieutenant Lysons and Private Fowler, following closely on his footsteps, killed one Zulu and dislodged another, who crawled away by a subterranean passage, and reappeared higher up the mountain. Assistance was now being rendered by the fire of Colonel Buller's men from above. Colonel Weatherley, whose loss up to this time was three dead and seven wounded, now moved down the hill to gain the track which he had lost, and reached the lower plateau of the mountain without further casualty. The bodies of Captain Campbell and Mr. Lloyd were carried half-way down the hill, and were there buried by a party under fire in a grave dug with hatchets and sword-bayonets, Colonel Wood reading a portion of the Burial Service the while.

With a view to ascertaining what progress Colonel Russell's column might have made, Colonel Wood now rode slowly round the mountain to the westward, stopping occasionally to administer stimulants to a wounded man who formed one of his party, and utterly unconscious that an immense Zulu force was moving from the left across his front. It was not until the little party had advanced half-way, under the centre of the mountain, that one of the natives saw, and explained by signs, that a large army was close upon them : directly afterwards a clear view of it was obtained, and it was found to be marching in five columns, with horns and dense chest, the normal Zulu attack formation.

Colonel Wood instantly despatched Lieutenant Lysons to Colonel Russell, informing him of the advent of this immense force, and directing him to form immediately on the Zunguin Neck. Colonel Russell had, however, from the position he had assumed on the lower plateau of the mountain, detected its advance some time previously, and had at once communicated the fact to Colonel Buller, whose movements on the higher plateau were completely hidden from him. Concluding, after waiting for a space of nearly two hours, that Colonel Buller's force had been able to return only by the way it had advanced, Colonel Russell retired to the foot of the mountain, and there received Colonel Wood's order. The 1st Battalion of Wood's Irregulars, and Oham's men, who had been capturing cattle, were already making for the Zunguin Neck, which is the eastern corner of the range: misapprehending its position, concerning which general doubt appears to have prevailed, Colonel Russell ordered them to abandon their spoil, and moved off in a contrary direction six miles to the western end of the mountain. The result was that their retreat was uncovered, and the Zulus, moving down upon them with great rapidity, killed about eighty of their number, and put to flight the rest.

In the meantime Colonel Buller had succeeded in clearing the heights of the mountain, though not without the loss of two gallant officers—Lieutenant Williams, of the Frontier Light Horse, and Baron Stentercron—in the assault. Having reached the summit, he despatched two companies of Wood's Irregulars down the mountain-side to clear out the retreating Zulus from the rocks and caves, and sent the remainder of the corps to collect the numerous cattle distributed over the plateau. These operations were successfully carried out.

It was not until after he had been some three hours on the summit of the mountain that Colonel Buller, riding eastward to see how matters were progressing in that direction, received Colonel Russell's message announcing the advent of the Zulu army. His position was now most critical, the route by which he had advanced in the morning being completely closed by the advancing force. Hastening back, he collected the scattered detachment on his way, and commenced a retreat down the western side of the mountain to the lower plateau, by the narrow and almost perpendicular path, over rocky steps in many cases only a few inches broad, and with spaces of three, four, and even five feet between them. No sooner was the descent commenced than the enemy emerged from their rocks and caves, and crowded on the rear of the retreating force. A rush was made, and the narrow gully was at once choked with a struggling mass of men and horses. In this retreat Colonel Buller "was enabled," wrote Colonel Wood, "by his great personal exertions and heroic conduct, not only to bring away all his men who had lost their horses, but also all his wounded who could make an effort to sit on their horses."

At the foot of the precipitous path a neck ran along between the krantz and the lower mountain, and over this the men who had got down safely retreated. Some of them went on at once, and got down into the plain by the west end of the lower mountain, but others halted on the slightly rising ground just across the neck, and opened fire on the Zulus so as to cover the retreat of those not yet down the krantz. The enemy, however, now rushed among those on the krantz with their assegais, and in the struggle which ensued many fell—amongst others Piet Uys, the gallant leader of the Dutch Burghers, who was assegaied whilst returning to assist his son. The main body, followed by the bulk of the enemy, made for the west end of the mountain, but Lieutenant Duncombe, of Wood's Irregulars, Lieutenant Smith, of the Frontier Light Horse, and Major Leet, who were in the rear, attempted to make their way down by the north side, and were at once pursued by a crowd of Zulus. When they had succeeded in descending some little distance, they suddenly found themselves upon the brink of a precipice, and were obliged to turn back towards the enemy in order to get clear of it. By the time this was accomplished the Zulus were almost up with them, firing and throwing their assegais. Lieutenant Duncombe was here shot down, and Lieutenant Smith, who was on foot, became too exhausted to be able to move farther; in another moment he must have been assegaied had not Major Leet stopped and lifted him up on a pack-horse he was riding, his own having been shot earlier in the retreat. The horse, being much exhausted, made slow progress; but the two riders managed to check their pursuers to some extent with their revolvers, and eventually to make their escape. Colonel Wood, who had gone with his escort to the Zunguin Neck, sent an order to Colonel Russell, who was then ascending the western end of the range, to proceed eastward and cover the movement of the natives into camp, which he did. On the Kambula Hill being reached, at 7 p.m., it was found that Captain Barton's party, and Commandant Weatherley's Border Horse, had been cut off whilst on Colonel Wood's track, and almost completely destroyed. Colonel Buller at once started, in heavy rain; and, after scouring the country for a distance of ten miles, was able to bring back seven men, the sole survivors.

Flushed with success, the Zulu army was not slow to follow up its advantage. Colonel Wood received intelligence that he would be attacked, and preparations were at once made for defending the camp and a neighbouring redoubt which, situated to the north-east, was armed with two guns, and held by three companies under Major Leet. Early in the forenoon of the 29th, Captain Raaf, who was out reconnoitering, fell in with one of Oham's men who had been overtaken by the Zulus, and who, not having been recognized by them as an enemy, had marched with their army to the Umvolosi, and had subsequently escaped: this man, giving detailed information concerning the enemy's movements, confirmed the intelligence that an attack was to be made upon the camp almost immediately.

About 11 a.m. dense masses of the enemy were seen approaching in five columns from the Zunguin range and the Umvolosi. Preparations for their reception were completed: two companies which were out woodcutting were recalled, the cattle were brought in and laagered to the south-east of the camp, and the troops took up their assigned positions.

At 1.30 p.m. the action commenced, the mounted riflemen under Colonels Buller and Russell sallying forth and engaging the right horn of the Zulu army on the north side of the camp. Being unable to check the advance of so enormous a body, the mounted men retired into the laager, the Zulus following them to within 300 yards of the intrenchment; at this juncture, however, so deadly a fire was poured into them by the 90th Light Infantry that their line wavered, and eventually spread out to the front and rear of the camp. The attack, checked on the left, now rolled round to the right front and right rear. Occupying a neighbouring hill, and well supplied with Martini-Henry rifles and ammunition, a body of the enemy opened so accurate an enfilade fire upon Captain Cox's company of the 13th Light Infantry, posted at the right rear of the laager, that it had to be withdrawn—an operation which was not accomplished before Captain Cox was severely wounded. As large numbers of the enemy, unseen by another company of the 13th, which held the front of the cattle laager, now made rapidly for the abandoned position, Colonel Wood ordered Major Hackett, 90th Light Infantry, with two companies, to advance over the slope to check them. The companies moved down to the rear of the laager, driving the Zulus from their immediate front; but the numbers opposed to them became so great, and the fire of the enemy so severe, that they were recalled shortly afterwards. In the attack, Lieutenant Bright, an accomplished young officer, fell mortally wounded, and while bringing the companies in, Major Hackett, their gallant leader, was completely disabled. Of the six seven-pounders of Major Tremlett's battery, two were posted in the redoubt to the north-east of the camp, and were admirably worked by Lieutenant Nicolson, R.A., until he fell mortally wounded; the remaining four, under Major Tremlett and his two subalterns, Lieutenants Bigge and Slade, were in a position on the ridge sloping from the redoubt to the camp. The Zulus in great numbers occupied every available spot in the neighbourhood of this position where the slightest cover could be obtained, and their fire, especially from the front and right flanks, was extremely severe. Several times they rose up together in a large body, as if by word of command, apparently with the intention of making a rush forward, but on each occasion they met with such a withering fire as to deter them from carrying out their object. Large numbers, evidently under the impression that they would find protecting cover, sped down to and occupied the deserted kraals of Wood's Irregulars, situated within 400 yards of the right front of the fort; on these a heavy fire was directed, and after the action they were found to be full of dead bodies.

At 5.30 p.m., seeing the attack was slackening, Colonel Wood took out a company of the 1st Battalion of the 13th Regiment to the right rear of the cattle laager to attack some Zulus who had crept into it, but who had been unable to remove the cattle; and took forward Captain Laye's company of the 90th Light Infantry to the edge of the krantz on the right front, whence they did great execution amongst a mass of retreating Zulus. The enemy made one final effort against the right rear of the camp, and then fled precipitately. Colonel Wood now ordered out the mounted men, who, under Colonel Buller, pursued the retreating foe with revengeful slaughter for a distance of seven miles.

The number of Zulus engaged in the attack was estimated to be 20,000, and no less than 700 of their dead were counted within half a mile of the camp. Of the British, 2 officers and 25 men were killed, and 4 officers and 63 men were wounded.

The column destined for the relief of Colonel Pearson's force at Etshowe had been organized in two brigades, which were constituted as follows:—1st Brigade: Lieutenant-Colonel Law, R.A., commanding. Naval Brigade of H.M.S. "Shah" and "Tenedos," except the Royal Marines of the "Shah," 350 men; 57th Regiment, 640; two companies of the Buffs, 140; five companies of the 99th Regiment, 430; five battalions of Natal Native Contingent, 1,200; mounted infantry, 70; mounted volunteers, 30; mounted natives, 130; native foot scouts, 150; Commissariat and Transport Department; Medical Department; total, 1,660 whites, 1,480 Native Contingent; grand total, 3,140 fighting men. Artillery, two 9-pounder guns, two 24-pounder rocket tubes, one Gatling gun. Attached to this divison of the column were the train of supplies for Etshowe (a month's supply for 1,200 men, about 25 waggons), and a train of supplies for both divisions of the column for ten days, about 25 waggons. 2nd Brigade: Lieutenant-Colonel Pemberton, 60th Rifles, commanding. Naval Brigade of H.M.S. "Boadicea," 190 men; Royal Marines, "Shah" and "Boadicea," 100; 60th Rifles, 540; 91st Highlanders, 850; 4th Battalion, Natal Native Contingent, 800; Commissariat and Transport Department; Medical Department; total, 1,680 whites, 800 Native Contingent; grand total, 2,480 fighting men. Artillery, two 24-pounder rocket tubes, one Gatling gun. Recapitulation: 3,340 whites, 2,280 natives; grand total, 5,620 fighting men.

On the morning of March the 29th the column left the banks of the Tugela, advancing by the coast road in order to avoid passing through bushy country until the last day's march. At every halt the precaution was taken to form a waggon laager and intrench it, and, owing to this and to the immense length of the baggage train and the necessity for keeping it together, the progress made was not rapid. The Amatakulu River was reached on the 30th, and the water being high, the whole of the following day was consumed in transferring the train across the stream, each waggon requiring no less than thirty-two oxen to draw it through; whilst this operation was proceeding, Captain Barrow, 19th Hussars, with a portion of his command, pushed on some twelve miles towards the Engoya Forest, and burnt the kraal of Inagwendo, a brother of the Zulu king. On April the 1st the column marched to the Ginghilovo stream, six miles distant, and an intrenched laager was there formed in a favourable position, within a mile of the Inyezane River. From this point the road to Etshowe, after crossing swampy ground, winds through a bushy and difficult country for some fifteen miles, for the last eight or nine of which the ground steadily ascends. The whole country is covered with very high grass, and is sufficiently undulating to cover considerable bodies of natives.

Etshowe could be plainly seen, and flash signalling was at once established. Before the laager was completed a heavy thunderstorm came on; rain fell again at nightfall, and continued until morning. The laager defences were, however, satisfactorily completed after dark. The north or front face was held by the 60th Rifles, the right flank face by the 57th Regiment, the left front face by the 99th Regiment and the Buffs, the rear face by the 91st Regiment; and each angle was manned by the Naval Brigade, Blue Jackets, and Marines—the Gatling of the "Boadicea" being on the north-east corner; two rocket-tubes, under Lieutenant

Kerr, on the north-west; two 9-pounder guns, under Lieutenant Kingscote, on the south-west; and one Gatling and two rocket-tubes, under Commander Brackenbury, on the south-east. The night passed without any alarm.

On the 2nd of April, the troops, as usual. stood to their arms at 4 a.m., at which hour a heavy mist shrouded the surrounding country. The mounted men were at earliest dawn scouting around, and at 5.45 reports came in simultaneously from them and from the picquets of the 60th and 99th Regiments that the enemy were advancing to the attack: no preparation was necessary, and no orders had to be given other than to saddle up the horses of the officers of the Staff.

At 6 a.m. the attack commenced. The Zulus advanced with great rapidity and courage towards the north front of the laager, firing incessantly, and taking advantage of the cover afforded by the undulations of the ground and the long grass; when within twenty yards of the intrenchment, however, they were met with a fusillade so heavy as to render their reaching it physically impossible, and their line wavered, paused, and finally broke. Within the laager Colonel Northey, 60th Rifles, had fallen mortally wounded; Colonel Crealock and Captain Barrow had received injuries, and Captain Molyneux and Lieutenant Courtenay had had their horses shot under them. The attack, checked on the north, now rolled round to the west or left face, at which point Lieutenant Johnson, 99th Regiment, was killed. Whilst it was being developed, a fresh body of the enemy appeared in sight and advanced against the rear, evidently anticipating that the defending force would prove insufficient to hold all the faces of the laager at the same time: fire was at once opened on them, but they obstinately held their ground, finding cover in the long grass and undulations.

It was now 7.30 a.m., and the Zulus, who, during one hour and a half, had obstinately attacked three sides of the laager, at last began to realize the hopelessness of attempting to pass through the zone of heavy fire with which their onslaughts were met. Lord Chelmsford now directed Captain Barrow, with the Mounted Infantry and Volunteers, who had been engaged in clearing the front face of the laager, to move across and attack the enemy's right flank. No sooner did they make their appearance than the Zulu retreat commenced. The Natal Native Contingent, who were formed within the intrenchment on the rear face, at once cleared the ditch, and with loud cheers rushed forward, led by Captain Barrow's horsemen; the pursuit was carried on for a distance of several miles, the enemy making a stand nowhere, and throwing away their arms to assist their flight. The number of Zulus estimated to have taken part in the attack was 11,000, of whom about 1,000 were killed; 471 of their dead were counted within a thousand yards of the intrenchment, and 200 more were shortly afterwards found in the neighbourhood. Of the English, eleven were killed and sixty-two wounded.

On the morning of April the 3rd, the day after the battle, a portion of the column was left as a garrison for the laager, and the remainder, carrying three days' supplies and escorting fifty-eight waggons of stores, moved off in compact order for Etshowe. The distance to be traversed was some fifteen miles, the streams were deep and the swamps heavy, and for the last eight or nine miles of the road—which had been in two places partly destroyed by the Zulus—the ascents were steep. Eventually the column neared its destination. As it appeared in sight Colonel Pearson, accompanied by some hundreds of his men, galloped out from the fort, amidst ringing cheers, to meet it. The long and weary waiting time, during which disease and death had wrought havoc in the ranks of the beleaguered, was well nigh spent. The hour of relief was at hand.

With the battles of Kambula and Ginghilovo, and the relief of Etshowe, the second period of the campaign may be said to have come to an end. Lord Chelmsford returned to Durban to organize the reinforcements which were continuing to arrive daily, for a final investment of the enemy's country; and was there met, on April the 9th, by the Generals and Staff Officers who had just landed. It was then decided that the old distribution of the forces should be broken up, and that two new columns, under Generals Crealock and Newdigate respectively, should be constituted as the 1st and 2nd Divisions of the Field Force, while Colonel Wood's Column should remain an independent command, henceforward to be known as the Flying Column. The 1st Division had for its objective the subjugation of the coast line from the south, with the possibility of afterwards advancing to Ulundi should occasion require; whilst the 2nd Division and the Flying Column, co-operating, were to march on Ulundi from the north-west. General Newdigate received instructions to start at once for Utrecht, and arrange a meeting with Colonel Wood, in order to select a site for an advanced depôt in the neighbourhood of the Doornberg Mountain, from which supplies were to be drawn both by his own Division and by Colonel Wood's Column. He arrived at the Kambula Camp on April the 22nd, and on the morning of the following day started with Colonel Wood to inspect the country in the neighbourhood of the Ihnlahgati Mountain, round the north side of which it was expected that the advance would be made. On this supposition, Conference Hill, a position on the Blood River, was selected as the site for the depôt, and, two days later, arrangements were made for sending a company of the Royal Engineers, the 94th Regiment, and a company of Major Bengough's Battalion of Native Infantry to erect a fortified post there. On April 29th, Lord Chelmsford and his Staff, with the Prince Imperial, paid a visit to Dundee, and on the following day held an inspection of the troops which had been gradually arriving. Detachments had been left at Pietermaritzburg, Durban, Ladismith, and Greytown, by the various regiments as they advanced, and convoys of supplies were being sent up from the base and from Helpmakaar.

On May the 2nd, General Newdigate marched with the 2nd Battalion 21st Regiment, the 58th Regiment, and Harness's Battery, to Landman's Drift, a position on the Blood River, and there formed a camp, with two redoubts; on the same day Lord Chelmsford, accompanied by the Prince Imperial, started for Balte's Spruits, leaving the head-quarter camp at Landman's Drift until the 6th, when it was moved to Utrecht. Colonel Wood's Column left the slopes of the Kambula, on which it had been stationed for upwards of three months, at daybreak on the 5th, crossed the Umvolosi, and encamped at Landman's Drift. The construction of the fortified post at Conference Hill was now progressing, and from this time until the end of the month every effort was made to forward to this spot the immense quantity of supplies which it was deemed necessary to accumulate before carrying out the projected advance on Ulundi. On May the 8th, intelligence arrived that a party of Zulus had crossed the river near the La Fuie Drift, and carried off cattle from the Natal natives. General Newdigate arranged to make a raid through the Bashee Valley, and destroy all the kraals in which Sirayo's men were in the habit of congregating—an operation which was successfully carried out by Bengough's Battalion and Bettington's Troop. On May the 12th, the right wing of the 17th Lancers, under Colonel Drury Lowe, and Major Le Grice's Battery of the Royal Artillery, arrived at Landman's Drift, and shortly afterwards the remainder of the Lancers, and the King's Dragoon Guards, under General Marshall, proceeded from Dundee to the same place.

The situation of affairs was now analogous to that which prevailed immediately after the occurrence of the disaster at Isandhlwana. Again the forces lay massed on the border ready to advance, and again they were hampered and delayed by the want of supplies and the inadequacy of transport. The difficulties to be overcome were great. Every pound of food both for man and horse had to be carried into the field, and every stick of firewood had to be hewn and brought into camp from, generally speaking, considerable distances.

On May the 19th General Marshall made a successful reconnaissance with the cavalry to the field of Isandhlwana. The bodies of the dead were roughly covered with stones, but, by the special request of the officers of the 24th, the duty of interring the remains of those of that regiment who had fallen was left to be performed by their comrades; every kraal in the vicinity of the ill-fated camp was burnt, and a route was reopened into the heart of Zululand.

On May the 24th, Lord Chelmsford and his Staff moved the head-quarters back from Utrecht to Landman's Drift. It was then decided that a more southerly route should be taken by the invading force than that at first projected, and that the 2nd Division should concentrate at Koppie Allein, a position on the Blood River, about twelve miles from Landman's Drift, and a like distance from Conference Hill. By May the 30th the concentration was completed. The Division was then composed of a Cavalry Brigade, under General Marshall, consisting of the King's Dragoon Guards, the 17th Lancers, and Shepstone's Basutos; the N/5 Battery Royal Artillery, under Major Harness, the N/6 Battery, under Major Le Grice, and an ammunition column, under Captain Alexander; and two brigades of infantry—the 1st, under Colonel Glyn, consisting of the 2nd Battalion 24th Regiment, the 58th Regiment, and Bengough's Natal Native Contingent; and the 2nd, under Colonel Collingwood, consisting of the 1st Battalion 24th Regiment, and the 94th Regiment.

On June the 1st the whole of the Division, with Lord Chelmsford and his Staff, crossed the Blood River, and marched to the Itelezi Hill. On this day the Prince Imperial, riding forward to make a sketch of the ground where the Division was to halt on the following day, was surprised and slain by a party of the enemy. On the 5th, a position some four miles beyond the Ityotyozi River was taken up, and on the same day Lord Chelmsford ordered General Marshall to advance with his brigade, and clear a district in which a large number of Zulus were congregated in the neighbourhood of the Upoko River. After marching a distance of eight miles the brigade came into action with some 2,000 of the enemy; they were so strongly ensconced amongst high rocks, however, and the country was so intersected with dongas, that the cavalry could not act with much effect. In this skirmish Lieutenant and Adjutant Cokayne Frith, 17th Lancers, was shot through the heart.

The Division and the Flying Column slowly made their way forward, garrisoning a long chain of fortified positions behind them as they advanced. Fort Newdigate, constructed on the Nondwini River, was commenced on June the 5th; Fort Marshall, on the Upoko and in the neighbourhood of Izipesi Hill, on the 18th; Fort Evelyn, on the Umlatoosi River, on the 23rd.

The Cavalry Brigade from the date of its arrival was constantly employed in reconnoitring, and the whole of the scouting for miles ahead and on the flanks of the Infantry fell to its lot. On General Marshall devolved the arduous and responsible duty of maintaining, with only one squadron of Dragoons, the communications, of securing the flanks of the invading force, and, generally, of taking charge of everything behind it. With no vehicles of transport of any kind excepting the Army Service waggons (with which nearly as much was consumed as they were capable of carrying), and such wrecked ox-waggons as he could secure from the field of Isandhlwana and repair, that officer succeeded in less than four weeks in supplying Forts Newdigate and Marshall with two months' provisions for the whole force.

On June the 30th, the invading force marched to within ten miles of the Umvolosi River, and there encamped. About mid-day two emissaries arrived from Cetchwayo, bearing the sword of the late Prince Imperial, and professing a desire to come to terms of peace. They were at once sent back with orders to inform the King that if he would send in, before the 3rd of July, the guns he had taken at Isandhlwana, as an earnest of his desire to surrender, Lord Chelmsford would abstain from burning his kraals.

On July the 1st, the advance was continued over a difficult country, the track passing through cactus and mimosa bush. After considerable labour on the part of the troops in clearing the road and levelling the drifts, the Column reached the Umvolosi River about 1 p.m. The enemy's picquets fell back on its approach; no opposition was offered, and by dusk the position taken up had been made perfectly defensible. On the ensuing day, the 2nd Division closed up to the Flying Column, and an entrenched camp, with a stone fort, was formed on such a plan as would enable it to be defended by a small garrison, and would leave the remainder of the force free to operate as might be deemed desirable. The Zulu army did not show itself during the day, and no messengers arrived from the King; a large herd of white cattle was observed, however, being driven from his kraal towards the camp, and it was subsequently ascertained that these had been sent by the King as a peace-offering, but had been turned back by one of his regiments.

On the morning of July the 3rd, Lord Chelmsford directed Colonel Buller to make a reconnaissance with his mounted men towards Ulundi, with a view to finding out a favourable position for the next halting place of the Column. The party crossed the river by the lower drift to the right of the camp, and was soon in possession of the high ground in front, and of the Undabakaombie Kraal. Having collected his men near the kraal from the thorny country near the river, Colonel Buller advanced rapidly towards Ulundi, passing Nondwengo on his right. He had reached the vicinity of the stream Untukuwini, about three-quarters of a mile from Ulundi, when he was met by a heavy fire from a considerable body of the enemy lying concealed in the long grass, which had been carefully plaited to trip up the horses. Wheeling about, Colonel Buller retired deliberately to the high ground near Nondwengo, suffering a loss of three men killed, notwithstanding the gallant exertions of himself and his officers to save them. In the meantime, large reinforcements of the enemy were to be seen advancing from all directions. Though they moved forward rapidly, and endeavoured to get round his flank, Colonel Buller was able to withdraw his force across the river, and to take back to Lord Chelmsford a report of the district reconnoitred, which subsequently proved to be of the greatest value. Throughout the night of the 3rd, the Zulus were moving about in large numbers, as testified by the sound of their war-songs, but no attack was made.

At 4 a.m., on the 4th, the troops were silently roused; the bugles, however, sounding the reveille at the usual hour, 5.15. Leaving the camp with a garrison of 763 Europeans and 203 natives, under Colonel Bellairs, D. A. G., Lord Chelmsford crossed the river at 6.45 a.m., with the remainder of his force—viz., 1,884 Europeans, and 540 natives of the 2nd Division, and 2,281 Europeans, and 465 natives of the Flying Column. Colonel Buller's mounted men, crossing by the lower ford, seized the high ground on the front without opposition.

The force advanced in a hollow square, the sides being formed by the 1st Battalion 13th Regiment, the 2nd Battalion 21st Regiment, the 58th, 80th, 90th, and 94th Regiment, the rear and flanks being covered by a squadron of the King's Dragoon Guards, the 17th Lancers, and the Mounted Irregulars; the ammunition, tool-carts, &c. moved in the centre, and the guns were placed in the angles, and in the centre of each square. Passing over a mile of very bushy ground, the force reached the high ground between the Undabakaombie and Nodwengo Kraals at 7.30 a.m. By this time the advance from camp was evidently observed, for dark clusters of men could be seen by the morning light on the hill-tops to the left and left front. To the right, where the largest number of the enemy were believed to be, but little could be seen, as the mist from the river and the smoke from the camp fires hung heavily over the bush below. Leaving the Undabakaombie Kraal, which was burnt by the rear guard, to the left, the column advanced to the position previously reported on by Colonel Buller; this was on high ground uncommanded from any point, with but little cover, beyond long grass, near it, and was some 700 yards from Nodwengo, and about the same distance from the stream which crosses the road half-way to Ulundi. At this point Lord Chelmsford wheeled the square to the right, with its front face towards Ulundi; it was then halted, and the faces formed fours outwards, the men in the fourth ranks filling the intervals between the men in the third, the first and second ranks kneeling, the remainder standing, and all with fixed bayonets. The portions of the Zulu army on the left and left front were now formed in good order, and were steadily advancing to the attack; masses also appeared from the thorny country on the right, and passed round Nodwengo and to the rear, thus completely encircling the column.

The battle commenced about 8.45 a.m. by the mounted men on the right and left becoming engaged. Slowly retiring until the enemy came within range, they passed into the square, which now opened fire with artillery and rifles. Shortly before 9 a.m. the Zulu army attacked the column on every side. Four of the Zulu regiments, taken by surprise by the early and silent advance, came on rapidly from the Nodwengo Kraal without any order in their movements. Hurrying up from their bivouacs, they had no time to form up separately, but advanced in a cloud to the attack from out of the cover of the kraal; the fire with which they were met, however, from the right face of the column, proved too heavy for them, and, failing to advance, the bulk of them rapidly passed to the right and joined another regiment which was now pressing up to the attack in a determined manner. Passing along a valley to the rear of the column, which afforded them complete shelter to a point within 150 yards of the right rear corner, the enemy collected rapidly, and made a dash at the guns situated between the 58th and 21st Regiments. Rushing forward with extraordinary bravery, they got within thirty yards of the line at this point, before the galling and destructive fire which was poured into them could stay their advance.

The fire of the enemy from shortly before 9 o'clock to 9.20 was very heavy, and many casualties occurred; it was returned, however, so effectively by the artillery and infantry that within half an hour signs of wavering in the attack became perceivable. Lord Chelmsford now directed Colonel Drury Lowe to take out the 17th Lancers. Passing through the rear face of the square, he led his regiment towards the Nodwengo Kraal, dispersing and killing those who had not time to reach its shelter or that of the bush below; then, wheeling to the right, charged through the remainder, who, in full flight, were endeavouring to reach the lower slopes of the mountains beyond. Numbers of the enemy in this direction, who had not taken part in the actual attack, were now firing, and, momentarily strengthened by those retreating, were enabled to pour in a considerable fusillade on the advancing Lancers below them. Captain Wyatt-Edgell, gallantly leading his troop, was here shot. The cavalry did not halt, however, until the whole of the lower ground was swept, and some 150 of the enemy killed. Many of those whom they had passed in their speed, and who had collected in a ravine to the rear, were attacked and destroyed by the Mounted Natives.

The flight of the Zulu army was now general; the slopes of the hills were, however, beyond the reach of the already fatigued cavalry, and Colonel Drury Lowe, having no fresh troops to support him, rallied his men. Meanwhile Colonel Buller had posted the Mounted Infantry so as to fire into the flank of the retiring enemy, and the remainder of his mounted men, making for the country beyond, killed some 450 in the pursuit. The nine-pounder guns were shortly afterwards moved from the rear and front faces of the square, and made excellent practice on the enemy retreating over the hills to the east between Ulundi and the Umvolosi. As soon as the wounded had been attended to, the force advanced to the banks of the stream near Ulundi, while the mounted men and cavalry swept the country beyond.

The estimated number of the enemy who took part in the attack was 25,000, of whom some 1,500 were killed. The British casualties were eighteen killed, and eighty-five wounded.

Ulundi was fired at 11.40 a.m. At 2 p.m. the force commenced its return march to the camp on the right bank of the Umvolosi, which it reached by sunset. Every military kraal undestroyed up to this time in the valley of the river was now in flames. Not a sign of the vast army which had made the attack in the morning was to be seen in any direction.

The 1st Division, or Coast Column, under General Crealock, though it had not been opposed by Zulus in the field, had contributed in no small measure to the eventual success of the campaign. The task that had been allotted to it by Lord Chelmsford was, to establish a series of fortified posts along the south coast of Zululand; to establish an advanced depôt of supplies for three months; to open a new base of supplies at Port Durnford from which to feed a force operating against Ulundi (should such an advance be required); to destroy the military kraal of Emangwene; to destroy the King's old military kraal at Undine; to enforce the submission of the Zulus throughout the whole of the district between St. Lucia Bay and the Tugela. In the face of very great difficulties, and with its ranks thinned day by day with disease and death, the Coast Column succeeded in the responsible duty of carrying out this programme to the letter.

The end was now at hand. With the battle of Ulundi the Zulu power completely broke down, and Cetchwayo was driven, a fugitive, into the bush. Lord Chelmsford, having accomplished the object of his advance, fell back with Wood's Column by the eastern road to Pietermaritzburg, and shortly after arriving there departed for England. Sir Garnet Wolseley, into whose hands the chief military and civil command in the eastern part of South Africa had been placed by the Home Government, and who had recently arrived in Natal, at once broke up the then existing organization of the forces, and, confident in the collapse of the Zulu power, ordered several of the regiments home. Small flying columns were organized for the pursuit of Cetchwayo, who, on August the 28th, was captured by Major Marter with a detachment of the King's Dragoon Guards. Meantime the Zulu chiefs had flocked in on all sides to tender their submission.

On the 1st of September—exactly six years from the day of Cetchwayo's accession to the throne—a great meeting was held, and a new constitution of Zululand was proclaimed by Sir Garnet Wolseley to the assembled warriors, amidst universal acclamations.

THE PRINCE IMPERIAL.

THE PRINCE IMPERIAL.

NAPOLEON EUGÈNE LOUIS JOHN JOSEPH BUONAPARTE, PRINCE IMPERIAL, who was killed in a reconnaissance near the Ityotyozi River, Zululand, on the 1st of June, 1879, was the only son of the Emperor Napoleon III. and the Empress Eugénie. He was born at the Palace of the Tuileries in Paris on the 16th of March, 1856, and passed the earliest years of his life in France. In the first days of his childhood his name was enrolled on the list of Grenadiers of the Imperial Guard, and he was promoted to the rank of corporal at six years of age. His education was carefully conducted under the superintendence of General Froissard, and in his studies, as in all manly exercises, which he pursued with keen zest, he early became proficient. In 1868 he visited Corsica, the cradle of the Buonaparte family, and attended the centenary festival of the annexation of that island to France. War having broken out in July, 1870, between France and Germany, the Emperor left Paris to join the army between Metz and Saarbrück, taking his son, then aged fourteen, and a sub-lieutenant in the Guards, with him. The Prince was present on the hills above Saarbrück during the engagement at their base, but was shortly afterwards sent away from the army in consequence of the reverses sustained by the French arms. The surrender of Napoleon III. as a prisoner of war after the battle of Sedan gave rise to the establishment of the French Republic, when the Empress Eugénie took refuge in England, where shortly afterwards the Prince, who had passed through Belgium, was conducted to her by Count Clary. Upon the termination of the war the Emperor was released from his captivity, and joined the Empress and the Prince in this country, taking up his residence at Chislehurst.

With a view to the education of the Prince, permission was obtained from Her Majesty's Government for him to enter the Royal Military Academy at Woolwich, which he joined in November, 1872. With respect to his studies, he was at first under a considerable disadvantage, from his imperfect knowledge of the English language; moreover, the death of the Emperor, his father, for whom he had the deepest reverence and the most devoted filial attachment—which occurred in January, 1873, and affected him very deeply—caused his temporary withdrawal from the Academy, so that he lost his first term. He afterwards succeeded, however, by his unremitting diligence and by the strong determination of his character, in overcoming the difficulty of the language; in each successive examination he obtained a higher place in his class, until at length, in February, 1875, in the final examination, he stood seventh by competition in a class of thirty-four—a position which would have entitled him to select service in either the Artillery or the Engineers, if it had been intended that he should enter the British army.

The Prince held the rank of corporal in the Cadet company, and was highly complimented by H.R.H. the Duke of Cambridge, at his inspection on February the 16th, 1875, for the manner in which he moved the battalion, and put it through the manual and platoon exercise: he also was the best rider in his class, thus giving early proof of a quality for which he afterwards became well known. The Governor of the Royal Military Academy, General Sir Lintorn Simmons, in a report addressed to the Duke of Cambridge, stated that "the Prince Imperial, by his invariable punctuality and exactitude in the performance of his duties, by his perfect respect for authority and submission to discipline, has set an example which deserves honourable mention."

After leaving the Academy, the Prince, in the autumn of 1875, joined a battery of field artillery under the command of Major Ward Assheton, R.A., and did duty with it as an honorary lieutenant at the manœuvres; by his kindly, genial nature, he made many fast friends among the officers, and became a great favourite with the men, for whose comfort and welfare, during a very wet season under canvas, he was always most thoughtful. He was also attached to a battery of field artillery during the manœuvres in the autumn of the following year, and subsequently travelled for a short time on the Continent. Returning to England, he took up his residence at Chislehurst, and there devoted himself to the study of history, of political economy, and of passing events, with the view of fitting himself for the high position to which he always conceived it probable that the voice of his country might call him.

When the news of the disaster at Isandhlwana reached England, and the hasty preparation and despatch of troops to the seat of war followed, the Prince considered that a good opportunity presented itself for making himself practically acquainted with the movements and operations of an army in the field, in a manner to which—as being removed from the complication of civilized politics—exception could not be taken by any European Power or political party, as might have been done had he joined either of the contending armies in the Turko-Russian, or even in the Afghan, war. He, moreover, longed to share the fatigue and risks of service in the field with several of his most intimate friends who had been his comrades in the Artillery, and had already gone to South Africa; and could not bear the thought of remaining at ease at home while they were serving their country in a war the result of which, as he said, could only tend to the advance of civilization. He therefore requested permission to join the army in South Africa, but this was refused him; he nevertheless left England on the 27th of February, 1879, with letters of introduction from the Duke of Cambridge and from the Secretaries of State for War and for the Colonies to Sir Bartle Frere and Lord Chelmsford, in the hope that he might be allowed to follow the movements of the army, and that his services might possibly be turned to some useful account by the General in command. He received no commission either from the Home or Local Government, but shortly after his arrival at Durban joined the General's Head-Quarters, and meeting Lord Chelmsford for the first time on the 9th of April, became his guest, and was nominally placed upon his staff.

A few days afterwards the Prince was attacked with fever, from which, however, he soon recovered: he then left Maritzburg, where he had been detained, in order to rejoin the Head-Quarters Staff as an extra aide-de-camp to Lord Chelmsford. On the 2nd of May he started with the General and some of his staff from Dundee, and marched *viâ* Landman's Drift and Balte's Spruit to General Wood's camp at Kambula, and thence by Conference Hill to Utrecht, where the remainder of the staff joined the General on the 7th. On the 8th of May Lord Chelmsford appointed Colonel Harrison, R.E., Assistant Quartermaster-General at Head-Quarters, to take charge of the whole of that department, with Lieutenant Carey, 98th Regiment, as Deputy-Assistant; and the same day requested the former to give the Prince some employment, as he was eager to be of use, and did not find enough occupation in his capacity of extra aide-de-camp. The Prince was accordingly employed by Colonel Harrison to collect and record information as to the distribution of troops, stores, &c. On the 13th he marched to Conference Hill, and started thence on the following day on a reconnaissance into a part of Zululand which was believed to be strongly held by the enemy. This reconnaissance was conducted by Colonel Harrison, under the escort of Colonel Redvers Buller, V.C., C.B., and about 200 officers and men of the Volunteer Horse.

The night of the 14th the party bivouacked at a deserted farm, and the next day pushed on, driving back some scouts, but not coming into close contact with the enemy. During the succeeding night the horses were kept saddled and bridled, and on the 16th the party reached General Wood's camp at Kambula. On the 17th they returned to Conference Hill, when Colonel Harrison, who was about to start on another reconnaissance, sent the Prince to rejoin Lord Chelmsford at Utrecht. The Prince, however, stopped on the road at Balte's Spruit, and sent a message to his lordship, begging permission to take part in the reconnaissance.

Colonel Harrison had started, and was already a mile or two on the Zulu side of the Blood River on the morning of the 18th, when the Prince, whose request had been granted, joined him, having galloped all the way alone from Balte's Spruit. The reconnoitring party on this occasion was under the personal command of Colonel Harrison, who expected to meet Colonel Buller in the course of the afternoon. It consisted of an officer and five men of the Natal Horse and an officer and twenty Basutos, in addition to the Prince, his servant, who was an old pensioner, and Lieutenant Carey. They failed to find Colonel Buller and his party. In the evening they bivouacked, taking every possible precaution, the setting sun having shown Zulus on the neighbouring hills.

Next morning, the 19th, the party were ascending a hill in search of a road when they were suddenly confronted by about sixty Zulus, who appeared lining the rocks on the top of the hill, and at once opened fire, at the same time adopting their usual tactics, sending men down the hill to the right and left to outflank the force they were attacking. Any hesitation at that moment might have endangered the whole party, but fortunately Captain Bettington, of the Natal Horse, who was leading, was equal to the occasion, and dashed straight up a steep path against the enemy's centre, followed by the Prince, Colonel Harrison, the few Europeans, and some of the Basutos, the remainder of whom at first hung back. The boldness of this onslaught brought success, the Zulus, who sustained some loss, turning and fleeing. The reconnaissance was continued throughout the day and the greater part of the following night, with occasional halts. On the morning of the 20th the party returned to Conference Hill, whence the Prince accompanied Colonel Harrison at once to Utrecht to report to Lord Chelmsford.

The Prince was much pleased with this employment: the night bivouac, the simple fare cooked by himself at the camp fire, the march by day, during which he took careful observations and notes, and the occasional gallops after some scout on a hill in front, all interested him exceedingly, and made him feel, as he himself said, as though he were doing real soldier's duty. The amount of work done and of country traversed during these few days, from the 13th to the 20th, show that he had quite recovered from his fever, and that he was determined to make himself useful to the utmost while taking a full share of the risks of the war.

After this, the talents of the Prince, who was a good draughtsman, were turned to useful account by the Assistant-Quartermaster-General, who employed him in compiling a map of the country from the reconnaissance sketches made by himself and others. On the 28th the force moved to Koppie Allein, on the Blood River, and on that and the two following days reconnaissances were made by Lieutenant Carey and other officers far into Zululand: large and small parties, and even single officers, went all over the country beyond the spot where the Prince was subsequently killed without seeing any of the enemy.

On the 31st of May the Prince, having asked Colonel Harrison, as was his constant daily practice, for more active work, was desired to go and report on the road and camping-ground for the 2nd Division, which was to march on the following day; and Lieutenant Carey, who volunteered to accompany him, was instructed to do so, with a native interpreter and an escort of six European troopers and six Basutos. The party thus detailed was considered sufficient for security, as the whole division was advancing in the immediate neighbourhood.

The Prince started accordingly at 9.30 a.m. with Lieutenant Carey and the escort of six Natal Horse, but unfortunately without the Basutos. A messenger was sent for these before the Blood River was crossed, but returned to say that they would join the escort on a ridge between the Incenzi and Itelezi Hills, some eight miles distant from the camp. The party accordingly rode on. After reaching the ridge they were overtaken by Colonel Harrison, to whom it was stated that they were waiting for the rest of the escort, the Basutos. Lieutenant Carey was occupied with Colonel Harrison for about half an hour, and after some further delay, during which Colonel Harrison and his party were more or less dispersed examining the ground for camping, the Prince, with Lieutenant Carey and the six troopers, went down from the ridge to a watercourse in the valley below. It appears that, although the Basutos are looked upon as the most essential part of a small escort, owing to their wonderful powers of sight and hearing, and their quick perception of danger, the Prince and Lieutenant Carey did not wait for those detailed to accompany them, nor did they take any of them from the scouts in front, but proceeded on their expedition. After a short time they reached a commanding and rocky range of hills overlooking the Ityotyozi River, and there dismounted and halted for half an hour, during which the Prince made this last entry in his note-book: "1.20. Extremity of the ridge between the Tombokole and Ityotyozi. Good camping-ground on slope south of Donga;" and sketched in beneath the entry a view of the country lying immediately beyond the very spot where, two hours and a half later, he was killed, and embracing outlines of the distant hills, against which he marked their names.

A kraal was sighted about a mile further on, and towards this the party descended, the Prince having observed that a stream which ran past it would enable them to water their horses, and make themselves some coffee. Between the kraal and the stream stretched a luxuriant growth of tambookie grass five or six feet in height, with—after the fashion of all deserted Zulu kraals—mealies and Kaffir corn interspersed. The dense covert did not, however, completely surround the kraal, for in front there was an open space, apparently used by the Zulus as a common cooking-ground. Here the party halted, and off-saddled for an hour. The huts betrayed no signs of recent occupation, and as Lieutenant Carey had been twice before in the neighbourhood without having seen a Zulu, and a third time three miles beyond the kraal, when he ascertained from the reports of a native woman that all the men had left for Ulundi, the position was considered a perfectly safe one, and no precautions whatever were taken. The horses having been turned into the grass, and the Kaffir sent to the stream for water, all the party sat down in the open space, and made themselves some coffee. It is reported that the Prince was tired, and lay down beside one of the huts, and that Lieutenant Carey reconnoitred the surrounding country with his telescope; the Kaffir meanwhile went off again to see that the horses kept together, and so the hour wore on. At this time some forty Zulus, concealed by a deep donga, must have been creeping on towards their victims. Stealing out of the donga, they appear to have made their way, completely concealed by the rank vegetation, along the water's edge. While thus in ambush they seem to have been surprised by the Kaffir, for one of them left his concealment, and, crossing the stream, was seen by him making off up the opposite hill. It was now about 3.40 p.m. The party caught their horses, and while saddling them were informed by the native, who had returned, that he had seen the Zulu; as he did not, however, appear to be concerned, no danger seems to have been apprehended.

The Prince, who is stated to have saddled-up first, waited until, in a soldier-like manner, he had asked the men, "Are you all ready?" and had received the reply, "Yes, sir," when he gave the order, "Prepare to mount." At this moment, suddenly, there burst from the cover a rifle-volley, and with a loud shout the Zulus rushed towards the party. The horses all swerved at the suddenness of the tumult, and some broke away. One of the escort was shot while still on foot, another directly he was mounted, and the rest fled precipitately. The Zulus started in pursuit, yelling and firing after the fugitives. The Prince's horse followed the others, and the Prince was seen holding the stirrup-leather with his left hand and the saddle with his right, trying to mount. The last man who seems to have seen him was a trooper named Letocq, who was lying across his saddle unable to get into it, and who, as he passed, cried out, "Dépêchez-vous, monsieur, de monter," so that, strange to say, the last words uttered by European lips which the poor Prince heard were in the same language which had first greeted him at his birth. He must have made one desperate effort to leap into the saddle with the help of the holster, and the holster must have given way. Sir Evelyn Wood, accompanying the Empress Eugénie on a visit to the fatal spot, twelve months afterwards, elicited the following details of the catastrophe from a party of eighteen Zulus who had taken part in the attack, and who were examined separately and out of sight of one another:—

"The attacking party numbered about forty, of whom twelve followed the

Prince, and either seven or eight were concerned immediately in his death. The Zulus, having nearly surrounded the party, fired and rushed on them as they were in the act of mounting. The Prince, not having succeeded in mounting, ran alongside of his horse until it broke away from him, on the hither bank of the donga, about 220 yards from the kraal where the party had off-saddled. The Prince followed his horse into the Donga, until closely pressed by his pursuers, when he turned upon them, in the words of the Zulus themselves, 'Like a lion at bay.' Struck by an assegai inside the left shoulder, he rushed at his nearest opponent, who fled out of the donga, and got behind another Zulu, who, coming up, fired at the Prince when only ten yards from him. The Prince returned the fire with his pistol, and faced his now rapidly increasing foes until, menaced from his right rear and struck by another assegai, he regained the level spot on which he had first stood in the donga, and where he was speedily surrounded. He then seized an assegai which had been thrown at him, for, in struggling with his terrified horse, his sword had fallen from its scabbard. He thus defended himself against seven or eight Zulus, who state that they did not dare to close on him, until exhausted he sank down on his hips."

After the fugitives had ridden some hundreds of yards they drew up for a moment on rising ground, and Lieutenant Carey had his attention drawn to the Prince's horse, which was seen galloping away by one of the men, who said that he feared the Prince was killed; they then rode on towards General Wood's camp, one of the troopers catching the horse on the way. After the party had gone some three miles, they met General Wood and Colonel Buller, who, looking through their glasses, were able to descry the Zulus leading away the horses they had captured—the trophies of their successful attack.

On the following morning a cavalry patrol under General Marshall left the camp between the Incenzi and Itelezi Hills at 7 a.m. to search for the Prince's body. They found it lying at the bottom of the donga, about two hundred yards north-east of the kraal. It was stripped of everything with the exception of a gold chain with medallions attached, which was still around the neck. The sword, revolver, helmet, and clothes were gone; but the spurs, and one sock, were discovered in the grass, which showed evident signs of a severe struggle. The body had seventeen wounds upon it, all in front, any five of which would have been, according to the testimony of Dr. Scott, who examined them, fatal,—thus proving, if further proof were needed, that the Prince had turned on his pursuers, and had fallen, after a desperate resistance, as a gallant and true soldier, with his face to the foe, fighting to the last. On examining his saddle it was found that the strap connecting the holsters had given way: this may account for his failure in mounting, which seemed so remarkable, as he was seldom known to use a stirrup for the purpose, but was always in the habit of vaulting into the saddle.

The Prince, during the short time he was with the Head-Quarters Staff of the army, in addition to the topographical work upon which he was employed, wrote several reports, which gave such proof of his powers of observation, of method in arranging his facts, of good judgment and originality of thought, that a staff officer who knew him, and had the best opportunities of judging of him, said that he was, notwithstanding his want of experience, one of the best staff officers with the army.

The remains of the Prince, which passed through the colony amidst expressions of universal sorrow, were borne to England in H.M.S. "Orontes," and were landed at Woolwich on the 10th of July. On the evening of the 11th they were escorted from Woolwich to the imperial residence at Chislehurst by a troop of the Royal Artillery. A military funeral, at which the Queen, the Ambassadors of the Court, and the principal dignitaries of the realm were present, took place on the following day, when the Prince's body was consigned to a temporary resting-place in the Roman Catholic Chapel of St. Mary's, Chislehurst, in which the remains of Napoleon III. were already deposited. The Prince of Wales, the Duke of Edinburgh, the Duke of Connaught, Prince Leopold, the Crown Prince of Norway and Sweden, the Duke of Cambridge, the Duke of Bassano, and M. Rouher acted as pall-bearers. Every regiment at Aldershot and all arms of the service were represented, and an immense concourse of all classes of the community testified by their presence to the estimation in which they held him who had given to their country all that he had to give—his service and his life.

WALTER GLYN LAWRELL,

Captain, 4th Hussars (Queen's Own).

WALTER GLYN LAWRELL,

CAPTAIN, 4TH HUSSARS.

CAPTAIN WALTER GLYN LAWRELL, who was killed at the storming of Sekukuni's stronghold, South Africa, on the 28th of November, 1879, was the eldest son of the Rev. John Lawrell, of Hampshire. He was born on the 10th of April, 1844, near Christchurch, and was educated at Charterhouse. Subsequently to his leaving school he obtained, and held for a short period, an appointment in the War Office. Competing at the Army Examination for direct commissions, he passed first in the list of successful candidates, and on the 8th of December, 1865, was gazetted to a cornetcy in the 9th Lancers. He served with that regiment at various home stations. In July, 1870, he obtained his troop.

In December, 1871, Captain Lawrell exchanged into the 4th Hussars, then stationed at Delhi. After serving in India for a period of seven years, he returned with the regiment, in January, 1879, to England. On the news of the disaster at Isandhlwana reaching this country in February, he immediately volunteered for the Cape: it was not, however, until three months later that his services were accepted. He embarked for South Africa at the latter end of June, but reached his destination too late to admit of his taking an active part in the Zulu war. Shortly after his arrival he was appointed orderly officer to Sir Baker Russell, a column under whom had been formed by Sir Garnet Wolseley to carry on hostile operations against the rebel chief Sekukuni, who, from his almost inaccessible fastness in the Transvaal, was defying the authority of the Government. In the successful assault made upon this stronghold on the 28th of November, Captain Lawrell, clambering over the jagged and boulder-strewn heights, had succeeded in reaching a ledge almost opposite to the mouth of the cave into which the enemy had retired, when a bullet struck him in the throat, killing him almost instantaneously.

In Captain Lawrell the service lost a most brave and valued officer; his brother officers, a well-loved companion; his men, a true friend and stanch supporter; and society, a gentleman of sense and honour, whose amiability and moral rectitude had gained for him the esteem of all.

Captain Lawrell married, in December, 1874, Mary, daughter of John Hamilton, Esq., of Tyne Court, Somersetshire.

THE HON. EDMUND VERNEY WYATT-EDGELL,

Captain 17th (Duke of Cambridge's Own) Lancers.

THE

HON. EDMUND VERNEY WYATT-EDGELL,

CAPTAIN, 17TH LANCERS.

CAPTAIN EDMUND VERNEY WYATT-EDGELL, who was killed in action at Ulundi on the 4th of July, 1879, was the eldest son of the Rev. Edgell Wyatt-Edgell, by his marriage with Henrietta, fourth Baroness Braye; was grandson of Mr. Wyatt-Edgell, formerly of Milton Place, Egham, and of Great Missenden; was heir-apparent to the barony of Braye, and represented in his own person the ancient and political family of the Earls Verney (this earldom is extinct), and also the elder branch of the Caves, of Stanford Hall, Leicestershire. He was born on the 16th of August, 1845, and was educated at Eton, and Christ Church, Oxford. He entered the army in 1866, being gazetted cornet in the 17th Lancers; became lieutenant, by purchase, in 1868; and obtained his troop in 1873. Captain Wyatt-Edgell spent much of his leisure time in study, especially of the Latin classics, of which he read even the most obscure; and he was considered one of the best French, as well as Latin, scholars in the army. During a winter's leave he rode through the whole length of Persia, and spent some time at Teheran; he completed his journey in safety, though quite unattended. On a vacancy occurring in the representation of the northern division of Northamptonshire, in 1877, through the death of Mr. Ward Hunt, he contested the seat in the Liberal interest, being opposed by Lord Burghley, who was returned. In February, 1879, he entered the Staff College, where, however, he was only destined to spend a fortnight.

Captain Wyatt-Edgell embarked with the 17th Lancers for Natal in the last days of the same February, shortly after the news of the disaster at Isandhlwana reached England. He landed at Durban soon after the battle of Ginghilovo and the evacuation of Etshowe, and, on the return of Lord Chelmsford with the relieving column to Natal, proceeded with the Lancers into the interior. With the right wing of the regiment, under Colonel Drury Lowe, he joined General Newdigate's division, then in course of formation, at Conference Hill, on the 11th of May, and subsequently served with his troop through the whole of the reconnoitring and other important duty on which it was employed during the advance of that force into the enemy's country.

On the morning of the 4th of July, the 17th Lancers covered the rear and flanks of the advancing column, and on the force being attacked by the enemy, passed into the hollow square in which it was formed. When the fire of the enemy slackened, Colonel Drury Lowe received orders to take out the regiment to strike the then wavering line. Passing through the rear face of the square, the regiment rode towards the Nodwengo Kraal, dispersing and killing those who had not time to reach its shelter; then, wheeling to the right, charged through the remainder, who, in full flight, were endeavouring to reach the lower slopes of the mountains beyond. Numbers of the enemy in this direction, who had not taken part in the actual attack, were now firing, and, momentarily strengthened by those retreating, were enabled to pour in a considerable fusillade on the advancing Lancers below them. It was at this moment that Captain Wyatt-Edgell, gallantly leading his troop, was shot through the head.

" The country has lost a very gallant officer." Such were the words of the Secretary of State for War when he announced to the House of Commons the victory at Ulundi; and the feeling which they expressed has found an echo in the hearts of all to whom Wyatt-Edgell was known. " A more gallant leader," wrote Colonel Drury Lowe, in his official account of the engagement, " never rode in a charge." He will long be remembered in the 17th Lancers for his genial kindness and manly bearing, and the wide circle of friends to whom he had endeared himself will be slow to forget the pleasantness of his ways.

Captain Wyatt-Edgell was by no means the first of his race who has met a soldier's death. At the battle of Edge Hill one of his ancestors, Sir Edmund Verney, standard-bearer to Charles I., was killed; and so firmly did he grasp the staff in death, that the hand had to be amputated before the flag could be released. John, second Lord Braye, fought at the battle of St. Quintin, and died, aged thirty-three, in 1557, from the wounds and exhaustion he had sustained; he was buried with much ceremony in Chelsea Church, where the tomb is still shown. Captain Wyatt-Edgell, had he survived five months, would have succeeded to the barony of Braye as fifth Lord—his mother dying on the 14th of November, 1879.

FREDERICK JOHN COKAYNE FRITH,

LIEUTENANT AND ADJUTANT, 17TH (DUKE OF CAMBRIDGE'S OWN) LANCERS.

FREDERICK JOHN COKAYNE FRITH,

LIEUTENANT AND ADJUTANT, 17TH LANCERS.

LIEUTENANT FREDERICK JOHN COKAYNE FRITH, who was killed at the Erzungayan Hill, near the Upoko River, Zululand, on the 5th of June, 1879, was the second son of Major Cokayne Frith, of Dover, by his marriage with Amelia, daughter of Christopher Kane, M.D., Surgeon-General in the Honourable East India Company's Service, and widow of John S. Denis de Vitré, of the Bombay Civil Service.

He was born at Oban, Argyllshire, on the 22nd September, 1858, and was educated at Mr. Harrison's school at Dunchurch, Warwickshire; and afterwards at Haileybury College, until 1874, when he was prepared for the examination for the army by Mr. John Le Fleming, of Tonbridge.

At the examination in December, 1875, he passed twelfth in the list of successful candidates; and, joining the Royal Military College, Sandhurst, as sub-lieutenant, at the age of seventeen, he passed out in the first class in the following year, and was gazetted on the 16th of February to the 17th Lancers. He had previously received a commission as sub-lieutenant in the Argyll and Bute Artillery Militia in November, 1875, which regiment, however, he never joined, owing to his having passed the army examination direct for Sandhurst in the following month. On succeeding to a lieutenancy in his regiment in 1878, his commission was antedated two years, in consequence of his having obtained a first-class certificate at Sandhurst.

In May, 1878, he joined the School of Musketry at Hythe, and there obtained a first-class certificate. On the 12th of February, 1879, within two years after joining, he was appointed adjutant of his regiment.

On reinforcements being sent out to South Africa, when the news of the disaster at Isandhlwana was received, Lieutenant Cokayne Frith embarked with his regiment at Southampton, in the s.s. "England," on the 26th February, 1879, for Natal. Landing at Durban, the 17th Lancers joined the forces under Lord Chelmsford, and advanced into Zululand with General Newdigate's column.

On the 5th of June a portion of the regiment, under Colonel Drury-Lowe, was engaged in their first skirmish with the enemy at the Erzungayan Hill, near the Upoko River, during which, while in the act of turning his horse at the side of his

Colonel, Lieutenant Cokayne Frith was shot through the heart. His body was taken into the camp on the Nodwini River, and buried the same evening, followed to the grave "by all his brother officers, and by most of the officers in camp, Lord Chelmsford, General Newdigate, and staff included."

Lieutenant Cokayne Frith was a young officer of much promise; active, hard-working, genial, and kind-hearted; he was a general favourite, not only with his brother officers, but with all who knew him; whilst to his own family the loss of so exemplary a son and brother is irremediable.

STUART SMITH,

Major, Royal Artillery.

STUART SMITH,

BREVET-MAJOR, ROYAL ARTILLERY.

MAJOR STUART SMITH, who was killed at Isandhlwana on the 22nd of January, 1879, was the second son of the Rev. Stuart Smith, of Ballintemple, in the county of Cavan, and his wife Henrietta, daughter of William Graham, Esq., of Lisburn in the county of Antrim. He was born at Dumlion Cottage, Ballintemple, on October the 6th, 1844, and was educated at the Royal School of Cavan, Dr. Stacpoole's school at Kingstown, co. Dublin, and the Royal Military Academy at Woolwich, from which he obtained his commission on the 24th of March, 1865.

In the following September he proceeded to India, where he served at various stations until 1876, when he returned to England with the A/A Battery, Royal Horse Artillery. On the 1st of October, 1877, he obtained his company.

Early in 1878 Captain Stuart Smith was posted to the N/5 Battery, Royal Artillery, and went with it to the Cape, where he was employed in the Kaffir war of that year. During the operations in the field, his name was repeatedly mentioned in despatches. Upon one occasion he rallied a force which had got into an ambuscade and become disorganized, and covered it with the fire of two guns, of which he was in command, until it could reform. In the course of the war he led for some time a body of European volunteers, of which he was appointed commandant. In November, 1878, Her Majesty conferred on him a brevet-majority for his distinguished services.

On the massing of the forces on the Natal frontier in view of the impending outbreak of the Zulu war, Major Stuart Smith proceeded with his company to the front, and, in command of two guns of the Royal Artillery, took part in the subsequent advance of Colonel Glyn's column, in January, 1879, into the enemy's country. In the disastrous encounter with the enemy which took place at Isandhlwana on the 22nd, he forfeited his life in performing an act of heroism for which, had he lived, he would surely have been decorated with the Victoria Cross, and which his grateful countrymen will be slow to forget. When the troops left in camp were overwhelmed by the countless hordes of the enemy, Major Stuart Smith calmly and intrepidly spiked his gun, and in doing so received his death-wound. Had he not delayed to perform this act he might, being a bold and skilful horseman, have managed to effect his escape. With characteristic generosity he deliberately chose to lay down his life in destroying the means of dealing death to his comrades.

FRANCIS BROADFOOT RUSSELL,

Major, Royal Artillery.

FRANCIS BROADFOOT RUSSELL,

BREVET-MAJOR, ROYAL ARTILLERY.

MAJOR FRANCIS BROADFOOT RUSSELL, who was killed at Isandhlwana on the 22nd of January, 1879, was the eldest son of Lieutenant-Colonel F. Russell, of the Madras Infantry. He was born in India on September the 4th, 1842. In 1861 he entered the Royal Military Academy at Woolwich, and, on March the 24th, 1865, obtained a commission in the Royal Artillery. He served in Malta and in Canada, and returning to England in 1869, passed through a course of gunnery instruction at Shoeburyness. In 1870 he proceeded to India, and thence to Aden, at which station he was placed in command of the Native Artillery. On the removal of that force to Upper Sind, he was appointed district-adjutant in Aden, and held the appointment for two years.

On obtaining his company in October, 1877, Captain Russell was ordered to join his battery at Pietermaritzburg, and being at that time the senior officer present, held command of it for some months. In November, 1878, he received his brevet-majority. Prior to the outbreak of the Zulu war he acted as district-adjutant on Colonel Pearson's staff, and was about to proceed to the front in that capacity when Lord Chelmsford's forces were massed on the Natal and Transvaal frontiers with a view to the invasion of Zululand; his services were, however, requisitioned to organize a rocket battery, in command of which he left Pietermaritzburg on the 22nd of December, 1878, to join Colonel Durnford's column.

Major Russell crossed the border into Zululand, with the rocket battery, on January the 21st, 1879, and arrived at the camp at Isandhlwana on the forenoon of January the 22nd, a short time after Colonel Durnford, who, with the rest of his force, had ridden on in advance. Immediately after his arrival in camp, Major Russell started in charge of his battery, escorted by a hundred Natal natives under Captain Nourse, with Colonel Durnford and his mounted men, to follow up the Zulus, who by that time had shown themselves in considerable force, and were slowly retiring. After the battery and its escort, distanced by the remainder of the force, had proceeded some three miles, Major Russell was apprised by one of the natives that the enemy were forming upon some neighbouring heights to the left. He immediately wheeled his battery round in the direction indicated, and, after ascending the hill-side, brought it into action. At the first discharge of the mortars, however, immense numbers of the enemy sprang up from the surrounding bush, where they had lain, within a hundred and fifty yards, completely hidden, awaiting the signal for onslaught. Major Russell was one of the first to fall: he met his death, sword in hand, at the head of his little force, striving manfully against the overwhelming odds with which he was beset.

FREDERICK NICOLSON,
Lieutenant, Royal Artillery.

FREDERICK NICOLSON,

LIEUTENANT, ROYAL ARTILLERY.

LIEUTENANT FREDERICK NICOLSON, who died at Kambula, on the 30th of March, 1879, from wounds received in action on the previous day, was the eldest son of Admiral Sir Frederick Nicolson, Bart., C.B., by his marriage with Clementina, daughter of the late James Loch, Esquire, M.P. He was born on the 16th of June, 1848, and was educated at the Rev. J. M. Brackenbury's school, at Wimbledon. In July, 1866, he competed in the examination for admission into the Royal Military Academy at Woolwich, and passed fifth out of a large number of candidates. On leaving the Academy at the end of his course, he elected to serve in the Artillery, and was gazetted to that regiment on the 13th of January, 1869.

After serving for a few months at Woolwich, chiefly in the Riding Establishment, Lieutenant Nicolson sailed for Bombay, in November, 1869, to join the D Battery of the 16th Brigade of Field Artillery. With this battery he served for about four years in India, and continued with it for some months after its return to England. In September, 1874, he was appointed to the Horse Artillery, and served in the Riding Establishment at Woolwich until, two years later, he was transferred to the Chestnut Troop.

In April, 1878, subalterns of Artillery were required for special service in South Africa, and a call was made from the Horse Guards for volunteers. Out of the large number of applicants who sent in their names, three were selected—Lieutenants Nicolson, Bigge, and Slade. On the arrival of these officers at the Cape, Lieutenant Nicolson was ordered to Natal, and thence to the Transvaal, where, in command of two seven-pounders, he took part in the expedition against Sekukuni, under Colonel Rowlands, V.C. Through his exertions, the equipment and organization of his guns, which were manned by artillerymen and men of the 80th Regiment, had been brought to a high state of efficiency, enabling them either to be carried on mule-back or drawn on wheels.

On the amalgamation of the two northern columns, shortly after the outbreak of the Zulu war, Lieutenant Nicolson joined Colonel Wood's force, near Utrecht. This force formed an entrenched camp at Kambula, which was attacked by a large Zulu army for five hours on March the 29th, 1879 While directing the fire of his guns from the parapet of Major Leet's redoubt, which was detached from the camp, Lieutenant Nicolson received the wound from the effects of which he died on the following day.

To the manner in which Lieutenant Nicolson did his duty until he fell, Colonel Wood's despatch bears witness. The high estimation in which he was held by all who knew him is fitly expressed in a notice which appeared in "The Times" of April the 24th, 1879: "Many will be ready to testify that among the gallant men whose loss we are now deploring there was not one of more conspicuous bravery, of more untiring energy and devotion to duty, than Lieutenant Nicolson."

ANTHONY WILLIAM DURNFORD,

COLONEL, ROYAL ENGINEERS.

ANTHONY WILLIAM DURNFORD,

COLONEL, ROYAL ENGINEERS.

COLONEL ANTHONY WILLIAM DURNFORD, who was killed at Isandhlwana on January the 22nd, 1879, was the eldest son of General E. W. Durnford, Colonel Commandant, Royal Engineers. He was born on May the 24th, 1830, and was educated chiefly in Germany. He entered the Royal Military Academy at Woolwich, in July, 1846, and obtained a commission as second lieutenant in the Royal Engineers on June the 27th, 1848; from Woolwich he proceeded to Chatham, and remained there until December, 1849, when he was ordered to Scotland, where he served at Edinburgh and Fort George. In October, 1851, he embarked for Ceylon, and upon his arrival was stationed at Trincomalee; there he gave so much assistance to Admiral Sir F. Pellew, relative to the defenceless state of the harbour, that the services he rendered were brought to the notice of the Master-General of the Ordnance by the Lords of the Admiralty. In 1855 he entered upon civil in addition to military duties, being appointed Assistant Commissioner of Roads and Civil Engineer to the Colony. Early in 1856 he proceeded to Malta, and was employed there as Adjutant until February, 1858, when he returned to England. After a short time spent at Chatham and Aldershot he proceeded to Gibraltar in December, 1860, in command of the 27th Company, and served there until August, 1864, when he again returned to England. In the latter part of the same year he embarked for China, but was landed at Ceylon, suffering from heat apoplexy, and was invalided home. From May, 1865, until 1870, he served at Devonport, and then for a short period at Dublin. At the end of 1871 he embarked for South Africa; upon his arrival he was employed for a short time at Cape Town and King William's Town, and then proceeded to Natal, where he formed one of the expedition that accompanied the Minister for Native Affairs into Zululand to be present at the coronation of King Cetchwayo in August, 1873. He subsequently acted as Colonial Engineer in addition to performing his own duties, and under his superintendence much valuable work was done for the Colony.

Colonel Durnford came prominently into public notice towards the close of 1873, at the time of the Langalibalele affair, when he was the senior officer of Royal Engineers in Natal. He was ordered to proceed by a forced night march to seize and hold the Bushman's River Pass, to prevent the escape of Langalibalele. It was supposed that he would be able to arrive there in one night, and he started at dark with the Karkloof Carabineers under Captain Barter, twenty men of the Natal Carabineers, and some twenty Basutos as guides. The greatest ignorance had prevailed as to the distance of the pass and the impracticableness of the way. Major Durnford found he had to cross an almost inaccessible mountain range, over 9,000 feet high, and to move along dangerous and most difficult ground. Nothing daunted, however, he pushed on, and although he lost many men too exhausted to proceed, and nearly all the pack-horses with rations and ammunition, and met with an accident by which his shoulder was dislocated and his head and body injured from his horse falling over a precipice, he yet struggled on in the hope that he might arrive in time to effect his object. He succeeded in reaching his destination at 5.30 a.m., on November 4th, 1873, having been dragged up the Giant's Castle Pass during the previous night by aid of a blanket, thirty-six hours instead of twelve after starting, with only thirty-eight rank and file left, and all exhausted from fatigue and want of food. No sooner had he formed across the mouth of the pass than he became aware that he was too late, and that the natives were not only in front of him, but on either flank. His orders were "not to fire the first shot;" so, attended only by his interpreter, he went forward to endeavour to persuade the natives to return peaceably. This, however, they refused to do, and the volunteers wavering, he at last reluctantly directed an orderly retreat to higher ground, from which he could still command the pass. On a heavy fire being opened upon his force, the retreat became a stampede : three of the Carabineers and one Basuto fell, the horse of the interpreter was killed, and Major Durnford, while endeavouring to reach its rider by leaping over a deep gully, in order to lift him on to his own horse, was surrounded and left alone, the interpreter being killed by his side. Shooting his assailants, who had seized his horse's bridle, he rode through the enemy, under a shower of bullets and assegais, receiving, besides several minor wounds, one from an assegai through the left arm, near the elbow, which severed the muscles and nerves, and from which he permanently lost the use of the limb. Rallying the Basutos and a few of the Carabineers, he covered the retreat of the force, which was pursued as far as the Giant's Castle Pass. The head-quarters camp was reached about 1 a.m. on the 5th. At 11 p.m. on that day, Major Durnford let out a volunteer party (artillery with rockets, fifty men of the 75th Regiment, seven Carabineers, and thirty Basutos) to the rescue of Captain Boyes, 75th Regiment, who had been sent out with a support on the 3rd, and was believed to be in great danger. Major Durnford had received such serious injuries that the doctor endeavoured to dissuade him from further exertion, but as those sent to his support were in danger, and he knew the country, he determined to go. He was lifted on to his horse and left amid the cheers of the troops in camp. Having marched all night—resting only from from 3 to 5 a.m.—his force met that of Captain Boyes about mid-day. For his conduct in this affair Major Durnford was thanked in Field Force Orders for his "courage and coolness."

In 1874 he patrolled the country, and carried out by means of natives the demolition of the passes in the Draakensberg Mountains in severe winter weather, restoring confidence among the colonists. For this service he received the written thanks of the Local Government.

In July, 1876, Colonel Durnford returned to England. He was mentioned in General Orders issued by General Sir A. Cunynghame, on quitting the Cape; was thanked by the Colonial Office for his services in Natal, and was recommended for a C.M.G. He was awarded a gratuity of one year's pay as a Major for the wounds he had received, and was subsequently granted a pension of £200 a year.

In February, 1877, Colonel Durnford again embarked for Natal. He was one of the commissioners on the disputed Zulu boundary, whose award restored to the Zulus a considerable portion of territory.

The engineer arrangements made before the commencement of the Zulu war, viz., raising, equipping, and training three companies of native pioneers, organizing two field parks, and providing complete bridge equipment for crossing the Tugela, were all the work of Colonel Durnford, and show the same earnestness of purpose and energy that have always distinguished him.

When war was declared against the Zulus, Colonel Durnford received the command of the No. 2 Column, consisting of three battalions Natal Native Contingent, of 1,000 men each, five troops of mounted natives (the Natal Native Horse), and a rocket battery under Captain Russell, R.A.

In a letter from one of his brother officers, written from the Cape just before the receipt of the news of his death, Colonel Durnford is thus alluded to:—"From long residence in the Colony, and from having commanded native contingents during former outbreaks, Colonel Durnford has great influence over the natives of Natal and Basutoland, many men coming hundreds of miles to serve under him."

The head-quarters of No. 2 Column were at Fort Buckingham. On January the 16th, 1879, Colonel Durnford was ordered to take a part of his force about thirty miles farther up the river to guard the frontier, as raids were expected, and a few days later to move up to Rorke's Drift. On January the 22nd he was ordered to move up to Isandhlwana, where the General had encamped on the 20th.

He arrived about 10.30 A.M. Zulus had been sighted moving about in the immediate neighbourhood of the camp, and one column of their force was reported to be retiring in the direction in which Lord Chelmsford had moved in the morning. Apprehending that this column was threatening to cut off the General's force from his camp, Colonel Durnford, with a portion of his mounted men, followed it. Two troops which he had previously sent on to reconnoitre a range of hills on the left and the valley beyond, after proceeding about five miles, met the Zulu army, numbering at least 20,000, and the officer in command at once rode back to warn the camp. Colonel Durnford and the force with him slowly retired before the advancing horde, fighting, in good order, on to broken ground and a watercourse in front of the camp, and formed to the right of the 24th Regiment. This position was held as long as the ammunition lasted; when it failed, Colonel Durnford withdrew the mounted men to the right of the camp, and galloped towards the 24th, to endeavour to concentrate the force. The Zulu army at this moment, dashing forward in the most rapid manner, surrounded the regiment, and the survivors retreated by the right rear. For months little was known of the later events of the fatal day, beyond the fact that firing was seen up to nearly four o'clock. Colonel Durnford's watch was by chance taken from his body at dawn on the 23rd; it had been injured, and had stopped at 3.40 p.m. On May the 21st, General Marshall made a reconnaissance to Isandhlwana. Colonel Durnford's body, surrounded by those of fourteen of the Carabineers and their officer, Lieutenant Scott, a few Mounted Police, and about thirty soldiers, was discovered at the mouth of the neck on the right of the camp: there the little force had made a last stand, and had given their lives away in order to afford their comrades in arms a chance of retreat; it must have been within fifty yards of them over the neck, that the rush was made to escape. Colonel Durnford's body was temporarily interred close to where he fell; it was subsequently removed, and buried with military honours at Pietermaritzburg, on October 12.

His commissions bore date as follows:—

Second Lieutenant	June 27, 1848.
First Lieutenant	February 17, 1854.
Second Captain	March 18, 1858.
First Captain	January 5, 1864.
Major	July 5, 1872.
Lieut.-Colonel	December 11, 1873.
Brevet-Colonel	December 11, 1878.

The following extract from a letter written a few days after the battle of Isandhlwana, by Sir Henry Bulwer, the Lieutenant-Governor of Natal, shows the estimation in which Colonel Durnford was held by those who knew him:—

"Colonel Durnford was a soldier of soldiers, with all his heart in his profession; keen, active-minded, indefatigable, unsparing of himself, and utterly fearless, honourable, loyal, of great kindness and goodness of heart.

"I speak of him as I knew him, and as all who knew him will speak of him."

WARREN RICHARD COLVIN WYNNE,

MAJOR, ROYAL ENGINEERS.

WARREN RICHARD COLVIN WYNNE,

BREVET-MAJOR, ROYAL ENGINEERS.

MAJOR WARREN RICHARD COLVIN WYNNE, who died at Fort Pearson, on the Natal frontier, on the 9th of April, 1879, was the eldest surviving son of Captain John Wynne, Royal Horse Artillery, of Wynnestay, county Dublin, by his marriage with Anne, daughter of Admiral Sir Samuel Warren, K.C.B., G.C.H. He was born on the 9th of April, 1843, at Collon House, County Louth, and was educated at the Royal Naval School, New Cross, where he carried off numerous prizes, including two silver medals for Classics and Mathematics. He passed out from the Royal Military Academy, Woolwich, fourth on the list of successful candidates, and elected to serve in the Royal Engineers. On the 25th of June, 1862, he was gazetted to a Lieutenancy in this corps. His first foreign service was at Gibraltar, where he remained for five years, and was appointed Acting Adjutant, an appointment which he held for four years. On his return to England he was appointed to the Ordnance Survey in December, 1871, and stationed at Guildford, from whence he was removed to Reading in November, 1875. In December, 1878, at a day's notice, he was given the command of the 2nd Field Company, then stationed at Shorncliffe, and under orders to proceed on active service to Natal, in view of the impending invasion of Zululand.

Captain Wynne embarked with his company on the 2nd of December, and, on arriving at Durban, at once proceeded to the Tugela mouth to join Colonel Pearson's column. The river having been crossed on the 12th of January, 1879, Captain Wynne laid out and built Fort Tenedos, a strong earthwork commenced on the 15th, and completed on the 17th, of January. He afterwards proceeded with the No. 1 column to Etshowe, taking part in the engagement on the Inyezane River, where his company was employed as light infantry. The following is an extract from his Diary, written at Etshowe:—

"*28th January.*—At 10 a.m., telegram received from General Lord Chelmsford, stating that he had found it necessary to retire to the frontier, that all former plans were given up, and that he left it entirely to Colonel Pearson's own discretion to retire upon the Tugela, or to hold his position. At a meeting of commanding officers, to which I was called, I found it had been pretty well determined to retreat at once, leaving all standing. The Fort being in a tolerably advanced state, I could not concur in this decision, looking upon such a retreat as hazardous in itself, and the moral effect of it much to be deprecated. I, therefore, was in favour of remaining and strengthening the position to the utmost. It was, however, a question of provisions and ammunition, and about the sufficiency of these for holding out there was some uncertainty. At this point Colonel Walker, A.A.G., and Captain MacGregor, D.A.Q.M.G., came in, and, being decidedly of the same opinion as myself, it was determined to remain."

So that to Captain Wynne in no small degree it was due that Fort Etshowe was held and a firm front shown to the Zulu forces for so many weeks, when a retreat to the Tugela mouth would have involved a deplorable loss of prestige to the British arms, and invited that invasion of Natal which it was the first object to prevent, and which another gallant Engineer Officer, Major Chard, had so effectively checked on the Buffalo River.

This view is confirmed by Colonel Pearson, who in his despatch wrote as follows :—

"Personally I was in favour at first of retiring; but, on further reflection, I judged that if we continued to hold the forward position in the country, nearly forty miles from the frontier, it might have a good moral effect, and even afford protection to that part of the colony immediately behind."

And Lord Chelmsford wrote in his despatch of the 10th of April, 1879 :—

"I am much indebted to Colonel Pearson for so tenaciously holding on to Etshowe after the bad news of the Isandhlwana affair had reached him. The occupation of that Fort . . . . . had, no doubt, a very powerful moral effect throughout South Africa."

The report drawn up by Captain Courtney from the diary of Captain Wynne, which appeared in despatches, bears testimony to the admirable manner in which the latter discharged his duties as Commanding Royal Engineer of the 1st Column, to the energy with which he set about the construction of the Fort, and the ready resource which met all difficulties as they arose, while he managed, in addition, to make a trigonometrical survey of the position. Captain MacGregor wrote from Etshowe :—"Wynne, our C.R.E., works from morning till night, always ready and cheerful, and making the best of the means at hand."

On the 12th of March he was taken ill with fever and was placed on the sick list, but he continued hopeful and patient, ever ready with his advice and suggestions.

On the relief of Etshowe he was moved in a cart to the Tugela River, but the frightful jolting over the rough roads proved too much for him, and he died near Fort Pearson on the anniversary of his birthday, at the age of thirty-six. He was buried on a hill-side cemetery overlooking the river and Fort Tenedos. A non-commissioned officer of the company, in a letter to his wife, wrote :—

"Every man in the company deeply regrets his death. I can safely say there is not a man but would have done anything for him, he was so respected by them. It was a sad sight to see our men standing over his grave with tears in their eyes. Captain Courtney was the only officer present (the others being up country), and he was so deeply cut up that he could hardly read the burial service."

Captain Courtney wrote from the Tugela camp :—

"His work at Etshowe will not soon be forgotten, and the enclosed extract from his diary will show that the stand made there was mainly due to his advice. That stand has cost him his life, humanly speaking, and he has died a soldier's death as truly as any man ever did. I have been under fire with him twice, and he was always cool and collected. He was only too devoted to his work, and on the 11th March, the morning after the attack mentioned in his diary, he had a walk of six miles and more in the hot sun, and I fear we must attribute his illness, partly at least, to this."

In the course of a speech made at Yeovil, shortly after his return to England, Colonel Pearson said :—

"I have been given credit for my skill in rendering our fort at Etshowe impregnable, but it was made so by Captain Wynne, my Commanding Engineer, and his brother officers, under whose directions we all worked. Captain Wynne died of an illness brought on by exposure, and by unflinchingly remaining at his duty when almost incapable of performing it."

The following announcement appeared in the "London Gazette" of the 5th May, 1880 :—

"Captain Warren Richard Colvin Wynne, Royal Engineers, to be Major, in recognition of his distinguished services during the Zulu campaign of 1878-1879. Dated 2nd April, 1879. Since deceased."

Major Wynne was twice married: first, in 1872, to Eleanor, seventh daughter of J. B. Turbett, Esq., of Owenstown, Dublin (who died in 1873); and, secondly, in 1876, to Lucy, eldest daughter of Captain Alfred Parish, R.N.R.

FRANCIS HARTWELL McDOWEL,
LIEUTENANT, ROYAL ENGINEERS.

FRANCIS HARTWELL MACDOWEL,

LIEUTENANT, ROYAL ENGINEERS.

LIEUTENANT FRANCIS HARTWELL MACDOWEL, who was killed at Isandhlwana on the 22nd of January, 1879, was the second and youngest son of Professor Macdowel, M.D., of the University of Dublin, and grandson of the late Rev. Francis Brodrick Hartwell, Vicar-General of the Isle of Man, and formerly a Major in the 6th Dragoon Guards. He was educated by the Rev. Mr. Cook, and subsequently at Dr. Stackpoole's at Kingstown. He possessed mathematical talents of a very high order, which were cultivated by Dr. Barry, a distinguished mathematical teacher in that school. Without any further special preparation he entered Woolwich as a cadet in 1868, at the age of seventeen years, obtaining eighth place in the list of successful competitors, out of 150 candidates. Passing out from the Academy in August, 1871, he was gazetted a lieutenant in the Royal Engineers. In 1873 he was appointed to the C (mounted) troop of the corps, and served with it at Aldershot for three years under Sir Howard Elphinstone, V.C.; after being stationed for a year at Chatham, he was ordered to South Africa, and sailed from Dartmouth for the Cape in October, 1877.

On his arrival in South Africa, Lieutenant Macdowel was sent by way of Durban to the Transvaal, and for two months was engaged in building a fort between Utrecht and Newcastle. In January, 1878, he was employed with Captain Clarke, R.A., in an extensive survey of the disputed territory between the Blood and Buffalo Rivers, during which he mapped a large tract of country. In June and July he was at Prætoria, and was engaged with Lieutenant Bradshaw, 13th Light Infantry, in an extended surveying expedition about the Amaswazi border. In September he joined the force under Colonel Rowlands, V.C., which was formed to operate against Sekukuni and his tribe, and was attached to the smaller division under Major Russell, 12th Lancers. On the expedition being abandoned in consequence of the inadequacy of the force in point of numbers, Lieutenant Macdowel, with a command of eighty men, was left in charge of Burgher's Fort for several weeks, in the vicinity of large bodies of the enemy. Almost all his horses having died, and fever having broken out amongst his men, he extricated his little force from its dangerous position, and, marching through the Waterfall Valley, ultimately reached Leydenburgh. On November the 14th he started to explore the Zulu border east of that town, and, after riding a distance of 250 miles in five days, and encountering considerable hardship, succeeded in bringing in much valuable information. Proceeding to Utrecht on his return, he was attached to Colonel Wood's Column, which was then in course of formation. On the day after his arrival he was sent with an interpreter to the Assegai River, to convey orders to the 13th Light Infantry : he was absent on this duty four days, riding 150 miles. On the day after his return he was sent to Helpmakaar, eighty miles distant, to inspect and report on some Royal Engineer stores, and on arriving at his destination, he found himself attached, in general orders, to Colonel Glyn's Column.

Lieutenant Macdowel was now entrusted with the engineering operations necessary to enable the Head-Quarter Column to cross the Buffalo River, and for the admirable way in which he carried these out in the face of great difficulties he was complimented by Lord Chelmsford in person. On the subsequent advance of the column into Zululand, he was sent on with it, in compliance with his own request, instead of being left at Rorke's Drift.

When Lord Chelmsford marched from Isandhlwana before daybreak on January the 22nd to search for the Zulu force supposed to exist some miles off to his right front, Lieutenant Macdowel, who was on Colonel Glyn's staff, was taken on with the advance ; about eleven o'clock in the forenoon, however, he was sent back with orders to the senior officer left in command, "to strike the camp and follow the General."

As the Zulu attack had by this time developed, it is probable that he had to fight his way through the enemy to deliver his orders. Soon afterwards he was seen by Lieutenant Higginson fighting side by side with Colonel Durnford, R.E., in the desperate charges that officer was making to repel the encircling Zulu forces. It would appear that when his chief fell, he threw in his lot with the companies of the 24th Regiment, for in an official letter to his relatives it is stated that "when he (Lieutenant Macdowel) was last seen, he was getting bandsmen, gunners, and others, together, and bringing up reserve ammunition to the fighting line of the 24th Regiment. A Zulu fired at him at close quarters, and he fell between the General's tent and the fighting line."

Colonel Black, 24th Regiment, after his visit to the field for the purpose of interring the dead, wrote : "We found and buried a body with R.E. officer's blue coat and trousers, unrecognizable otherwise. From the uniform I believe that this was the mortal part of that good young fellow Macdowel."

THE HON. RONALD GEORGE ELIDOR CAMPBELL,

Captain, Coldstream Guards.

THE HON. RONALD GEORGE ELIDOR CAMPBELL,

CAPTAIN, COLDSTREAM GUARDS.

CAPTAIN RONALD GEORGE ELIDOR CAMPBELL, who was killed in action on the Zlobane Mountain on the 28th of March, 1879, was the second son of the Earl of Cawdor, by his marriage with Sarah Mary, second daughter of Lieutenant-General Cavendish. He was born on December the 30th, 1848, and was educated at Eton. He entered the army in 1867, being gazetted to the Coldstream Guards as ensign on the 25th of December. In 1871 he became lieutenant and captain, and on the 19th of August in the same year was appointed adjutant, which appointment he held until October, 1878.

Captain Campbell embarked for South Africa in November, 1878, and on arriving there was appointed staff officer to Colonel Wood, whose column was at that time in course of formation on the Transvaal frontier, preparatory to the invasion of Zululand. Crossing the Blood River with this force on the 6th of January, 1879, Captain Campbell was present throughout its various operations during the two months following, accompanying Colonel Wood, in his capacity of staff officer. On the morning of the 28th of March he took part in the attack on the Zlobane Mountain, and fell, gallantly fighting, in the assault. The following passage, taken from Colonel Wood's despatch to Lord Chelmsford, describes the manner in which he met his death: "We soon came under fire from an unseen enemy on our right. Ascending more rapidly than most of the Border Horse, who had got off the track, with my staff and escort I passed to the front, and, with half-a-dozen of the Border Horse, when within a hundred feet of the summit, came under a well-directed fire from our front and both flanks, poured in from behind huge boulders and rocks. Mr. Lloyd fell mortally wounded at my side, and as Captain Campbell and one of the escort were carrying him on a ledge rather lower, my horse was killed, falling on me. I directed Colonel Weatherly to dislodge one or two Zulus who were causing us most of the loss; but, as his men did not advance rapidly, Captain Campbell and Lieutenant Lysons, and three men of the 90th, jumping over a low wall, ran forward, and charged into a cave, when Captain Campbell, leading in the most determined and gallant manner, was shot dead. . . . Mr. Lloyd was now dead, and we brought his body, and that of Captain Campbell, about half-way down the hill, where we buried them, still being under fire." In another of his official despatches Colonel Wood wrote of Captain Campbell: "He was an excellent staff officer, both in the field and as regards office work; and having shown the most brilliant courage, lost his life in performing a gallant feat." Again, in a private letter, bearing date January the 29th, Colonel Wood wrote: "I never saw a man play a more heroic part than he did yesterday."

Captain Campbell married, in 1872, Katherine, daughter of Bishop Claughton, now Bishop of St. Albans.

ROBERT JOHNSTON BARTON,
CAPTAIN, COLDSTREAM GUARDS.

ROBERT JOHNSTON BARTON,

CAPTAIN, COLDSTREAM GUARDS.

CAPTAIN ROBERT JOHNSTON BARTON, who was killed in action at the base of the Zlobane Mountain, on the 28th of March, 1879, was the fourth son of the late T. J. Barton, Esquire, D.L., of Glendalough, county Wicklow. He was born in Dublin, on the 20th of February, 1849, and was brought up at first for the navy, passing through the prescribed course on board the "Britannia." On leaving the training-ship he did not, however, enter the service, but continued his education at the Blackheath Proprietary School, from whence, after a few years, he proceeded to Sandhurst. On the 14th of September, 1866, he obtained a commission in the 9th Lancers, then quartered at the Island Bridge Barracks, Dublin; was gazetted lieutenant on the 2nd of May, 1868; obtained his company on the 26th of March, 1873; and in the following December exchanged into the Coldstream Guards. He was for four years aide-de-camp to the late Lieutenant-General Sir Hope Grant, while that distinguished officer was in command of the Aldershot Division, and was on terms of the closest intimacy with him until his death.

In February, 1878, Captain Barton volunteered for the Gaika campaign, then in progress, and was on the point of embarking for South Africa when permission was refused him in consequence of European complications. In the following May Lord Chelmsford applied for more officers to be sent out, mentioning him, among others, by name: he again volunteered, and being one of those selected by the authorities at the Horse Guards, left England on the last day of the month. On arriving at Cape Town he was immediately appointed second in command of the Frontier Light Horse, which then consisted of 200 men; and from the day of his appointment to that of his death was the right-hand man of their gallant commander, Colonel Buller, V.C.

In the various operations of his incessantly active corps throughout the earlier phases of the Zulu war, Captain Barton performed much distinguished service, being repeatedly marked out for special commendation in despatches. In the attack on the Zlobane, immediately after the summit of the mountain was carried, he was detached with thirty men to bury the body of an officer killed in the assault. Shortly afterwards an immense Zulu army crossed the flat to cut off the retreat of the main body of the column. Joined by about fifty-four of the Border Horse, Captain Barton and his party attempted to cut through the 20,000 men opposed to them, but failed, and beset by the enemy, the survivors lost most of their horses. Captain Barton, however, still mounted, with a few others, managed to make his way through the encircling horde and reach the flats, whence he might have made his escape had he not been too chivalrous to ride on while dismounted men were being assegaied: though his horse was knocked up, and though he was warned of the danger he was incurring, he continued to carry a man whom he had taken up and placed behind him, and was last seen alive so doing.

Captain Barton was a universal favourite, and his untimely death caused the greatest grief in his regiment. On the 23rd of April the following regimental order was made:—"The commanding officer wishes to express the sorrow which he and all ranks must have felt at hearing the loss the regiment has sustained by the deaths of Captains Campbell and Barton, killed in action at the Cape in the performance of that duty for which they had so gallantly volunteered. All who knew them are aware of their merits, and it is superfluous for the commanding officer to say how well they performed their professional duties, and how popular they were in the regiment." Colonel Evelyn Wood, in his despatch from Kambula, bearing date March the 30th, wrote:—"Captain Barton, commanding the Frontier Light Horse, was always most forward in every fight, and was as humane as he was brave. On the 20th of January one of Umsabe's men, whom Captain Barton wished to take prisoner, fired at Captain Barton within two yards, the powder marking his face. When last seen on the 28th he was carrying on his horse a wounded man." Colonel Buller, in his official account of the engagement, wrote:—"Captain Barton is also a great loss; active, energetic, and intrepid, he was an excellent officer, and devoted to his profession." In a private letter, too, he briefly summarizes the characteristics of his late comrade in the following words: "A more perfect gentleman, a more generous man, a braver soldier it has never been my lot to know."

THE HON. HUGH RODOLPH GOUGH.

CAPTAIN THE HON. H. RODOLPH GOUGH.

CAPTAIN HUGH RODOLPH GOUGH, who died in the Military Hospital at Herwen on the 19th of April, 1879, was the third son of the Right Honourable Viscount Gough, of Lough Cutra Castle, county Galway, and a grandson of the hero of Goojerat. He was born in Ireland on the 11th of January, 1856, and was educated for the army. A commission in the Coldstream Guards being given him by Sir William Codrington, he entered that regiment in 1875, and served with it until the latter end of 1878.

On preparations being hastened forward at that time with a view to the impending invasion of Zululand, he embarked for South Africa, and reaching Cape Town early in December, at once proceeded to Natal. Shortly after arriving there, he was offered by Commandant Nettleton a captain's commission in the 2nd Regiment of the Natal Native Contingent—a corps recently raised by that gallant officer in the Cape Colony, and destined to form part of Colonel Pearson's column of the army of invasion, then in course of formation at the Lower Tugela Drift. He at once accepted the offer, and joining the 2nd Battalion of the regiment at Durban on the day of its disembarkation, proceeded with it in its march to the frontier.

Captain Gough took part in the advance of the column, in January, 1879, into the enemy's country, and was present at the battle of Inyezane on the morning of the 22nd, and the subsequent occupation of Etshowe. When the news of the disaster at Isandhlwana reached the garrison on the 28th, the intrenchments were far advanced: they were, however, of but limited extent, being intended for only 1,000 infantry, and there being, consequently, no space either for the mounted troops or the two battalions of the 2nd Regiment Natal Native Contingent, they were ordered back to the Tugela at an hour's notice. The country was of the roughest description, the distance to be covered forty miles, and the probability of an attack being made by an overwhelming force of the enemy, considerable. It is perhaps worthy of record that Gough, with characteristic generosity, gave up his horse on the way to non-commissioned officers, marching more than half the distance. The journey was accomplished in less than fifteen hours, the little force reaching the Tugela at 2.30 a.m. on the 29th.

In the month of February, Captain Gough, having pressing business to transact, obtained six days' leave of absence while the regiment was being reorganized, and proceeded to Durban: there he fell ill, and was laid up for several weeks. Before he should have left his bed he was met in Durban, and remonstrated with, by General Lord Chelmsford, who, arriving at Stanger shortly afterwards, informed Commandant Nettleton that "young Gough was going about too early." The Commandant immediately wrote to him, telling him not to think of rejoining the regiment until his strength was restored, and shortly afterwards bade him follow the advice of the medical officers and go to Pinetown to recruit. At that time preparations for the departure of the force destined for the relief of Etshowe were being rapidly pushed forward.

The column commenced its advance on the 29th of March, and reached the Inyone River on the evening of that day. To the astonishment of their commanding officer, Gough, Davis (who had also been sick at Durban), and Dawnay arrived at the camp at dusk, having ridden through from Durban—a distance of eighty-two miles—in less than two days. Gough, who had suffered badly *en route*, was not allowed to take duty, much as he desired to. On the 31st of March he was again severely attacked with dysentery, and at the instance of his commanding officer was ordered to take to one of the waggons: there he remained until the column reached the Ginghilovo Stream, all that was possible to be done for his comfort being done. On the morning of the battle which ensued at the position taken up by the column —the 2nd of April—it so happened his company was, with part of the 91st Highlanders, close to the waggon in which he was sheltered. "The moment the alarm sounded," wrote Commandant Nettleton, in a letter to Viscount Gough, bearing date June the 15th, "the poor fellow, weak as he was, staggered out and took command of the company. I need not say how he behaved, but I was astonished to learn after the action that he had actually led his men over the shelter-trench, when the cheer was started and the charge sounded. My own post was some hundred yards to the right of the ground covered by his company, so that until the action was over and the regiment had returned from pursuit, I had not the least notion that he had even left the waggon."

The excitement and exertion proved too much for his enfeebled frame, and utter collapse followed. He was moved in the first week in April, with the sick and wounded, to the Lower Tugela, and thence to the Base Hospital at Herwen, some twelve miles inland: there he grew worse and worse, and in spite of tender nursing, and the solicitous care of Surgeon-Major Dudley, the medical officer who attended him, he died on the 19th of April.

"Throughout the force," wrote Commandant Nettleton in his letter to Viscount Gough, "all who knew my late friend felt most forcibly that they had lost a right good fellow and pleasant companion, whilst the service had lost a splendid soldier. That was the universal opinion. He was more than true to the soldierly instincts of his race. I never met a man so wedded to the army service, and had his sad fate been a different one, he must have made his mark during this campaign, which affords such scope for dash and gallantry."

Captain Gough's remains were interred in the cemetery at Stanger, a spot where those of many of his comrades had already found a last resting-place.

HERBERT JOHN MAINWARING WILLIAMS,
Captain, 3rd Regiment (The Buffs).

HERBERT JOHN MAINWARING WILLIAMS,

CAPTAIN, 3RD REGIMENT (THE BUFFS).

CAPTAIN HERBERT JOHN MAINWARING WILLIAMS, who died at Etshowe on the 12th of March, 1879, was the second son of the Rev. Richard Williams, J.P., Rector of Roggiett with Llanvihangel Roggiett, Monmouthshire, his mother being the eldest daughter of Ambrose Philips Mainwaring, Esquire, of Chambers Court, Worcestershire. He was born at Leamington on the 28th of September, 1838, and was educated at Cheltenham, and by a private tutor. Obtaining his commission without purchase, he entered the army in 1859, being gazetted to an ensigncy in the 2nd Battalion of the 4th Regiment (King's Own). He served with that corps at Corfu, at Malta, and in Canada, from whence he returned to England in 1867. In 1871 he retired on temporary half-pay.

Captain Williams was brought in again to serve in September, 1877, joining the 41st Regiment (The Welsh). Being desirous to see more foreign service, and hoping to be enabled to take part in the Kaffir war, then in progress in South Africa, he exchanged, in August, 1878, into the 2nd Battalion of the "Buffs." Before he arrived at the Cape, however, his regiment had been ordered to join the force which, with a view to the impending invasion of Zululand, was being massed on the Natal frontier. Joining his battalion at the Lower Tugela Drift, on the 2nd of December, he proceeded with Colonel Pearson's column, to which his regiment was attached, on its advance into Zululand on the 12th of January, 1879. He was present at the battle of Inyezane on the morning of the 22nd, and marched into Etshowe on the following day. In the long and anxious time which succeeded the arrival of the column at this position, throughout the wearisome routine which fell to the lot of the beleaguered force, Captain Williams, though in indifferent health, pre-eminently distinguished himself by his kindly ways and cheerful demeanour. Enfeebled by exposure, and without medical necessaries, he was unable to rally against the fever with which he was stricken, and died while heliographic messages were being flashed to the garrison by the force preparing for its relief.

Captain Williams was a thorough soldier and a general favourite; ready to undergo any fatigue or hardship, self-sacrificing to a degree: he was a keen sportsman too, and readers of the " Field " will miss with regret the graphic accounts of his shooting expeditions in Canada and other quarters of the globe which he was in the habit of contributing to the pages of that Journal.

Captain Williams married, in February, 1871, Wilhelmina, daughter of Thomas Brittain, Esquire, of Chester.

CHARLES EVELYN MASON,

LIEUTENANT, 3RD REGIMENT (THE BUFFS).

CHARLES EVELYN MASON,

LIEUTENANT, 3RD REGIMENT (THE BUFFS).

LIEUTENANT CHARLES EVELYN MASON, who died at Herwen on the 7th of April, 1879, was the fourth and youngest son of G. W. Mason, Esquire, of Morton Hall, Retford, Notts, and Marianne Atherton, his wife, daughter of Captain J. G. Mitford, E.I.C.S. He was born on the 27th of January, 1855, at Langharne, Carmarthenshire, South Wales. Early in 1866 he went to a preparatory school at East Sheen, the head master of which was Mr. Waterfield; thence he was removed to Repton, where he remained for several years. He proceeded to Brussels, in 1872, in order to perfect his knowledge of French; and on his return commenced reading at Captain Lendy's establishment at Sunbury. Competing in the Army Examination, in August, 1874, he passed first in the list, taking nearly 2,000 marks more than the second successful candidate. Being allowed to choose his regiment in consequence of his success, he selected the "Buffs," and at the end of September joined his battalion at Mullingar.

In May, 1875, Lieutenant Mason proceeded with his regiment to Mauritius, where he remained stationed until immediately prior to the outbreak of the Zulu war. Owing to his health having been greatly impaired by the climate during his three years' service in the island, he was then offered the charge of the invalids who were about to be sent home; but, being unwilling to lose any opportunity of seeing active service, he declined the offer, and embarked with his regiment on its departure for South Africa.

On his arrival in Natal, Lieutenant Mason at once proceeded with his regiment to join Colonel Pearson's column, which was then in course of formation on the Lower Tugela, and subsequently took part in the advance of that force into Zululand. He was present at the battle of Inyezane on the 22nd of January, and after the column had arrived at Etshowe was ordered back to Fort Tenedos on the Tugela, in charge of empty waggons. From Fort Tenedos he was sent, with several companies of his regiment, to occupy St. Andrew's, a deserted mission station in Zululand, a few miles over the frontier. He was seized with fever a few days afterwards, was taken to the Military Hospital at Herwen, New Gelderland, and died there after an illness of a few days.

GEORGE ROWLEY JOHN EVELYN,
2ND LIEUTENANT, 3RD REGIMENT (THE BUFFS).

GEORGE ROWLEY JOHN EVELYN,

SECOND LIEUTENANT, 3RD REGIMENT (THE BUFFS).

SECOND LIEUTENANT GEORGE ROWLEY JOHN EVELYN, who died at Etshowe on the 30th of March, 1879, was the eldest son of Colonel George P. Evelyn, of Hartley Manor, Dartford, Kent, by his marriage with Esther Emiline, daughter of Lewis Phillips, Esq., and grand-daughter of the Rev. Phillip Phillips, of Frankfort-on-the-Maine. He was born in London on the 12th of August, 1857, and was educated at the East Sheen School, under Mr. Waterfield's head-mastership, and at Mr. Brackenbury's, at Wimbledon; he also went through a course of instruction at the Royal Agricultural College, Cirencester. In 1875 he obtained a commission in the Royal Surrey Militia, and on the 24th of November, 1877, was gazetted a second lieutenant in the "Buffs."

Leaving England on the 26th of January, 1878, he joined his regiment in Natal. After being for a few months with the head-quarters at Maritzburg, he was detailed to join the detachment then stationed at Mauritius: shortly after his arrival in the island, however, the detachment was ordered to rejoin the head-quarters, and he accompanied it back to Natal.

On arriving at Durban, Second Lieutenant Evelyn at once proceeded, with his company, to join Colonel Pearson's column, which was then in course of formation on the Lower Tugela, and subsequently took part in the advance of that force into Zululand. He was present at the battle of Inyezane on the morning of the 22nd of January, and, on the following day, marched with his company into Etshowe. He served in the defence of that position until nearly the end of February, when the fever and dysentery from which he had been for some days suffering mastered him, and he was obliged to go on the sick-list. Without medicine or medical comforts, and with barely the necessaries of life, his recovery was hopeless; and he died on the evening of the 30th of March. He was buried on the following day in the small cemetery outside the fort. A wooden monument was erected at the head of his grave by the men of his company, by whom he was much beloved; and an inscription was cut in it by three officers of the regiment, who, in spite of hard duty, found time during the few remaining days of the siege to show this mark of esteem for their late comrade.

Second Lieutenant Evelyn was a very promising young officer, and devoted to his profession; fond of all field sports, in which he excelled; a bold rider; a skilful draughtsman. He had endeared himself to all with whom, during his brief life, he had come in contact.

GEORGE ASTELL PARDOE,

LIEUTENANT, 13TH REGIMENT (PRINCE ALBERT'S LIGHT INFANTRY).

GEORGE ASTELL PARDOE,

LIEUTENANT, 13TH LIGHT INFANTRY.

LIEUTENANT GEORGE ASTELL PARDOE, who died in General Newdigate's camp on the Umlatoosi River, on July 14th, 1879, of wounds received at the battle of Ulundi, was the second son of Edward Pardoe, Esq., of Amberwood, Christchurch, Hampshire, formerly Captain 15th and 82nd Regiments, and his wife Harriet, daughter of William Astell, Esquire, M.P., of Everton, Bedfordshire. He was born on the 5th of September, 1855, at Brighton, and was educated at Cowes, Isle of Wight, under the Rev. Arthur Watson, M.A., and at Eton. He passed the competitive examination for entrance to the Royal Military College at Sandhurst, on the 11th of February, 1875, taking a high place, and obtaining his commission, at the same date, on the unattached list. After a year spent at Sandhurst he was gazetted to the 13th Light Infantry, and in May, 1876, joined the 1st Battalion of that regiment in South Africa. Lieutenant Pardoe carried the colours of the 13th Light Infantry at Prætoria, when the reading of the Queen's proclamation on the annexation of the Transvaal took place. Soon afterwards he was invalided home in consequence of a dangerous illness, but rejoined his regiment in South Africa before the commencement of the campaign against Sekukuni in 1878, in which it served, and in which he twice narrowly escaped being shot in the bush.

Lieutenant Pardoe was with Colonel Evelyn Wood's column throughout the whole of its operations on the Transvaal frontier, and during its subsequent advance into Zululand. At the very commencement of the battle of Ulundi, he was shot in both thighs. Though most skilfully and tenderly treated and nursed both by the surgeons and his brother officers, hemorrhage recommenced at the end of ten days, and amputation of the left leg became the only possible means of saving his life. The shock was, however, too great for his system: he never rallied afterwards, but died on his way to the Base hospital at Utrecht. His body was carried to Fort Marshall, and was there buried on the day after his death. By the thoughtful kindness of those in command at the time, a cairn and wall of rough stones protect his grave; a cross has since been erected on the spot by his brother officers to his memory. His character cannot be better described than by quoting from a letter written by one of them:—"A more honourable, high-minded, generous young fellow did not exist: he was a favourite with everyone, from the Colonel down to the youngest bugler." A mural tablet which has been placed in Highcliffe Church, near Christchurch, by friends in the neighbourhood, also testifies to the estimation in which he was held, and to the sorrow caused by his early death.

Descended from an Essex family, Lieutenant Pardoe is the third of his name who during the present century has died on active service. In 1810, George Pardoe, Royal Navy, fell in an engagement off Palamos on the Spanish main, and in 1814 his brother, Ensign Edward Pardoe, Grenadier Guards, was severely wounded at the siege of Bergen-op-Zoom, and in the following year killed at the battle of Waterloo.

JAMES HENRY SCOTT DOUGLAS,

Lieutenant, 21st Regiment (Royal Scots Fusiliers).

JAMES HENRY SCOTT DOUGLAS,

LIEUTENANT, 21ST ROYAL SCOTS FUSILIERS.

LIEUTENANT JAMES HENRY SCOTT DOUGLAS, who was slain at Kwamagwasa, Zululand, on June 30th, 1879, was the eldest son of Sir George Henry Scott Douglas, of Springwood Park, Kelso, Baronet, M.P. for Roxburghshire, and Doña Mariquita Juana Petronila Sanchez de Piña, his wife. He was born at Edinburgh on May the 27th, 1853, and passed his early years at Springwood Park. In 1864 he went to school at Blackheath, under Mr. R. C. Powles, and thence proceeded to St. Leonards, where he was prepared by the Rev. J. Wright for Winchester. He entered Winchester early in 1869, and whilst there became a member of the school corps of Rifle Volunteers; thence he proceeded to Llanwenorth, where he was prepared by the Rev. G. Faithfull for the University. On February 29th, 1872, he received from the Duke of Buccleuch a commission as Lieutenant in the Queen's Regiment of Light Infantry Militia, which he joined at Dalkeith for the training of that year. In October he began his studies at Trinity College, Cambridge, and in the following spring passed his previous examination, thereby qualifying himself for a commission in the army as University Candidate; having, however, commenced to read for the Historical Tripos, and being anxious to more effectually complete his education, he abstained from availing himself of the qualification. About this time he enrolled himself in the University Volunteers, and shortly afterwards became a Sergeant of that corps. At the close of the long vacation of 1875 he had the misfortune to meet with a severe fall from his horse, which brought on concussion of the brain; he was thereby prevented from taking part in the final examination for the Tripos, but the examiners were so convinced, by his previous work, of his attainments, that they conferred on him the B.A. degree with honours.

On April the 1st, 1875, he was gazetted to the 19th Regiment, but being anxious to serve with a Scotch corps, he was transferred to the 21st Royal North British Fusiliers, joining that regiment at Portsmouth in January, 1876. Shortly afterwards he passed most creditably through a course of garrison instruction, his commanding officer testifying to the manner in which he excelled in tactics and military law. From the School of Musketry at Hythe he came out with an extra first-class certificate: he also obtained a first-class instructor's certificate at the School of Army

Signalling at Aldershot; and on his return to his regiment, performed the duty of officer-instructor to it.

Lieutenant Scott Douglas, accompanying his regiment, left Queenstown for Zululand in February, 1879, and arrived at Durban on March the 29th. Proceeding to the front, he was appointed Chief of the Signalling Staff of the 2nd Division of the Field Force, and, applying himself ardently to his difficult and important duties, he succeeded in a short time in establishing a line of communication, by means of flags and the heliograph, from the most advanced post to the rearmost. On the morning of June 30th, he was employed with his signalling party at Entonganeni: before noon a mist came on which obscured the sun and prevented the working of the heliograph, and shortly afterwards an important message arrived which Lord Chelmsford was desirous to have forwarded to Sir Garnet Wolseley. Lieutenant Scott Douglas, with his signalling party and an escort, immediately set out to carry it to Fort Evelyn, twenty miles distant; but finding the condition of the horses to be so bad as to preclude the possibility of escape in the event of the enemy being met with in force, he decided not to risk the safety of so large a party, and rode on with only his orderly, Corporal Cotter of the 17th Lancers. Upon his arrival at the fort, the officer who commanded it, observing the fatigued condition of the horses and the unsettled appearance of the weather, urged him to pass the night there; but knowing, by the nature of the messages he had forwarded, that the army was to march for Ulundi at daybreak on the following morning, he preferred to return. The start for Entonganeni was made at 3 p.m., and about an hour afterwards a dense fog came on and shrouded the surrounding country. The track, at all times difficult to follow, branches off towards the deserted mission-station of Kwamagwasa: in the obscurity the two horsemen accidentally took the wrong path, and it was not until they arrived at the mission-station that they discovered their mistake. Hard by this spot, where they dismounted to refresh their horses, they were observed and surprised by a body of some five hundred Zulus, who were marching to join Cetchwayo at Ulundi. Lieutenant Scott Douglas was able to discharge five chambers of his revolver, and then fell pierced to the heart by an assegai. His body was found some days afterwards by Brigadier-General Wood, lying near to that of Corporal Cotter, who had also stood his ground most gallantly: the two were buried, with military honours, side by side, in graves marked by crosses and sheltered by a luxuriant growth of the wild cactus.

"Of the soldierlike, manly bearing and social virtues of Lieutenant Scott Douglas," wrote Colonel Collingwood, 21st Royal Scots Fusiliers, "I, his commanding officer, cannot speak too highly. He was the ideal type of an officer and a gentleman in the highest sense in which that term can be applied."

HENRY BURMESTER PULLEINE,

LIEUTENANT-COLONEL, 24TH REGIMENT (2ND WARWICKSHIRE).

HENRY BURMESTER PULLEINE,

LIEUTENANT-COLONEL, 24TH REGIMENT (2ND WARWICKSHIRE).

LIEUTENANT-COLONEL HENRY BURMESTER PULLEINE, who was killed at Isandhlwana on the 22nd January, 1879, was the eldest son of the Rev. Robert Pulleine, rector of Kirkby Wiske, near Thirsk, Yorkshire, by his marriage with Susan, eldest daughter of H. Burmester, Esq., of Wandsworth, and grandson of Colonel Henry Percy Pulleine, of Crakehall, Yorkshire, of the Scots Greys. He was born at Spennithorne, Yorkshire, on the 12th of December, 1838, and was educated at Marlborough College, Wilts, and the Royal Military College, Sandhurst, where he obtained various prizes. On the 16th of November, 1855, he was gazetted to an ensigncy, without purchase, in the 30th Regiment, which he joined at Fermoy, in Ireland, and afterwards was quartered at Parkhurst, Isle of Man, Dublin, and other home stations. On leaving the Isle of Man he received a testimonial from the leading men in the island, expressing regret at the departure of the detachment under his command and commendation of the good behaviour of the men during their stay. In June, 1858, he was gazetted to a lieutenancy in the 2nd Battalion 24th Regiment (then being raised), and served at Sheffield, at Aldershot, and afterwards in Mauritius, where he became a captain by purchase in 1860. For nearly four years he held an appointment in the Commissariat Department, and was very highly spoken of by Commissary-General Routh and others for unusual ability and industry.

After two years spent at home on leave and at the depôt at Buttevant and Sheffield, he rejoined the regiment at Rangoon, and also served at Secunderabad. In 1871 he received his majority by purchase into the 1st Battalion, then at Malta, where he acted for four months as deputy quartermaster-general, and received commendation from the General, Sir Alford Horsford, for the way in which this duty was performed. He was for three years with his regiment at Gibraltar, whence he proceeded with it to South Africa, and served at Cape Town and King William's Town, receiving, in 1877, his brevet lieutenant-colonelcy.

About this time the troubles in the Transkei first began, and in consequence of the estimation in which the abilities of Lieutenant-Colonel Pulleine were held by His Excellency General Sir A. Cunynghame, he was, on the occasion of the war in

Galekaland, called upon to raise two frontier corps, one of infantry, subsequently called "Pulleine's Rangers" (afterwards the Transkei Rifles), and the other of cavalry, subsequently called the Frontier Light Horse. So ably was this service executed, although under many difficulties, that both these corps, under the able officers appointed to command them, were brought to such a state of efficiency as to be enabled, in the short space of two months, to take the field. This was in no small degree owing to the zeal and assiduity of Lieutenant-Colonel Pulleine, and to his thorough knowledge of interior economy and the rules of the service, in addition to the peculiar qualities which he possessed of enjoying the good wishes and feelings of the civil communities in whatever station he might be quartered.

Lieutenant-Colonel Pulleine served with his regiment in the Transkei for nearly three months, and then, in September, 1878, in view of the impending hostilities with the Zulus, returned to embark for Natal; on arriving there he was selected to command at the city of Durban, an appointment of much difficulty, requiring not only the utmost zeal and energy, but great tact. He then succeeded Colonel Pearson as commandant at Pietermaritzburg, and for nearly two months was an energetic President of the Remount Depôt, purchasing horses for the troops. These appointments, however, he relinquished, and applied to be allowed to rejoin his regiment, declining to act upon a suggestion of the General's that he should retain them a short time longer; upon his so doing, Lord Chelmsford sent him a letter, thanking him for his services, and speaking in high terms of the way in which his duties had been performed.

Lieutenant-Colonel Pulleine set off in high spirits, riding with his groom and a pack-horse, and by dint of covering long distances each day, succeeded in reaching the head-quarter column at the camp on the Buffalo River on the 17th of January, 1879. On the morning of the 20th the column advanced to Isandhlwana. In the disastrous encounter with the enemy which ensued on the 22nd, Lieutenant-Colonel Pulleine fell doing his duty, endeavouring to his utmost to obey the orders he had received.

Lieutenant-Colonel Pulleine married, in 1866, Frances Katherine, daughter of Frederick Bell, Esq., J.P., of Fermoy, Ireland, and leaves a son and two daughters.

WILLIAM DEGACHER,

Captain, 24th Regiment (2nd Warwickshire).

WILLIAM DEGACHER,

CAPTAIN, 24TH REGIMENT (2ND WARWICKSHIRE).

CAPTAIN WILLIAM DEGACHER, who was killed at Isandhlwana on the 22nd of January, 1879, was the third son of the late Walter Henry Degacher, Esq., of St. Omer, France. He was born on the 4th of April, 1841, and was educated at the Imperial College, St. Omer, and Rugby. In May, 1859, he was gazetted ensign to the 2nd Battalion of the 24th Regiment; became lieutenant in August, 1862; and obtained his company in December, 1868. He served with his battalion at various home stations, in Mauritius, at the Mediterranean stations, and in South Africa, where he took part in the expedition to the Diamond Fields, under Sir Arthur Cunynghame, in 1876. On returning to Cape Town at the latter end of the year he proceeded home on leave.

Shortly after arriving in England, Captain Degacher formed an intention to retire from the service. In consequence, however, of the Kaffir war breaking out about this time, he volunteered for active service; and, his request being acceded to, again embarked for South Africa.

In October, 1878, in view of the impending outbreak of hostilities with the Zulus, the 24th Regiment was ordered to Natal to join the Head-Quarter Column of the army of invasion, then concentrating at Helpmakaar. Taking part in the subsequent advance of that force in January, 1879, Captain Degacher commanded the 1st Battalion of the regiment on the crossing of the Buffalo on the 10th, and in the storming of Sirayo's stronghold in the Bashee Valley on the 12th,—his eldest brother, Lieutenant-Colonel Henry Degacher, C.B., being at the same time, by a remarkable coincidence, in command of the 2nd Battalion. Captain Degacher subsequently advanced with the column to Isandhlwana, and, in the disastrous encounter with the enemy which ensued on the 22nd, was in command of the battalion, Lieutenant-Colonel Pulleine being in command of the troops. No authentic record of his death exists—a fact from which it would seem probable that he fell shortly after the three companies were driven in, in the last despairing rally which took place before the retreat towards Fugitives' Drift became defined. Of one thing his countrymen may rest assured—that he fell fighting gallantly to the last.

Captain Degacher married, in March, 1877, Caroline, daughter of General Webber Smith, C.B.

WILLIAM ECCLES MOSTYN,

CAPTAIN, 24TH REGIMENT (2ND WARWICKSHIRE).

WILLIAM ECCLES MOSTYN,

CAPTAIN, 24TH REGIMENT (2ND WARWICKSHIRE).

CAPTAIN WILLIAM ECCLES MOSTYN, who was killed at Isandhlwana on the 22nd of January, 1879, was the only son of the late Rev. George Thornton Mostyn, M.A., formerly Incumbent of St. Thomas's, in the town of St. Helen's, Lancashire, and afterwards of St. John's, Kilburn, by his marriage with Charlotte, daughter of the late William Eccles, Esquire, of Glasgow. He was born in Glasgow on the 27th of November, 1842, and was educated at Rugby. On the 29th of July, 1862, he was gazetted to an ensigncy in the 24th Regiment, which he joined at Aldershot. He served with his battalion at various stations in Great Britain and Ireland, in British Burmah, in India, at Malta, at Gibraltar, and at the Cape of Good Hope, where he acted for some time as Aide-de-Camp to General Cunynghame; and throughout the Kaffir war of 1878 he performed many arduous and important duties.

In November, 1878, Captain Mostyn proceeded with the regiment to Natal, to join the force which, with a view to the impending invasion of Zululand, was then being concentrated on the frontier. On the 9th of January, 1879, his company marched from Pietermaritzburg to join the Head-Quarters, which, six weeks earlier, had left the capital, and formed part of Glyn's column at Helpmakaar. The company reached Isandhlwana on the 21st. In the battle which ensued at that position on the 22nd, Captain Mostyn moved the men under his command out of camp to the support of another company of his battalion which, under Lieutenants Cavaye and Dyson, had engaged the enemy on a steep hill about a thousand yards distant, to the left. A few minutes after his arrival on the hill, his company extended and entered into action, supported on the right by a small body of the Native Infantry. Shortly afterwards, the enemy appeared in great force in the rear, and the two companies fell slowly back, keeping up firing. After descending the hill, which was rocky and precipitous, they formed in extended order at a distance of about four hundred yards from it; but their ammunition running short, and the enemy, heavily reinforced, pressing on rapidly, they continued to retire until within three hundred yards of the position occupied by the Native Contingent. Shortly afterwards, that body retreated, rushing past the companies in the utmost disorder, and laying open their right and rear. The men scarcely had time to fix their bayonets, before the enemy were among them, using their assegais with fearful effect. Captain Mostyn fell fighting gallantly at the head of his company. In his death, those to whom he was known sustained a severe loss, his frank disposition and extreme amiability having much endeared him to all with whom he had come in contact.

GEORGE VAUGHAN WARDELL,
CAPTAIN, 24TH REGIMENT (2ND WARWICKSHIRE).

GEORGE VAUGHAN WARDELL,

CAPTAIN, 24TH REGIMENT.

CAPTAIN GEORGE VAUGHAN WARDELL, who was killed at Isandhlwana on January the 22nd, 1879, was the second son of Major Wardell, who served for forty-three years in the 66th Regiment, the 93rd Highlanders, and the Royal Canadian Rifles. He was born at Toronto, Canada, on February the 21st, 1840, and was educated in that country and in England, passing the direct examination for a commission in the line from Kensington School. Gazetted to an ensigncy in the 2nd Battalion 24th Regiment, on May the 14th, 1858, he joined that corps at Bury, and, after serving at Sheffield and Aldershot, embarked with it for Mauritius in March, 1860. He there became a lieutenant by purchase, on July the 23rd, 1861, and there being a scarcity of officers of the Commissariat Department in the island, he acted for nearly two years as Deputy Assistant Commissary-General. In 1865 the battalion proceeded to Burmah, where he remained with it until the middle of 1867, when he proceeded to England on leave, and was afterwards attached to the depôt at Sheffield and Preston.

In 1870 Captain Wardell exchanged into the 1st battalion of his regiment, and served with it for three years at Malta and Gibraltar, obtaining his company on January the 10th, 1872. After being two years at the Brigade Depôt at Brecon, he embarked in May, 1875, in charge of drafts, to rejoin the head-quarters of his regiment, which had been sent to the Cape of Good Hope. In 1876 he went in command of a detachment to St. Helena, where he was quartered more than a year; on his being recalled to the Cape, the governor of the island issued a general order expressing warm approval of the exemplary behaviour of the non-commissioned officers and men, against whom no single complaint had been made, and stating that by the departure of Captain Wardell he lost a valued friend. Rejoining his regiment in 1877, he accompanied it up the country to King William's Town, and, on the Galeka outbreak taking place, was again detached with a hundred men of the 24th, with about three hundred Burghers, Mounted Police, and Natives, to guard the drift, or ford, across the Great Kei River at Impetu. He there constructed a redoubt named by him Fort Warwick (in allusion to the county of his regiment), which afforded shelter to the neighbouring farmers and their families. After holding this post for three or four months, much harassed and more or less surrounded by the Kaffirs, his communications were at last entirely cut, and he had to be relieved early in January, 1878, by a strong force under Colonel Lambert, 88th Regiment. A sketch of this relief appeared in the "Illustrated London News." For this service Captain Wardell received commendation from Sir Arthur Cunynghame, the Lieutenant-General Commanding, who appointed him commandant of the Kei Road and Kabousie stations, with a force of five hundred colonial troops under him. Besides keeping open the communications, he was there incessantly employed in forwarding supplies to the front. Upon the arrival of Lord Chelmsford to take command, he was superseded by a field-officer of another regiment, and rejoined his own corps in the Trans-Kei, where he served against the Galekas until they were completely subjugated.

In November, 1878, the 24th Regiment was ordered to Natal, to join the force being prepared to act against the Zulus in the event of their refusing to comply with the terms of Sir Bartle Frere's ultimatum. Disembarking at Durban, Captain Wardell marched with his company through Maritzburg to Helpmakaar, where he was encamped for a month. Upon the expiration of the period of grace allowed to the Zulus, he was advanced, in command of two companies, to Rorke's Drift, in order to cover the working parties employed in making the ford practicable for artillery and heavy ox-waggons, and in constructing pontoons for conveying the infantry across. On January the 11th, 1879, Colonel Glyn's column, to which both battalions of the 24th Regiment belonged, crossed the Buffalo River into Zululand, and on the following day Captain Wardell, whose company had been the first to pass over, was engaged in a skirmish with outlying parties of the enemy. After being encamped at the Bashee Valley, the column advanced on January the 20th to a new position at the foot of the Isandhlwana Hill. In the attack on the camp at that place on the 22nd, Captain Wardell was slain. Some Natal Carabineers who escaped from the massacre, reported that they saw him, surrounded by his company, making a most desperate stand against the savage foe; and in Lieut.-Colonel Black's description of the field as he found it when he buried the dead five months afterwards, it is stated that over sixty men of the 24th Regiment were found in one spot, together with the remains of Captain Wardell and two other officers who could not be recognized.

Captain Wardell was a thorough soldier; strong, active, and fearless; beloved by his men, and of high repute amongst his brother officers. He married in 1867, at Mauritius, Lucy Anne Charlotte, daughter of Captain Russell, R.N. His father, Major Wardell, served for five years in the Royal Navy before entering the army, and was present at the capture of Java (medal and clasp) in 1811; he also lost his right arm in 1820, from the effects of a wound received whilst in the naval service.

REGINALD YOUNGHUSBAND,

CAPTAIN, 24TH REGIMENT (2ND WARWICKSHIRE).

REGINALD YOUNGHUSBAND,

CAPTAIN, 24TH REGIMENT (2ND WARWICKSHIRE).

CAPTAIN REGINALD YOUNGHUSBAND, who was killed at Isandhlwana on the 22nd of January, 1879, was the fourth son of the late Thomas Younghusband, Esquire, formerly Captain H.E.I.C.S., and lately for very many years a resident of Weymouth, Dorset, by his marriage with Pascoa Georgina, only daughter and co-heiress of Joseph Barretto, of Calcutta, and Portland Place, Regent's Park, London, Esquire. He was born on the 16th of January, 1844, at Bath. Gazetted to an ensigncy in the 2nd Battalion of the 24th Regiment on the 20th of August, 1862, he served with that corps in Mauritius; in Burmah, where he accompanied the British expedition to Mandalay in September, 1867; and in India. He returned with his regiment to England in 1872, and shortly afterwards was appointed Instructor of Musketry, an appointment which he held for four years.

Having obtained his company on the 14th of March, 1876, Captain Younghusband was ordered to the Cape, two months later, to join the 1st Battalion of his regiment. Early in 1878 he returned to England on leave, but embarked again for South Africa in the month of July, to take part in the suppression of the Galeka outbreak. Shortly after his arrival at the Cape his regiment was ordered to Natal to join the force which, with a view to the impending invasion of Zululand, was being concentrated on the frontier.

Colonel Glyn's column, to which both battalions of the 24th Regiment were attached, crossed the Buffalo River on the 11th of January, 1879, and on the following day Captain Younghusband was engaged, with his company, in the reduction of Sirayo's stronghold. Moving through the Bashee Valley, the column encamped, on the 20th of January, under the Isandhlwana Hill. In the disastrous encounter with the enemy which ensued at this position on the 22nd, Captain Younghusband was slain. A bandsman of the 24th Regiment, who escaped from the massacre, reported that he saw him making a desperate stand at the last. With three men of his company he turned a waggon into a rifle-pit, and defended it as long as his ammunition lasted. When the last cartridge was fired, Captain Younghusband shook hands with his men, and then made a desperate attempt to cut his way through the encircling horde of the savage foe. A son of the chieftain

Sirayo, who surrendered at the close of the war, and who was interrogated as to the details of the battle, stated, with reference to what occurred in the neighbourhood of the waggons: "A very brave man was killed near one of them. I don't know whether he was an officer or not, for when I saw him after he was killed his coat had been taken off him, but he had a red stripe on his trowsers, and he had brown gaiters. He was a very tall man, and as we were rushing over the camps he jumped on to an empty waggon with a gun, and kept firing away first on one side and then on another, so that no one got near him. We all saw him and watched him, for he was high up on the waggon, and we all said what a brave man that was! I think he was an officer. All those who tried to stab him were knocked over at once or bayoneted. He kept his ground for a very long time; then someone shot him." The informant adds that those in camp best qualified to decide agreed that this officer was Captain Younghusband.

It is believed that the body of Captain Younghusband was recognized by Major Tongue, lying near to that of Major White. when Colonel Glyn temporarily reoccupied the ill-fated camp on the night of the battle; and the remains were identified and buried by Colonel Black, 24th Regiment, on his visit to the field five months afterwards.

Captain Younghusband married, in February, 1878, Evelyn, second surviving daughter of Richard Davies, Esquire, of the "Vigia," Madeira, and Jerez de la Frontera, Spain.

The family of Younghusband is of very old Northumbrian origin, having been located near Bamburgh before the Conquest. Tradition derives its name and descent from Oswald, the tenth son of Ida, the Flamebearer (A.D. 559). The prefix "Young" having been assumed at an early period by the descendants of the Saxon Oswalds, Oswys, and Osbans, for the sake of distinction, the name gradually became corrupted—"Young-Oswin," "Young-Osban," "Younghosban," to the present form of spelling it.

TEIGNMOUTH MELVILL,

Lieutenant and Adjutant, 24th Regiment (2nd Warwickshire).

TEIGNMOUTH MELVILL,

LIEUTENANT AND ADJUTANT, 24TH REGIMENT (2ND WARWICKSHIRE).

LIEUTENANT AND ADJUTANT TEIGNMOUTH MELVILL, who was killed on the Natal shore of the Buffalo River, in the neighbourhood of Isandhlwana, on the 22nd of January, 1879, was the younger son of Philip Melvill, Esq., late Secretary in the Military Department to the East India Company, by his marriage with Eliza, daughter of Colonel Sandys, of Lanarth, Helston. He was born in London on the 8th of September, 1842, and was educated at Harrow, Cheltenham, and Cambridge, where he graduated B.A. in February, 1865. He entered the army in the same year, and on the 2nd of December, 1868, was gazetted to a lieutenancy in the 1st Battalion of the 24th Regiment. He joined that corps in Ireland, and afterwards proceeded with it to Malta, to Gibraltar, where he was appointed adjutant, and, in January, 1875, to the Cape. Whilst in South Africa he passed the examination for entrance into the Staff College, and in January, 1878, was ordered home to join that establishment.

On hearing of the outbreak of fresh hostilities among the native tribes in Cape Colony, Lieutenant Melvill immediately expressed his willingness to rejoin his regiment: he was ordered out accordingly, and arrived at King William's Town at the end of February. He served with his corps through the whole of the suppression of the Galeka outbreak, performing many arduous and important duties.

Immediately prior to the outbreak of the Zulu war, Lieutenant Melvill proceeded with his regiment to join the Head-Quarters Column, which was then in course of formation on the Natal frontier. Taking part in its subsequent advance into Zululand, he was present at the reduction of Sirayo's stronghold in the Bashee Valley, on the 13th of January, 1879. The following account of the manner in which he met with his death on the day of the fatal attack on the camp at Isandhlwana is taken from a special despatch written by Colonel Glyn, describing the saving of the colours of the 24th Regiment, bearing date February the 21st, 1879:—

"It would appear that, when the enemy had got into the camp, and when there was no longer any hope left of saving it, the Adjutant of the 1st Battalion of the 24th Regiment, Lieutenant Teignmouth Melvill, departed from the camp on horseback, carrying the colour with him in hope of being able to save it.

"The only road to Rorke's Drift being already in possession of the enemy, Lieutenant Melvill and the few others who still remained alive struck across country for the Buffalo River, which it was necessary to cross to reach a point of safety. In taking this line, the only one possible, ground had to be gone over which, from its ruggedness and precipitous nature, would under ordinary circumstances, it is reported, be deemed almost utterly impassable for mounted men.

"During a distance of about six miles Lieutenant Melvill and his companions were closely pursued, or, more properly speaking, accompanied by a large number of the enemy, who, from their well-known agility in getting over rough ground, were able to keep up with our people though the latter were mounted; so that the enemy kept up a constant fire on them, and sometimes even got close enough to assegai the men and horses. Lieutenant Melvill reached the bank of the Buffalo, and at once plunged in, horse and all; but being encumbered with the colour, which is an awkward thing to carry even on foot, and the river being full and running rapidly, he appears to have got separated from his horse when he was about half-way across. He still, however, held on resolutely to the colour, and was being carried down stream when he was washed against a large rock in the middle of the river. Lieutenant Higginson, of the Natal Native Contingent, who had also lost his horse in the river, was clinging to this rock, and Lieutenant Melvill called to him to lay hold of the colour. This Lieutenant Higginson did, but the current was so strong that both officers with the colour were again washed away into still water. In the meantime, Lieutenant Coghill, 1st Battalion 24th Regiment, my orderly officer—who had been left in camp that morning, when the main body of the force moved out, on account of a severe injury to his knee, which rendered him unable to move without assistance—had also succeeded in gaining the river-bank in company with Lieutenant Melvill. He too had plunged at once into the river, and his horse had carried him safely across; but on looking round for Lieutenant Melvill, and seeing him struggling to save the colour in the river, he at once turned his horse and rode back into the stream again to Lieutenant's Melvill's assistance.

"It would appear that now the enemy had assembled in considerable force along their own bank, and had opened a heavy fire on our people, directing it more especially on Lieutenant Melvill, who wore a red patrol jacket; so that when Lieutenant Coghill got into the river again his horse was almost immediately killed by a bullet. Lieutenant Coghill was thus cast loose in the stream also, and notwithstanding the exertions of both these gallant officers, the colour was carried off from them, and they themselves gained the bank in a state of extreme exhaustion.

"It would appear that they now attempted to move up the hill from the river-bank towards Helpmakaar, but must have been too much exhausted to go on, as they were seen to sit down to rest again. This, I sorely regret to say, was the last time these two most gallant officers were seen alive.

"It was not for some days after the 22nd that I could gather any information as to the probable fate of these officers. But immediately I discovered in what direction those who had escaped from Isandhlwana had crossed the Buffalo, I sent, under Major Black, 2nd Battalion 24th Regiment, a mounted party who volunteered for this service, to search for any trace that could be found of them. This search was successful, and both bodies were found where they were last seen, as above indicated. Several dead bodies of the enemy were found about them, so that they must have sold their lives dearly at the last.

"I cannot conclude this report without drawing the attention of his Excellency the Lieutenant-General Commanding, in the most impressive manner which words can command, to the noble and heroic conduct of Lieutenant and Adjutant Melvill, who did not hesitate to encumber himself with the colour of the regiment, in his resolve to save it, at a time when the camp was in the hands of the enemy, and its gallant defenders killed to the last man in its defence; and when there appeared but little prospect that any exertions Lieutenant Melvill could make would enable him to save even his own life. Also, later on, to the noble perseverance with which, when struggling between life and death in the river, his chief thoughts to the last were bent on the saving of the colour.

"In conclusion, I would add that both these officers gave up their lives in the truly noble task of endeavouring to save from the enemy's hands the Queen's colour of their regiment; and, greatly though their sad end is to be deplored, their deaths could not have been more noble or more full of honour."

The two bodies were buried where they were found, and a stone cross was erected over the spot by Sir Bartle Frere and the members of his staff, bearing the following inscription:—

"In memory of Lt. and Adj. Teignmouth Melvill and Lt. Nevill J. A. Coghill, 1st Batt. 24th Regt., who died on this spot, 22nd Jany., 1879, to save the Queen's Colour of their Regiment." On the other face is inscribed: "For Queen and Country—Jesu, mercy."

Immediately after the receipt of Colonel Glyn's despatch in England, an official letter was sent to Mr. Melvill from the Horse Guards, expressing the sympathy of the Field-Marshal Commanding-in-Chief, and intimating that the Victoria Cross would have been conferred on Lieutenant Melvill had he survived his noble effort. The following notification appeared in a Supplement to the "London Gazette" of the 1st of May, 1879:—

"MEMORANDUM. Lieutenant Melvill, of the 1st Batt. 24th Foot, on account of the gallant efforts made by him to save the Queen's Colour of his Regiment after the disaster at Isandhlwana; and also Lieutenant Coghill, 1st Battalion 24th Foot, on account of his heroic conduct in endeavouring to save his brother officer's life, would have been recommended to Her Majesty for the Victoria Cross had they survived."

Lieutenant Melvill was married in February, 1876, and leaves a widow and two sons.

FRANCIS PENDER PORTEOUS,
Lieutenant, 24th Regiment (2nd Warwickshire).

FRANCIS PENDER PORTEOUS,

LIEUTENANT, 24TH REGIMENT (2ND WARWICKSHIRE).

LIEUTENANT FRANCIS PENDER PORTEOUS, who was killed at Isandhlwana on the 22nd of January, 1879, was the eldest son of the late James Porteous, Esq., of Jamaica, by his marriage with Emily, daughter of G. S. Kemble, Esq. He was born on the 26th of March, 1847, and was educated at the Rev. A. Jessop Helston's, in Cornwall; Mount Radford School (Dr. Roper's), Exeter; and Dr. Carter's, in Jersey. Proceeding to Sandhurst, he passed through the prescribed course, and was gazetted, in March, 1866, to the 1st Battalion of the 24th Foot: he joined the regiment at the Curragh, Ireland, and subsequently proceeded with it to Malta, to Gibraltar, and, in January, 1875, to the Cape, having meanwhile, in December, 1869, obtained his lieutenancy by purchase. In 1877 he was appointed instructor of musketry to his battalion. Throughout the Kaffir war of 1878 he served as garrison-adjutant at King William's Town.

In November, 1878, in view of the impending hostilities with the Zulus, the regiment was ordered to Natal, to join the Head-Quarters Column of the army of invasion, then concentrating at Helpmakaar. Taking part in the subsequent advance of that force, in January, 1879, into the enemy's country, Lieutenant Porteous was present at the reduction of Sirayo's stronghold in the Bashee Valley, and afterwards proceeded with the column to Isandhlwana; in the disastrous encounter with the enemy which ensued at that position on the 22nd, he fell fighting gallantly at the head of a company of which he had been temporarily placed in command.

Lieutenant Porteous was a thorough soldier, noble and generous in disposition, devoted to his profession. "He was a great favourite of mine, and much beloved by all in the regiment," wrote his commanding officer. His loss is deeply mourned by all who knew him.

CHARLES D'AGUILAR POPE,
LIEUTENANT, 24TH REGIMENT (2ND WARWICKSHIRE).

CHARLES D'AGUILAR POPE,

LIEUTENANT, 24TH REGIMENT (2ND WARWICKSHIRE).

LIEUTENANT CHARLES D'AGUILAR POPE, eldest son of the Rev. J. P. Pope, Assistant Chaplain, H.E.I.C.S., was born on the 23rd of August, 1849. He was educated at Bath, where he obtained various certificates at the Oxford and Cambridge local examinations. In 1865 he entered Sandhurst, and passing out in 1868 was gazetted to the 2nd Battalion of the 24th Regiment. He became lieutenant in 1871, and shortly afterwards embarked for Madras, where he served for three years. Returning from India to England in 1876, he passed most creditably through a course of garrison and gunnery instruction, and from the School of Musketry at Hythe came out with an extra first-class certificate.

In February, 1878, Lieutenant Pope embarked for South Africa, and, arriving at the Cape, served with his battalion through the Kaffir war of that year. In the following November he proceeded with the regiment to Natal to join the force being prepared to act against the Zulus in the event of their not complying with the terms of Sir Bartle Frere's ultimatum. He took part with the regiment in the subsequent advance of Colonel Glyn's column in January, 1879, into the enemy's country, and was present at the reduction of Sirayo's stronghold in the Bashee Valley. On the fatal 22nd of January, the day on which he met with his death, Lieutenant Pope was on picquet duty, and commanded his company. The following extract from his diary, which, kept up to the very hour of his death, was subsequently picked up in the battle-field, speaks highly for his cool self-possession:—

"At 4 P.M. N. N. C. mounted troops and 4 guns off. Great firing—believed to be by 1/24th. Alarm sounded. Three columns Zulus and mounted men on hill, E. Turn out! 7,000 men E.N.E., 4,000 of whom go round Lion's Kop. Durnford's Basutos arrive and pursue with rocket battery. Zulus retire everywhere. Men fall out for dinner."

And while the men fell out for dinner the right horn of the Zulu army, 7,000 strong, crept round the Kop, and the "three columns" swarmed down the face of it. Several survivors of the massacre which followed testify to the remarkable self-possession with which Lieutenant Pope encouraged his men, and restrained their wasteful fire when the trying order "to retire" was given; and the record of the part he played on the fatal day is supplemented by a statement made by an induna who was present at the slaughter. The Zulu reported that, when surrounding the 24th at the Neck at Isandhlwana, two officers (subsequently ascertained to have been Lieutenants Pope and Godwin-Austen), with pieces of glass in their eye, came forward, shooting at him with their revolvers. One fell from a gunshot, and the other kept firing his revolver at the induna, grazing the right side of his neck with one bullet, the left side with another, and wounding him in the leg with a third. The induna then flung an assegai, which entered the officer's breast. The officer, with a supreme effort, almost succeeded in pulling out the weapon (at this point in his statement the Zulu writhed his body in pantomime of the movements of the officer), but the induna fell on him, and instantaneously finished his work with another assegai.

Lieutenant Pope was a favourite with both officers and men. Besides being an excellent linguist, he was an accomplished draughtsman, and many of his sketches are to be seen in the pages of the "Graphic," and on the walls of the officers' guard-room at Chatham. On the spot at Isandhlwana where he fell, which was first marked by a sergeant of the 2-24th Regiment with a meat-scale, an iron cross, conveyed there by the Bishop of Pietermaritzburg, is about to be erected to his memory.

CHARLES WALTER CAVAYE,

Lieutenant, 24th Regiment (2nd Warwickshire).

CHARLES WALTER CAVAYE,

LIEUTENANT, 24TH REGIMENT (2ND WARWICKSHIRE).

LIEUTENANT CHARLES WALTER CAVAYE, who was killed at Isandhlwana on the 22nd of January, 1879, was the third son of General Cavaye, H.M.I.F., by his marriage with Isabella, daughter of the late Major T. F. Hutchinson. He was born on the 29th of May, 1849, at Rajkote, India, and was educated at the New Academy, Edinburgh, and afterwards at the University of that city, where he graduated M.A. in 1867. During 1871 he was at the Royal Military College at Sandhurst, and on the 30th of December of that year was gazetted sub-lieutenant to the 24th Regiment. Joining the 1st Battalion in March, 1872, at Gibraltar, he served with it during the whole of the time it was at that place, and embarked with it, early in 1875, on its departure for the Cape of Good Hope. In 1876 he was with a detachment of the 1-24th at St. Helena; he remained at that station until 1877, when he rejoined the head-quarters of the battalion. In the following year he served with his corps through the whole of its operations in the Gaika and Galeka war.

In November, 1878, in view of the impending hostilities with the Zulus, the 24th Regiment was ordered to Natal, to join the Head-Quarters Column of the army of invasion, then concentrating at Helpmakaar. Taking part in the subsequent advance of that force, in January, 1879, into the enemy's country, Lieutenant Cavaye was present at the storming of Sirayo's stronghold in the Bashee Valley, and afterwards proceeded with the column to Isandhlwana. In the disastrous encounter with the enemy which ensued at that position on the 22nd, he was in command of the company which had been detached at 10 a.m., and which engaged the enemy on a steep hill about a thousand yards distant from, and to the left of, the camp. The enemy appearing in great force in the rear, the company, supported by Captain Mostyn's, slowly retired. About four hundred yards from the hill they again formed in extended order; but their ammunition running short, and the Zulus, heavily reinforced, pressing on rapidly, they continued to fall back until within three hundred yards of the position occupied by the Native Contingent. Shortly afterwards they were surrounded by countless hordes of the enemy, and overwhelmed. It is believed to have been at this juncture that Lieutenant Cavaye fell: his remains were recognized on the return of the main body of the column to the camp on the night of the 22nd, and were subsequently interred with those of the eight hundred of his countrymen who shared his fate.

The last letter received from Lieutenant Cavaye by his family was one sent from Helpmakaar, bearing date 1st of January, written in the highest spirits, and testifying to his enjoyment of the hardships of campaigning. He was a promising and popular officer, and his loss is keenly felt by those of his comrades who survive him.

EDGAR OLIPHANT ANSTEY,

LIEUTENANT, 24TH REGIMENT (2ND WARWICKSHIRE).

EDGAR OLIPHANT ANSTEY,

LIEUTENANT, 24TH REGIMENT (2ND WARWICKSHIRE).

LIEUTENANT EDGAR OLIPHANT ANSTEY, who was killed at Isandhlwana on the 22nd January, 1879, was the third son of G. A. Anstey, Esquire, of Harley Street, London. He was born at Highercombe, South Australia, on the 18th of March, 1851, and was educated at Rugby. Proceeding to Sandhurst, he passed successfully through the prescribed course, and in March, 1873, was gazetted to a lieutenancy in the 1st Battalion of the 24th Regiment. He joined the regiment at Aldershot; embarked with it in May, 1874, for Gibraltar; and thence proceeded, six months later, to the Cape.

Lieutenant Anstey was engaged with his corps in the suppression of the Galeka outbreak, throughout which he performed distinguished service. He commanded his company in two several actions, and for his conduct on both occasions was mentioned in despatches. He was subsequently ordered to hold Pullen's Farm, and was enabled to successfully fortify that position.

In November, 1878, Lieutenant Anstey proceeded with the regiment to Natal, to join the force then being concentrated on the frontier with a view to the impending invasion of Zululand. On the 9th of January, 1879, Captain Mostyn's company, to which he was attached, marched from Pietermaritzburg to join the headquarters, which, six weeks earlier, had left the capital, and formed part of Glyn's column at Helpmakaar. The company reached Isandhlwana on the 21st. In the disastrous encounter with the enemy which ensued at that position on the 22nd, Anstey was engaged, under Captain Mostyn, at the commencement of the engagement, on the hills to the left of the camp. No accurate record of his death exists, but it is believed that he fell towards the latter end of the engagement, in the last desperate rally made by the three companies of his battalion to the east of the camp.

Lieutenant Anstey's remains were subsequently recovered from the battle-field by his brother, Captain Anstey, R.E., under whose superintendence they were conveyed to England, and interred in the family vault in Woking Cemetery.

NEVILL JOSIAH AYLMER COGHILL,
LIEUTENANT, 24TH REGIMENT (2ND WARWICKSHIRE).

NEVILL JOSIAH AYLMER COGHILL,

LIEUTENANT 24TH REGIMENT (2ND WARWICKSHIRE).

LIEUTENANT NEVILL JOSIAH AYLMER COGHILL, who was killed on the Natal shore of the Buffalo River, in the neighbourhood of Isandhlwana, on the 22nd of January, 1879, was the eldest son of Sir John Joscelyn Coghill, Bart., of Drumcondra, county Dublin, and nephew of the Right Rev. Lord Plunket, Bishop of Meath. He was born on the 25th of January, 1852, in Dublin, and was educated at Haileybury, after which he was for two years in the County of Dublin Militia. Having passed the examination for direct appointment to the army in 1871, he received a commission in the 24th Regiment, passed through Sandhurst, and, after serving for a short time in England, went out with the regiment to Gibraltar. From Gibraltar he proceeded to the Cape, and was there appointed Aide-de-Camp to General Sir Arthur Cunynghame, with whom he shortly afterwards made a tour of inspection through the whole colony and the adjacent country, including Natal, Griqualand, the Orange Free State, and the Transvaal. Shortly after he returned to Cape Town the Gaika and Galeka war was declared. He went through the whole of that campaign, still continuing as Aide-de-Camp to Sir Arthur Cunynghame, and was mentioned in despatches. He subsequently returned to England with his General on the latter being replaced by General Thesiger, afterwards Lord Chelmsford.

On preparations being made for the invasion of Zululand, Lieutenant Coghill at once hurried back to the Cape. Shortly after arriving there he was appointed Aide-de-Camp to Sir Bartle Frere, and travelled with him to Pietermaritzburg, where he obtained leave of absence to join his regiment at the front. He was there appointed extra Aide-de-Camp to Colonel Glyn, who was in command of the column to which the 24th Regiment was attached, and continued to hold the appointment until the day of his death. The last letter received from him by his family was written in the highest spirits, just after the successful attack upon Sirayo's kraal; in it he expressed the general opinion that, after all, the campaign would be a short one, and that in a month the war would be reduced to the proportion of mere guerilla work—driving the beaten enemy from the bush. So far as can be gathered from official accounts, and from the letters received from his brother officers, Lieutenant Coghill's share in the action which ensued at Isandhlwana, was as follows:—Some days previously to the 22nd of January he had strained an already injured knee, and when it was arranged that the reconnoitring force under Lord Chelmsford and Colonel Glyn should start early on the morning of that day, he was desired to remain quietly in camp, instead of accompanying the party as he would otherwise have done. In a letter received from Colonel Glyn, that officer wrote that he left him shortly before daybreak quietly sleeping in his tent. The next that is heard of him is in the account given by Captain Young, who, towards the end of the battle, succeeded in cutting his way through the encircling horde of the enemy. He saw Coghill, who was a splendid horseman and well mounted, desperately fighting, but unable to make his way through the opening through which he (Captain Young) escaped. It is clear, however, that he did manage to break through the line, for he was shortly afterwards seen by Lieutenant Higginson, of the Natal Native Contingent. That officer reported that while struggling in the Buffalo River, having lost his horse, he saw Lieutenant Melvill in the deep swift stream, with the colours. Higginson was at this time clinging to a rock, and contrived, by seizing the colours, to draw Melvill into calm water. At this moment Coghill, who had got out on the Natal side, and was breasting the hill, perceived their condition, and turning his horse rode back into the river to their assistance. Immediately afterwards his horse was shot; nevertheless the three contrived to reach the bank, and, according to Lieutenant Higginson's report, "managed to get about 100 yards up the hill, when Coghill called out, 'Here they are after us.' They had both revolvers, and I had nothing to defend myself with, so I told them to fire. We waited till they got to about thirty paces, and then fired. Two men fell, who were in front. Then Melvill, who was very much done up, said he could go no farther, and Coghill said the same. I thought I would have one more struggle for life, though my horse had kicked me on the leg very badly, so I got past them, and got on top of the hill."

A few days afterwards their dead bodies were discovered some three or four hundred yards from the river, behind some large boulders, surrounded by more than a dozen dead Zulus. They were buried where they lay, and a stone cross was erected over the spot by Sir Bartle Frere and the members of his staff, with the following inscription: "In memory of Lt. and Adj. Teignmouth Melvill and Lt. Nevill J. A. Coghill, 1st Batt. 24th Regt., who died on this spot 22nd Jany., 1879, to save the Queen's Colour of their Regiment." On the other face is inscribed: "For Queen and Country—Jesu, mercy."

The official despatch of Colonel Glyn to Lord Chelmsford, bearing date February 21st, 1879, concludes with the following words:—

"Similarly would I draw his Excellency's attention to the equally noble and gallant conduct of Lieutenant Coghill, who did not hesitate for an instant to return unsolicited, and ride again into the river under a heavy fire of the enemy, to the assistance of his friend, though at the time he was wholly incapacitated from walking, and but too well aware that any accident that might separate him from his horse must be fatal to him.

"In conclusion, I would add that both these officers gave up their lives in the truly noble task of endeavouring to save from the enemy's hands the Queen's colour of their regiment; and greatly though their sad end is to be deplored, their deaths could not have been more noble or more full of honour."

An official letter, bearing date April the 21st, 1879, received by Sir Joscelyn Coghill from the Horse Guards, concludes as follows:—

"His Royal Highness (the Field-Marshal Commanding in Chief) in communicating this despatch to you desires me to assure you of his sincere sympathy with you in the loss of your son, whose gallant death in the successful endeavour to save the colour of his regiment has gained the admiration of the army.

"It is gratifying to his Royal Highness to inform you that if your son had survived his noble effort, it was her Majesty's intention to confer upon him the Victoria Cross, and a notification to that effect will be made in the 'London Gazette.'"

In a supplement to the "London Gazette" of the 1st of May, 1879, the following notification appeared:—

"Memorandum. Lieutenant Melvill, of the 1st Battalion 24th Foot, on account of the gallant efforts made by him to save the Queen's colour of his regiment after the disaster at Isandhlwana, and also Lieutenant Coghill, 1st Battalion 24th Foot, on account of his heroic conduct in endeavouring to save his brother officer's life, would have been recommended to her Majesty for the Victoria Cross had they survived."

JAMES PATRICK DALY,

Lieutenant, 24th Regiment (2nd Warwickshire).

JAMES PATRICK DALY,

LIEUTENANT, 24TH REGIMENT (2ND WARWICKSHIRE).

LIEUTENANT JAMES PATRICK DALY, who was killed at Isandhlwana on the 22nd of January, 1879, was born in March, 1855. He was educated at Oscott, and at the Rev. E. Barney's establishment, at Gosport. After leaving school he served for two successive years with the Galway Militia. On the 28th of February, 1874, he was gazetted to a lieutenancy in the 1st Battalion of the 24th Regiment; and, having joined that corps at Gibraltar, embarked with it at the latter end of the same year for the Cape.

Lieutenant Daly served with his battalion through the Gaika and Galeka campaign of 1877, performing many arduous duties. In November, 1878, he proceeded with the regiment to Natal, to join the force then being prepared to act against the Zulus in the event of their refusing to comply with the terms of Sir Bartle Frere's ultimatum. On the 9th of January, 1879, Captain Mostyn's company, to which he was attached, marched from Pietermaritzburg to join the headquarters, which, six weeks earlier, had left the capital, and formed part of Glyn's column at Helpmakaar. The company reached Isandhlwana on the 21st. In the disastrous encounter with the enemy which ensued at that position on the 22nd, Daly was engaged, under Captain Mostyn, at the commencement of the engagement, on the hills to the left of the camp. No accurate record of his death exists, but it is believed that he fell towards the latter end of the engagement, in the last desperate rally made by the three companies of his battalion to the east of the camp.

Lieutenant Daly was a most promising young officer. His genial disposition had endeared him to all who knew him.

GEORGE FREDERICK JOHN HODSON,

Lieutenant, 24th Regiment (2nd Warwickshire).

GEORGE FREDERICK JOHN HODSON,

LIEUTENANT, 24TH REGIMENT (2ND WARWICKSHIRE).

LIEUTENANT GEORGE FREDERICK JOHN HODSON, who was killed at Isandhlwana on the 22nd of January, 1879, was the second son of Sir George Hodson, Bart., of Holybrooke, Bray, County of Wicklow, and of Green Park, Westmeath. He was born in Dublin on the 26th of November, 1854, and was educated at Haileybury College, Hertfordshire. On the 28th of February, 1874, he was gazetted to a lieutenancy in the 1st Battalion of the 24th Regiment, and joined that corps at Aldershot. In the following May he embarked with his regiment for Gibraltar, and thence proceeded, six months later, to the Cape.

Shortly after his arrival in South Africa, Lieutenant Hodson was appointed Aide-de-Camp to Sir Bartle Frere. He subsequently served as orderly officer to Colonel Glyn throughout the Gaika and Galeka campaign of 1877, during the arduous prosecution of which his name was more than once mentioned in despatches. At the conclusion of the campaign he returned to his duties with Sir Bartle Frere, and held his appointment until November, 1878, when his regiment was ordered to Natal in view of the impending invasion of Zululand.

Lieutenant Hodson took part with his regiment in the subsequent advance of the Head-Quarter column, in January, 1879, into the enemy's country, and was present at the storming of Sirayo's stronghold in the Bashee Valley on the 13th of January, 1879. In the disastrous encounter which ensued at Isandhlwana, on the 22nd, he was one of the first who fell, it is stated, in the last desperate rally made by the three companies of his battalion to the east of the camp.

CHARLES JOHN ATKINSON,

Lieutenant, 24th Regiment (2nd Warwickshire).

CHARLES JOHN ATKINSON,

LIEUTENANT, 24TH REGIMENT (2ND WARWICKSHIRE).

LIEUTENANT CHARLES JOHN ATKINSON, who was killed in action at Isandhlwana, on the 22nd of January, 1879, was the eldest son of the late Adam Atkinson, Esq., of Lorbottle, Northumberland, and Charlotte Eustatia, his wife, only daughter of the late John Collett, Esq., sometime M.P. for Cashel, in Ireland. He was born on the 27th of May, 1855, and was educated at Eton. Passing the examination for direct appointment, he was gazetted, in February, 1874, sub-lieutenant in the 1st Battalion of the 24th Regiment, and joining that corps at Aldershot he proceeded with it, in May, to Gibraltar; there he served until the following December, when he embarked with the battalion for the Cape. In February, 1877, he was gazetted to a lieutenancy.

After being quartered for two years and a half in South Africa, Lieutenant Atkinson saw active service, the regiment being ordered to the front on the outbreak of the Kaffir war of 1877-78. He served with his corps through the whole of that campaign, performing many important duties, and assisting materially in the arduous task of clearing the country of the enemy. At the action of Quintena, on the 7th of February, 1878, he commanded a company, and greatly distinguished himself. He was mentioned by Major Upcher, the officer in command, for his conduct on that occasion, and also by General Sir A. Cunynghame in his despatch of the 28th of March.

In November, 1878, Lieutenant Atkinson proceeded with the regiment to Natal to join the force being prepared there to act against the Zulus in the event of their refusing to comply with the terms of Sir Bartle Frere's ultimatum. He took part in the subsequent advance of Colonel Glyn's column, in January, 1879, into the enemy's country, and was present at the storming of Sirayo's stronghold in the Bashee Valley. He then proceeded with the column to Isandhlwana, and in the disastrous encounter with the enemy at that position fell in the execution of his duty—it is believed, in the last desperate rally of the three companies to the left front of the camp.

Lieutenant Atkinson was a most promising young officer, a great and general favourite in the regiment, and well loved beyond it. By others besides the sadly diminished roll of his comrades, his loss is keenly felt and deeply deplored.

HENRY JULIAN DYER,

Lieutenant, 24th Regiment (2nd Warwickshire).

HENRY JULIAN DYER,

LIEUTENANT AND ADJUTANT, 24TH REGIMENT (2ND WARWICKSHIRE).

LIEUTENANT AND ADJUTANT HENRY JULIAN DYER, who was killed at Isandhlwana on the 22nd of January, 1879, was the eldest son of Henry Julian Dyer, Esquire, and Emma, his late wife, eldest daughter of the late Francis Glass, Esquire, of Beckenham, Kent; and grandson of the late James Holland Dyer, Esquire, of Blackheath, Kent. He was born on the 21st of October, 1854, at Red Hill, Surrey, and was educated at the Institute Taplin, Lohnstein-on-Rhine. He entered the army in 1876, being gazetted to a Lieutenancy in the 2nd Battalion of the 24th Regiment in October of that year. Joining his corps at Dover, he served with it at that station and at Chatham, and in 1877 successfully passed through the School of Musketry at Hythe. On the 2nd of February, 1878, he embarked with the regiment for South Africa, where, after arriving, he served through the whole of the operations in connection with the suppression of the Galeka outbreak.

In November, 1878, Lieutenant Dyer proceeded with the regiment to Natal, to join the force being prepared to act against the Zulus in the event of their refusing to comply with the terms of Sir Bartle Frere's ultimatum. While at Durban, he held an appointment as principal officer. He took part with the regiment in the subsequent advance of Colonel Glyn's column into the enemy's country in January, 1879, and was present at the storming of Sirayo's stronghold in the Bashee Valley. On the morning of the 22nd of January, he left Isandhlwana with the main body of the column, under Lord Chelmsford; but subsequently rode back on special service with Major Smith, Captain Gardner, and Lieutenant Griffith, to convey the General's order to advance the camp. Arriving at the very crisis of the tragedy which was being enacted, Lieutenant Dyer yet managed to make his way to his company: he was seen on horseback, in the thick of the engagement, directing his men where to fire, and he fell doing his duty to the last. Colonel Degacher, 24th Regiment, in a letter written at Rorke's Drift, bearing date 27th of January, 1879, making reference to the loss he had personally sustained on the fatal day, said: "They all (viz., his brother, Major Smith, Lieutenant Griffith, and Lieutenant Dyer) died like gentlemen: not one of them, although they might have done so, left their men." On revisiting the ill-fated camp five months after the battle, for the purpose of burying the dead, Colonel Black found Lieutenant Dyer's body, pierced to the heart with an assegai, and lying in a group with those of sixty others who had formed a rallying-point in the retreat and fought desperately to the end.

In the death of Lieutenant Dyer a promising career was brought to an untimely close. "He would have made," wrote one of his comrades, "a first-rate officer. The men of his regiment would have done anything for him."

FREDERICK GODWIN-AUSTEN,

LIEUTENANT, 24TH REGIMENT (2ND WARWICKSHIRE).

FREDERICK GODWIN-AUSTEN,

LIEUTENANT, 24TH REGIMENT (2ND WARWICKSHIRE).

LIEUTENANT FREDERICK GODWIN-AUSTEN, who was killed at Isandhlwana on the 22nd of January, 1879, was the fourth surviving son of Robert Alfred Cloyne Godwin-Austen, Esq., D.L., J.P., F.R.S., of Shalford House, Surrey, and Maria Elizabeth, his wife, only daughter of the late General Sir Henry Thomas Godwin, K.C.B. (Peninsula, Waterloo), of the 9th and 41st Regiments, commanding-in-chief in both the first and second Burmese wars. He was born on the 3rd of August, 1853, at Chilworth Manor, Surrey, and was therefore in his twenty-sixth year at the time of his death. He entered the army in February, 1875, and was first posted to the 2nd West India Regiment, with which he served in the West Indies and on the Gold Coast. Exchanging into the 2nd Battalion of the 24th Foot in 1877, he joined that corps at Chatham, proceeded with it to South Africa, and served through the Kaffir war of 1878.

Lieutenant Godwin-Austen proceeded with the 24th Regiment to Natal, to join the force being prepared to act against the Zulus in the event of their refusing to comply with the terms of Sir Bartle Frere's ultimatum. He took part with the regiment in the subsequent advance of Colonel Glyn's column, in January, 1879, into the enemy's country, and was present at the storming of Sirayo's stronghold in the Bashee Valley. An induna who was present at the massacre at Isandhlwana on the 22nd, subsequently gave a minute description of the deaths of two officers, since ascertained to have been Lieutenants Godwin-Austen and Pope, who fell on that fatal day. The Zulu stated that when surrounding the 24th Regiment at the Neck at Isandhlwana, two officers with pieces of glass in their eye came forward, shooting at him with their revolvers. One fell dead from a gunshot, and the other kept firing his revolver at the induna, grazing the right side of his neck with one bullet, the left side with another, and wounding him in the leg with a third. The induna then flung an assegai, which entered the officer's breast. The officer, with a supreme effort, almost succeeded in pulling out the weapon (at this point in his statement the Zulu writhed his body in pantomime of the movements of the officer); but the induna fell on him, and finished his work with another assegai.

Lieutenant F. Godwin-Austen was the third of his name who has served in the 24th Regiment, his two elder brothers being Lieutenant-Colonel H. H. Godwin-Austen, who served in it from 1852 to 1861, and Captain A. G. Godwin-Austen, at present serving, who was with it through the last Kaffir war, in which he was wounded.

THOMAS LLEWELYN GEORGE GRIFFITH,
SUB-LIEUTENANT, 24TH REGIMENT (2ND WARWICKSHIRE).

THOMAS LLEWELYN GEORGE GRIFFITH,

SUB-LIEUTENANT, 24TH REGIMENT (2ND WARWICKSHIRE).

SUB-LIEUTENANT THOMAS LLEWELYN GEORGE GRIFFITH, who was killed at Isandhlwana on the 22nd of January, 1879, at the age of twenty-one, was the eldest son of the Rev. Thomas Llewelyn Griffith, M. A. (of Pen y Nant, near Ruabon, North Wales, and Rector of Deal, Kent), and Mary Moncreiff, his wife, daughter of the late Brevet-Major George St. Vincent Whitmore, Royal Engineers.

He was born on the 8th of October, 1857, at Chadlington, Oxon, of which village his father was then curate in charge; and was educated at Marlborough College. Belonging on his mother's side to a family long well known in the army, he early showed a decided wish for a military life; and accordingly, having been prepared for its requirements at the Priory at Croydon, and having passed his Army examination successfully, as well as those at Sandhurst and Edinburgh, where he was temporarily attached to the 78th Highlanders (Ross-shire Buffs), he was duly gazetted to a sub-lieutenancy in the 2nd Battalion 24th Regiment, in September, 1877. His commission was antedated a twelvemonth, to September, 1876, his name having been ninth on the list at the final Army Examination which entitled him to be placed on the second class in order of merit.

Joining his regiment at Chatham in October, 1877, he afterwards embarked with it, on the 1st of February, 1878, for the Cape. He served with his corps through the whole of its subsequent operations in the suppression of the outbreak in Kaffraria, seeing much service, and repeatedly winning the praise and commendation of his superior officers, as evincing much promise in all branches of his profession.

In November, 1878, Lieutenant Griffith proceeded with the regiment to Natal, to join the force being prepared there to act against the Zulus in the event of their refusing to comply with the terms of Sir Bartle Frere's ultimatum. He took part with the regiment in the subsequent advance of Colonel Glyn's column into the enemy's country in January, 1879; and was present at the storming of Sirayo's stronghold in the Bashee Valley. On the morning of the 22nd of January, he left Isandhlwana with the main body of the column under Lord Chelmsford, but subsequently rode back on special service with Major Smith, Captain Gardner, and

Lieutenant Dyer, to convey the General's order to advance the camp. Arriving at the very crisis of the tragedy which was being enacted, Lieutenant Griffith joined his company, and fell in the discharge of his duty. Colonel Black, visiting the battle-field five months afterwards for the purpose of burying the dead, found the bodies of some sixty officers and men lying in a group, giving evidence of their having gathered together and fought desperately to the last. Among them were the remains of Captain Wardell, Lieutenant Dyer, and a captain and subaltern of the 2-24th, the latter, it is believed, being the mortal part of young Griffith.

In addition to much real talent, Lieutenant Griffith possessed a disposition so bright and sunny, and was endowed with a helpfulness so ready and genial, that he was beloved by all who knew him; and his early death called forth a deep regret, more widely spread than could have been anticipated from the shortness of his life. A memorial lectern in the parish church of Deal (St. Leonard's) marks the estimation in which he was held by those round his own home, having been placed there by friends in his father's parish and the neighbourhood.

EDWARDS HOPTON DYSON,

2ND LIEUTENANT, 24TH REGIMENT (2ND WARWICKSHIRE).

EDWARDS HOPTON DYSON,

2ND LIEUTENANT, 24TH REGIMENT (2ND WARWICKSHIRE).

SECOND LIEUTENANT EDWARDS HOPTON DYSON, who was killed at Isandhlwana on the 22nd of January, 1879, was the son of Major Edwards Dyson, of Denne Hill, Canterbury, by his marriage with Caroline Agnes, daughter of John Stuart Jerdan, Esq., of London. He was born on the 23rd of January, 1858, and was educated in France, Germany, and at Wimbledon School. He subsequently entered the Royal Military College at Sandhurst, and passing out early in 1878 was gazetted to a 2nd lieutenancy in the 1st Battalion of the 24th Regiment, on the 11th of May of that year; he at once embarked for the Cape, and on his arrival joined his corps at King William's Town.

In November, 1878, Lieutenant Dyson proceeded with the regiment to Natal, and, disembarking at Durban, marched with it to Helpmakaar to join the force being prepared to act against the Zulus in the event of their refusing to comply with the terms of Sir Bartle Frere's ultimatum. He took part with the regiment in the subsequent advance of Colonel Glyn's column into the enemy's country in January, 1879, and was present at the storming of Sirayo's stronghold in the Bashee Valley. He then accompanied the regiment to Isandhlwana, and, in the disastrous and untoward encounter with the Zulus which ensued on the 22nd, shared the fate of the officers and men of the regiment who fell. The following extract from a private letter written to his father gives some clue to the manner in which he met his death :—

" The last person who saw your son and escaped, that I can find, was Captain Essex, 75th Regiment, acting transport officer. He tells me that just before the Zulu horns got round our flanks and the last overwhelming rush was made, Dyson was with one section of his company, which was in skirmishing order to the left-front of the camp. He gave him orders to retire, and I believe, from another witness, that he and all his company rejoined the main body without loss. The five companies were then together in line, giving volley after volley into dense masses of Zulus at only 150 yards' range. The men were laughing and chatting, and thought they were giving the blacks an awful hammering, when suddenly the enemy came down in irresistible numbers from the rear; the left and right flanks came in with a rush, and in a few moments all was over."

REGINALD WILLIAM FRANKLIN,
LIEUTENANT, 24TH REGIMENT (2ND WARWICKSHIRE).

REGINALD WILLIAM FRANKLIN,

LIEUTENANT, 24TH REGIMENT (2ND WARWICKSHIRE).

LIEUTENANT REGINALD WILLIAM FRANKLIN, who died at Helpmakaar on the 20th of February, 1879, was the youngest son of Major-General C. T. Franklin, C.B., late R.A. He was born on the 23rd of October, 1859, and was educated at Cheltenham College. He entered Sandhurst in February, 1878, and in the following May was gazetted to the 2nd Battalion of the 24th Regiment, which he joined shortly afterwards at the Cape.

In November, 1878, Lieutenant Franklin proceeded with his regiment to Natal, to join the force being prepared to act against the Zulus in the event of their refusing to comply with the terms of Sir Bartle Frere's ultimatum. He took part in the subsequent advance of Colonel Glyn's column into the enemy's country in January, 1879, and was present at the storming of Sirayo's stronghold in the Bashee Valley. On the morning of the 22nd he was absent from Isandhlwana with the main body of the column under Lord Chelmsford. On the return of that force to the devastated camp on the evening of the same day, he "led the company," to use the words of his captain, "as steadily as if he had been an old soldier, although an attack was momentarily expected, and few hoped to save their lives." A fortnight later Lieutenant Franklin was attacked with fever: he was removed to Helpmakaar, in the hope that change and a purer atmosphere might restore him; but his strength had been too severely tried by the hardships and fatigue of the preceding weeks, and on the night of the 20th of February he passed peacefully away.

Though not dying in the field of battle, Lieutenant Franklin none the less gave up his life in the service of his country. After his death his Colonel wrote a letter very strongly in his praise, assuring his father that he possessed all the qualities likely to form a fine soldier, and ending with the words, "Your boy was everything I could possibly desire." With all his brother officers he was a favourite, and the men of his company had become fond of him, in spite of the shortness of the time he had been with them.

Before his death, which occurred within nine months of his being gazetted to his regiment, Lieutenant Franklin had no less than twenty subalterns below him—an instance of promotion the rapidity of which would seem to be unique.

FRANCIS FREEMAN WHITE,

Staff Paymaster and Hon. Major, 24th Regiment (2nd Warwickshire).

FRANCIS FREEMAN WHITE,

PAYMASTER AND MAJOR, 24TH REGIMENT (2ND WARWICKSHIRE).

MAJOR FRANCIS FREEMAN WHITE, who was killed at Isandhlwana on the 22nd of January, 1879, was the second son of Benjamin Finch White, Esquire, of Rath Cahill, King's County, Ireland. He was born on the 5th of February, 1829, and was educated by the Rev. H. Tyrrel, curate of Shinrone, King's County. He obtained a direct commission by purchase in February, 1850, being gazetted to an ensigncy in the 1st Battalion of the 24th Regiment, and proceeded to the depôt of the corps at Chatham in the following April; shortly afterwards he embarked for India to join the head-quarters of the regiment, then in Bengal. In May, 1854, he became Lieutenant by purchase, and in July, 1856, Paymaster. He served with the regiment through the Indian mutiny, performing many arduous and important duties, and subsequently obtained the medal. In 1859 he returned from India to England, where he remained until 1866, when he again proceeded abroad with the regiment; he was stationed with it for four years at Malta and Gibraltar, and embarked with it, at the latter end of 1874, for the Cape.

Major White served with his battalion in South Africa through the Gaika and Galeka campaign of 1877, from the commencement of the outbreak until its suppression. In November, 1878, he proceeded with the regiment to Natal to join the force being prepared to act against the Zulus in the event of their refusing to comply with the terms of Sir Bartle Frere's ultimatum. He took part with the regiment in the subsequent advance of Colonel Glyn's column, in January, 1879, into the enemy's country, and was present at the storming of Sirayo's stronghold in the Bashee Valley. He then accompanied the regiment to Isandhlwana, and in the disastrous encounter with the enemy at that position on the 22nd of January, shared the fate of the bulk of his gallant corps: he fell in harness doing his duty in the fighting line of skirmishers, and much aiding in the defence by bringing ammunition to replenish the exhausted pouches.

In the death of Major White the country lost a gallant and able servant. He was the oldest officer in his battalion, having served with it without intermission, from the 15th of February, 1850, till the day of his death, and he was justly beloved not only by his brother officers and the men of the regiment, but by all who knew him.

Major White married, in 1874, Agnes, daughter of the late Captain Tracey, R.A.

EDWARD BLOOMFIELD,
QUARTER MASTER, 24TH REGIMENT (2ND WARWICKSHIRE).

EDWARD BLOOMFIELD,

QUARTERMASTER, 24TH REGIMENT (2ND WARWICKSHIRE).

QUARTERMASTER EDWARD BLOOMFIELD, who was killed at Isandhlwana on the 22nd of January, 1879, was born on the 7th of November, 1835, and was consequently in his forty-fourth year at the time of his death. When a lad of eleven years of age he enlisted in the Scots Fusilier Guards. He was transferred to the 2nd Battalion of the 24th Regiment on its formation, and accompanied it to Mauritius, to Burmah, and to India. After twenty-two years' honourable service, he was promoted, in 1868, from the rank of Colour-Sergeant to that of Sergeant-Major, an appointment which met with wide-spread satisfaction, and on the occasion of which his comrades took the opportunity of presenting to him some small token of their regard. "We have been in the company with you several years, and have never had cause to wish you aught but well," wrote the men of the K Company, with other kindly words which appear to have come straight from their hearts as they went straight to his. He returned from India to England in 1873, when he obtained the good conduct medal, and in September of the same year was promoted from the rank of Sergeant-Major to that of Quartermaster. On his promotion being announced in the "London Gazette," the following paragraph appeared in the Battalion Orders of the regiment, bearing date September the 26th, 1873:—"During the number of years Quartermaster Bloomfield has been in the Battalion, he has ever performed his duty with the greatest zeal and ability, and to the entire satisfaction of his commanding officers; and it is his highly meritorious service which has secured for him such a distinguished mark of the Queen's favour." He again embarked from England with the regiment in February, 1878, for the Cape, and, after arriving there, served through the whole of the operations in connection with the suppression of the Galeka outbreak, performing the arduous duties which fell to his lot with the zeal and ability for which he was distinguished.

In November, 1878, Quartermaster Bloomfield proceeded with the regiment to Natal to join the force being prepared to act against the Zulus in the event of their refusing to comply with the terms of Sir Bartle Frere's ultimatum. He took part with the regiment in the subsequent advance of Colonel Glyn's column, in January, 1879, into the enemy's country, and was present at the storming of Sirayo's stronghold in the Bashee Valley. He then accompanied the regiment to Isandhlwana, and in the disastrous encounter with the enemy at that position on the 22nd of January, shared the fate of the officers and men of the regiment who fell. He was killed while discharging his duty with that cool steadfastness which characterized him, being in the act of serving out to the men, in the thick of the engagement, the cartridges which enabled them to make their last desperate stand against the savage foe.

On the announcement of Quartermaster Bloomfield's death being made, many letters from unexpected sources, testifying to his worth, and bearing record of his acts of simple, unostentatious kindness in the past, were written, the burden of each and all being that those who had known him had never—to use words already quoted—had cause to wish him aught but well. "He was a stanch soldier, a warm-hearted friend, and a good husband and father," wrote Captain St. Aubyn, late of the 2-24th,—a brief summary of his character which is supplemented by words written in a letter to the "Times" by Major-General Ross, during whose command the Quartermaster obtained his rank: "A more upright, conscientious man I am sure never existed."

If one soldierly attribute may be said to have distinguished Bloomfield more than another, it is that he was intensely thorough: that which he laid his hand to he did cheerfully and with all his might.

JAMES PULLEN,

Quarter Master, 24th Regiment (2nd Warwickshire).

JAMES PULLEN,

QUARTERMASTER, 24TH REGIMENT (2ND WARWICKSHIRE).

NO accurate account of this officer's antecedents prior to his entry into Her Majesty's service can at present be obtained. He joined the 24th Regiment, as a private, in the year 1851. After nineteen years' honourable service in various quarters of the globe, he was promoted, in 1870, whilst at Malta, to the rank of Colour-Sergeant; and in 1873, whilst at Gibraltar, was appointed Sergeant Instructor of Musketry.

Sergeant Pullen proceeded with the regiment, at the latter end of 1874, to the Cape, and served with it at its various stations in the Colony. From May to November, 1876, he acted as Sergeant-Major to the detachment of his corps which formed part of the expedition to Griqualand West. In July, 1877, he was promoted to the rank of Quartermaster, and served with his battalion in that capacity throughout the Kaffir war of 1877-1878.

In November, 1878, he proceeded with the regiment to Natal, on its embarkation for that country in view of the impending hostilities with the Zulus. He took part, in January, 1879, in the subsequent advance of Glyn's column into the enemy's country, and was present at the storming of Sirayo's stronghold in the Bashee Valley. In the disastrous encounter with the enemy at Isandhlwana on the 22nd, he was last seen leading a party of twenty men, and was heard to say: "Come on, my lads! Follow me, and let us turn their flank." He went out with this party towards the hills to the left of the position, and steadfastly performed his duty of serving out ammunition until the line retired on the camp.

Quartermaster Pullen was a well-conducted, intelligent soldier, most zealous in the performance of his duties. He was a good shot and keen sportsman too—attributes which, perhaps, contributed not a little to the popularity which he enjoyed amongst his brother officers and his men.

CECIL CHARLES WILLIAMS,

Lieutenant, 58th Regiment (Rutlandshire).

CECIL CHARLES WILLIAMS,

LIEUTENANT, 58TH REGIMENT (RUTLANDSHIRE).

LIEUTENANT CECIL CHARLES WILLIAMS, who was killed in the retreat from the Zlobane Mountain, on the 28th of March, 1879, was the third son of the late John Williams, Esquire, of the Cedars, Didsbury, Manchester. He was born on the 28th of July, 1855, and was educated at Dr. Brackenbury's Military School, at Wimbledon. Passing the examination for direct appointment in 1873, he was gazetted, in August, to a lieutenancy in the 58th Regiment, then in India. He was sent temporarily to the 23rd Welsh Fusiliers, at Aldershot, where he remained until the 58th returned, when, joining it at Portsmouth, he proceeded with it to Aldershot, and thence to Dover. While the regiment was quartered at that town he passed creditably through a course of musketry instruction at Hythe.

On preparations for the invasion of Zululand being hurried forward at the latter end of 1878, Lieutenant Williams succeeded in obtaining orders to proceed to South Africa. Leaving the regiment at Dover, he embarked for the Cape, from whence, after arriving, he proceeded to Natal and the Transvaal. He joined Colonel Wood's column at Utrecht, and there remained for a time actively employed in discharging duties connected with the transport service. On the 7th of February, 1879, he was nominated staff officer to Major W. Knox Leet, commandant of Wood's Irregulars. Throughout the remainder of the month and during March he saw much service, accompanying his corps in the constantly recurring reconnaissances in which it was employed with the Mounted Volunteers, and winning golden opinions by the able manner in which he discharged the duties which fell to his lot. Colonel Buller, in a despatch to Lord Chelmsford reporting the operations in the Intombi Valley, wrote:—"Wood's Irregulars fought well, owing much, I think, to the admirable way in which they were led by Major Leet, Lieutenant Williams, and Captain Hook."

On the 28th of March, Colonel Wood, carrying out Lord Chelmsford's instructions to cause a diversion of the enemy's attention from the column which was about to advance to the relief of Etshowe, made an organized attack on the Zulu stronghold of the Zlobane Mountain. Setting out with his corps on the morning of the 27th, Lieutenant Williams marched with it across the Zunguin hills, where it was joined by a force under Colonel Buller destined to ascend the eastern acclivity of the mountain. With this force the 2nd Battalion of the corps advanced, but Lieutenant Williams, in consequence of his intimate knowledge of the country, was left with the 1st Battalion and Oham's men to act as a guide to a second body, under Lieutenant-Colonel Russell, of the 12th Lancers, shortly expected from Kambula. This force advanced at daybreak on the 28th, and succeeded in occupying the lower of the two eminences which together form the Zlobane Mountain. While Oham's men, who were attached to the Irregulars, were proceeding with a large capture of cattle, in accordance with an order received, towards the Zunguin Neck, their flank was laid open to the attack of an immense body of the enemy. In the desperate encounter which ensued, Lieutenant Williams, who had volunteered to accompany this party, fell fighting gallantly at the head of his men. In an official despatch bearing date March the 30th, Colonel Wood wrote:—"He evinced on this, as on other occasions, marked courage."

Lieutenant Williams's remains were found about six weeks afterwards where he fell, and were buried with military honours, Colonel Wood himself reading the funeral service at the grave.

FRANCIS VERNON NORTHEY,

Lieutenant-Colonel, 60th Regiment (King's Royal Rifle Corps).

FRANCIS VERNON NORTHEY,

LIEUTENANT-COLONEL, 60TH RIFLES.

LIEUTENANT-COLONEL FRANCIS VERNON NORTHEY, whose death, on the 6th of April, 1879, was caused by a bullet-wound received in the battle of Ginghilovo, was the youngest surviving son of the late Edward Richard Northey, Esquire, of Woodcote House, Epsom, Surrey, by his marriage with Charlotte Isabella, second daughter of the late General Sir George Anson, M.P., K.C.B., niece of Viscount Anson, and first cousin of the first Earl of Lichfield. He was born in 1836, and was educated at Eton. Entering the army in March, 1855, he was gazetted to an ensigncy in the 60th Rifles; and, after serving at various stations in Great Britain, embarked with that regiment for India. He served throughout the Oude campaign of 1858, being present at the capture of Fort Mittowlie and the action of Biswah, for which he was granted a medal. He also served in the Red River expedition of 1870, under Sir Garnet Wolseley, and gained a brevet-majority for the manner in which he performed his arduous and important duties.

On the news of the disaster at Isandhlwana reaching England, the 3rd Battalion of the 60th Rifles received orders to embark immediately for South Africa. Landing at Durban in the third week in March, 1879, Lieutenant-Colonel Northey at once proceeded with his battalion to the front to join the Etshowe relieving column, then in course of formation on the Lower Tugela, and took part in the subsequent advance of that force into Zululand. In the action which ensued on the morning of the 2nd of April, at Ginghilovo, the 60th Rifles held the front face of the laager, and bore the brunt of the first desperate onslaught of the enemy. Lieutenant-Colonel Northey fell mortally wounded at the head of his battalion, and, though treated with surgical skill, expired on the fourth day after the battle.

In the death of Lieutenant-Colonel Northey the country lost a most valuable officer. He was devoted to his profession, and in him were combined in a high degree the best qualities of an English soldier with a thorough knowledge of his work. Throughout the four battalions of his regiment he was loved and respected by officers and men alike. Strict, firm, and exceedingly just in all matters of discipline, he was ever ready with a word of sympathy and encouragement for any one who needed it, and by his gentle courtesy and kindly bearing he endeared himself to all with whom he came in contact. Fond of all manly sports, he was an excellent cricketer, having been captain of the Eton Eleven in 1854; he kept up his play to the last, and was well known in the army as one of the best captains of a team.

Lieutenant-Colonel Northey married, in 1869, Charlotte, daughter of Lieutenant-Colonel Gzowski, of Toronto, Canada, now A.D.C. to Her Majesty.

HENRY LOWTH FARMER,
LIEUTENANT, 60TH REGIMENT (KING'S ROYAL RIFLE CORPS).

HENRY LOWTH FARMER,

LIEUTENANT, 60TH REGIMENT (KING'S ROYAL RIFLE CORPS).

LIEUTENANT HENRY LOWTH FARMER, who died at Fort Pearson on the 20th of September, 1879, was the sixth son of the late William Francis Gamul Farmer, Esq., of Nonsuch Park, Cheam, Surrey, by his marriage with Matilda, daughter of Robert Wilkinson, Esq. He was born at Nonsuch Park, on the 28th of December, 1850. His education was commenced at Cheam School, under the head-mastership of the Rev. R. S. Tabor; thence he proceeded, in September, 1864, to Eton, where he passed with credit through the vicissitudes of a public school career, throwing his heart into the execution of that to which he set his hand, and winning golden opinions alike of his masters, by his strict conscientiousness, and of his house-fellows, by his manliness and pleasant ways. Having quitted Eton at the latter end of 1868, he competed in 1869 in the Midsummer army examination for direct commission, and took a high place in the list of successful candidates. He was gazetted to an ensigncy in the 60th Rifles on the 8th of April, 1870, and joining the 1st Battalion of the corps at Ottawa, served with it during the remainder of the time it was quartered in Canada, and subsequently at various home stations.

On the news of the disaster at Isandhlwana reaching England in February, 1879, Lieutenant Farmer was one of the first to volunteer for South Africa; but his services were not accepted until three months later, when, resigning the appointment of Instructor of Musketry, which he held at the time, he embarked with others to fill up the vacancies which had been caused by death and sickness in the 3rd Battalion of the corps, at that time on service in Zululand. He arrived at the front just in time to take part in the expedition which resulted in the capture of the Zulu king. During this expedition he began to feel the effects of the violent alternations in the temperature, and of the exposure and fatigue to which his harassing duties subjected him. He was shortly afterwards stricken with enteric fever, which necessitated his being removed from Ulundi to the hospital at Fort Pearson, where hopes of his recovery were, for a time, entertained. A fatal relapse, however, occurred, and in spite of the unceasing care and attention of those about him, he passed away, painlessly and peacefully, on the night of the 20th of September. He was buried by the side of his brother-officer and friend, Arthur Baskerville Mynors, on the southern shore of the Tugela, where crosses have been erected to their memory.

Lieutenant Farmer's loss is keenly and widely felt. An excellent son and brother, a firm friend, and, in his profession, a most conscientious and promising officer, whose many acts of kindness to his men only came to light when the hand that had wrought them was cold in death, he was loved and esteemed by all with whom, during his short life, it had been his lot to come in contact.

ARTHUR CLYNTON BASKERVILLE MYNORS,

2ND LIEUTENANT, 60TH REGIMENT (KING'S ROYAL RIFLE CORPS).

ARTHUR CLYNTON BASKERVILLE MYNORS,

2ND LIEUTENANT, 60TH REGIMENT (KING'S ROYAL RIFLE CORPS).

SECOND LIEUTENANT ARTHUR CLYNTON BASKERVILLE MYNORS, who died at Fort Pearson, Natal, on the 25th of April, 1879, was the second son of Robert Baskerville Mynors, Esq., of Evancoyd, Kington, Herefordshire, by his marriage with Ellen Gray, daughter of the Rev. Edward Higgins, of Bosbury House. He was born on the 17th of August, 1856, at Evancoyd. His education was commenced at Cheam, Surrey, under the head-mastership of the Rev. R. S. Tabor; and from thence he proceeded, in January, 1870, to Eton. The subjoined record, extracted from the "Eton College Chronicle" of June the 20th, 1879, furnishes the main features of his subsequent short career:—

"In Memoriam.

"Never has it befallen us to have to record, in such quick succession, the loss of those, alas! the memory of whose school lives is still fresh amongst us. For none of these will more keen regret be felt than for Arthur Clynton Baskerville Mynors, Lieutenant, 3rd Battalion 60th Rifles, who succumbed to dysentery on April 25th, at Fort Pearson, Natal. He had been present at the battle of Ginghilovo and the relief of Etshowe. On the 14th of April he was seized with dysentery, which never quitted its hold upon him. On the 23rd he was sent up to Fort Pearson on the Tugela, in hopes that the change might benefit him; but he sank on the 25th, and died at 7 p.m. on that day in the tent of Colonel Hopton, of the 88th Regiment, tended in his last moments by friendly hands, and, as recorded by one who was present, 'With a bright smile on his face, and the hope of heaven on his lips.' His was a loving, bright nature, and a simple faith: a combination of qualities that makes it possible for joy to dwell in the soul amidst the torture of such a terrible disease as dysentery, and in the very presence of death itself. His life here was always joyous—a fearless, keen boyhood, spent *sans peur et sans reproche.* He came to Eton in January, 1870. Many will remember him as, fleet of foot and of lasting powers, winning the Mile and the Steeplechase in 1874, and the Walking Race in 1875. As master of the Beagles in 1875 he showed himself to possess all the qualities of a keen sportsman, with an instinctive knowledge of the craft. He left at Election, 1875. He afterwards joined the Oxford Militia, and at the beginning of 1878 obtained a commission in the 60th Rifles. During the short year that he had been with his battalion he had become a general favourite with both officers and men ; for he had all the qualities of a good soldier and a leader of men, combined with a perfect temper, thorough unselfishness, and a genial, cheery manner. Truly a son of whom, while thus mourning his early death, Eton may speak with tenderness and pride. His grave is on a grassy slope, amid some waving palm-trees, looking down towards the sea, over the lovely valley of the Tugela."

MARMADUKE STOURTON,
CAPTAIN, 63RD REGIMENT (WEST SUFFOLK).

MARMADUKE STOURTON,

CAPTAIN, 63RD REGIMENT (WEST SUFFOLK).

CAPTAIN MARMADUKE STOURTON, who died at Pietermaritzburg, on the 18th of April, 1879, was the eldest son of the late Hon. William Stourton, of Yorkshire, by his marriage with Catherine, daughter of Edmund Scully, Esq., of Bloomfield, co. Tipperary. He was born on the 14th of January, 1840, and was educated at Downside College, near Bath; at Namur, in Belgium; and at Stonyhurst College, Lancashire. Entering the army in May, 1861, he was gazetted to an ensigncy in the 8th Foot, and served with that regiment at Malta, at Gibraltar, in India, and at the depôt in England. He became Lieutenant in 1864, and obtained his company in 1870, in which year he exchanged into the 63rd Regiment. He shortly afterwards embarked with that corps for India, and served there at various stations for several years.

On the news of the disaster at Isandhlwana reaching England in February, 1879, Captain Stourton, who was at the depôt of his regiment at Ashton-under-Lyne, immediately volunteered for South Africa. He was selected as a special service officer to take up duty with the 24th Regiment, and was sent out, on the 1st of March, in the transport "Clyde." The vessel was wrecked in St. Simon's Bay, but owing to the admirable discipline which prevailed, no lives were lost, and all the troops were safely landed on the coast. Arriving shortly afterwards at Durban, Captain Stourton proceeded in charge of drafts of the 24th Regiment to Pietermaritzburg. During the morning of the 18th of April he marched a distance of twelve miles, and was the cheeriest of the party—singing, bugling, and keeping up the spirits of the men in every possible way; but the afternoon's advance commenced with an exceedingly steep ascent, on surmounting which he gasped for breath. Turning to an officer of the Artillery, he said: "I feel my life-blood ebbing away. I am nearly done." Instead of falling out, he continued with the column in its march up another trying hill to the camp. When the bugle sounded "Halt," he had just sufficient strength left to give his word of command, and then fell fainting to the ground. Within an hour afterwards, in spite of every exertion made by his comrades, his prophecy had been fulfilled, and his gallant spirit had passed away.

Though Captain Stourton's death did not take place in the battle-field, he none the less rendered up his life in the service of his country. In spite of physical weakness he struggled on, a brave example to his men; and when his work was accomplished, he simply lay down and died. His remains were buried, with military honours, in the camp cemetery at Pietermaritzburg. The officers and men of the draft with which he had served erected a stone over the grave, and a tablet is about to be placed to his memory in St. Mary's Catholic Church, Ryde, Isle of Wight, by the officers of the 63rd Regiment.

Captain Stourton married, in 1870, Marie, daughter of William Franks, Esq.

DAVID BARRY MORIARTY,
CAPTAIN, 80TH REGIMENT (STAFFORDSHIRE VOLUNTEERS).

DAVID BARRY MORIARTY,

CAPTAIN, 80TH REGIMENT (STAFFORDSHIRE).

CAPTAIN DAVID BARRY MORIARTY, who was killed at Myer's Drift on the Intombi River on the 12th of March, 1879, was the sixth son of James Moriarty, Esq., of the Grange, Kilmallock, county Limerick, and Mary Catherine Bridget Barry, his wife. He was born on the 6th of March, 1837, and in the earliest years of his life it was his parents' intention that he should eventually go to the bar; he early showed, however, a marked inclination for the sea, notwithstanding which he accepted from the Earl of Harewood, when but sixteen years old, a lieutenancy in the 6th West York Militia. On the 19th of December, 1857, he was gazetted to an ensigncy in the 2nd Battalion of the 6th Regiment, which, with the co-operation of (now) General Fraser, had just been raised—Moriarty having materially assisted by bringing over more than a hundred men. In July, 1859, he succeeded to his lieutenantcy; and in April, 1870, obtained an unattached company.

Captain Moriarty served with his regiment at the Mediterranean stations of Gibraltar, Corfu, and Zante; and subsequently at the depôt for a period, after returning home. Just as he was on the point of leaving Colchester to rejoin the 2nd Battalion of the regiment, then in Jamaica, he was offered an exchange into the 1st, which was under orders to proceed to Jersey; accepting the offer, he joined the Battalion at its destination, and served with it in the Channel Islands for a period of twelve months. The regiment subsequently proceeded to Ireland. In December, 1867, he embarked at Queenstown with the 1st Battalion, under Colonel Creagh Osborne, for Bombay, and, arriving at that station, subsequently proceeded to Kurrachee, and up the Indus, *viâ* Mooltan and Lahore, to Rawul Pindee, Punjaub. In 1868 he was engaged in the Hazara campaign, and for his services obtained the medal and clasp.

In January, 1876, Captain Moriarty was gazetted to the 80th, and joined that regiment at Singapore. Whilst stationed at Fort Canning he assisted in quelling a very serious riot among the Chinese. At the latter end of the year the officer commanding the regiment received intimation that three companies were to be held in readiness to proceed to Mauritius, to relieve the detachment of the Buffs, then stationed at that island. Captain Moriarty's company was one of the three selected as being available on the conclusion of the Perak war, and subsequently embarked with two others under Colonel Amiel. On the detachment arriving at the island, however, the French authorities would not sanction its landing, in consequence of measles having broken out amongst the troops in the course of the voyage; it was, therefore, ordered on, by the Colonel in command of the station, to Port Natal. Arriving at the Bluff, it went through the form of fifteen days' quarantine, and then, pending further orders, proceeded to Durban.

In the meantime the annexation of the Transvaal had been decided upon, and, in view of the proclamation to that effect being made, the three companies were ordered on to Newcastle. In December, 1877, Captain Moriarty left Fort Amiel for Utrecht, the authorities deeming it necessary, in consequence of the disturbed state of political affairs in South Africa, to send part of the detachment to guard the Zulu border, and serve as a body-guard to the Administrator, Sir Theophilus Shepstone, who was at that time negotiating the boundary question with the Zulu king. In August, 1878, Captain Moriarty proceeded to take part with his company in the Sekukuni campaign of that year, under Colonel Hugh Rowlands; and during the brief period for which hostilities were continued, did excellent service, holding an important post to the north-west of the enemy. On the suspension of operations in consequence of the lateness of the season, he proceeded with his own and another company to Derby, where he was joined by the other three companies of the 80th—the whole, under Major Tucker, forming a portion of the Transvaal column of the army of invasion, then being concentrated on the Zulu border. The column subsequently marched to Lüneberg, and there Captain Moriarty was selected for the perilous and important service of escorting convoys of stores, on their way from Derby, through that portion of the route which passes between the mountain fastnesses then occupied by Manyonyoba, on the one side, and Umbellini on the other. This duty he at first performed with—in addition to two companies of the 80th—a proportion of mounted men and natives; in the last days of February, however, these latter were taken away to join Colonel Wood's column, at Kambula. On the 7th of March he left Lüneberg, with the two companies, to escort a convoy of eighteen waggons, some of which were reported to be broken down on the further shore of the Intombi. He reached the river the same day, but, in consequence of its flooded state, was unable to ferry across all the heavily-laden vehicles by nightfall on the 11th. Before daybreak on the 12th the party was surprised and attacked by the enemy in overwhelming numbers and with disastrous effect. Captain Moriarty, emerging from his tent, made desperate efforts to cope with the vast horde with which he was instantly beset. He managed to slay three Zulus (Manyonyoba's sons) before he was struck with an assegai, and then made his way, dealing death right and left with the three weapons which he had hastily snatched up, to the left face of the laager. There he received a rifle-ball in the chest, and, falling forward, was heard to exclaim, "I'm done! Fire away, my men! Death or glory!" A second assegai then finished off the dreadful work which the bullet had failed to complete.

On the afternoon of the day on which Captain Moriarty fell, his body was found by the detachment which was instantly despatched from Lüneberg on the news of the disaster reaching the station. It was stripped of clothing, but was in no way mutilated, and the face, which was turned to the ground, wore a perfectly calm and peaceful expression. The remains, together with those of the rest of the gallant band who fell, were subsequently removed to Lüneberg, and were there interred, with military honours, in the little cemetery which adjoins the German Missionary Station, two willows being planted to mark off the grave.

Captain Moriarty was a soldier of soldiers; brave, simple, and tender-hearted; well beloved by his men as by his brother officers. Socially he was of a somewhat reserved disposition, yet courteous to a degree, and never happier than when dispensing hospitality. His tall and commanding presence will long be missed in the places which knew it. His genial acts of kindness will not soon be forgotten by the many who received them at his hands.

JOHN THIRKILL

Lieutenant 88th Regiment (Connaught Rangers)

JOHN THIRKILL,

LIEUTENANT, 88TH REGIMENT (CONNAUGHT RANGERS).

LIEUTENANT JOHN THIRKILL, who died at Herwen, Natal, on the 22nd of April, 1879, was the only son of the late Rev. Thomas P. Thirkill, M.A., and the last of his name. He was born in Ireland on the 25th of June, 1851, and was educated at the Somersetshire College, Bath, and Clifton College. He passed the examination for direct commissions in July, 1870, and, after serving for two years in the Monmouthshire Militia, joined the Connaught Rangers at Aldershot in the spring of 1872. When the regiment proceeded to the Cape, he was stationed chiefly at Wynberg, where he fulfilled his duties as Instructor of Musketry—an appointment for which he had previously qualified at Hythe. He first saw active service in 1877, taking part in the Gaika and Galeka campaign of that year, and behaving throughout, according to the testimony of those present, with great gallantry.

On preparations being commenced in 1878 for the prosecution of the impending Zulu war, Lieutenant Thirkill, fearing that his own regiment might not be engaged in active service, endeavoured by every means in his power to procure some appointment that would take him to the front. Through the interest of Colonel Bellairs, Deputy Adjutant-General, he was appointed, in December, 1878, transport officer, and was sent immediately to Durban: there he fulfilled the difficult duties awarded to him until early in January, 1879, when he joined Colonel Pearson's column at the Lower Tugela. He took part in the subsequent advance of that force into Zululand, and was present at the battle of Inyezane on the 22nd of January, and at the entry of the column into Etshowe on the following day. During the siege he earned golden opinions from all by his carefulness and perseverance in the performance of his duties, and his unflagging energy and cheerfulness under the most trying circumstances. He was mentioned by Lord Chelmsford in despatches, and Colonel Pearson and other officers bore testimony to his unceasing attention and efficiency. Though he had been for some time previously in failing health, it was not until the day of the relief that he consented to go upon the sick list. On leaving Etshowe he nevertheless remained in charge of transport waggons, and was in consequence obliged to travel very slowly under a burning sun. One of the vehicles broke down in a drift, and he insisted on remaining behind to see it properly extricated. The prolonged exposure to the heat proved too much for his enfeebled frame: he was stricken with fever, and a fortnight afterwards, in spite of the tender nursing of his soldier servant, and the care lavished on him by his comrades, passed away quietly at the hospital at Herwen, to the heartfelt grief of his brother officers and of all who knew him.

Naturally brave, generous, and devoted, very fond of his profession, and a most promising young officer, Lieutenant Thirkill was universally and deservedly popular. "He was beloved by all," wrote one of his comrades; "he has been mourned as having been one of the most popular and beloved officers that ever joined the Rangers." Colonel Pearson, besides testifying to his public worth in his official report on Etshowe, wrote, in a private letter, as follows:—"The poor boy Thirkill, whom you mention, was as gallant a young fellow as ever wore the British uniform. From all I heard he must have been a great favourite in his regiment, as he was with us all at Etshowe."

A monumental tablet to the memory of Lieutenant Thirkill has been erected in the parish church of Ross, Herefordshire, by the officers, non-commissioned officers, and men of the Connaught Rangers.

GEORGE SANDHAM,

CAPTAIN, 90TH REGIMENT (LIGHT INFANTRY).

GEORGE SANDHAM.

CAPTAIN, 90TH LIGHT INFANTRY.

CAPTAIN GEORGE SANDHAM, who died in camp at Kambula, Zululand, on the 31st of March, 1879, was the eldest son of Lieutenant-General Sandham, late of the Royal Artillery, of Rowdell, Pulborough, Sussex, by his marriage with Mary Georgina, daughter of Robert Gear, Esquire, of Oxford Square, Hyde Park; and grandson of Major Sandham, late of the Royal Artillery, an officer who shared in the glories of Waterloo. He was born on the 21st of September, 1847, and was educated at Bradfield College, near Reading. In 1867 he obtained a cadetship at the Royal Military College, where his gentlemanly bearing and kindly nature caused him to be generally liked. It was a source of satisfaction to all connected with the establishment when, at the end of the prescribed course of study, his name appeared second in the A list.

Soon after leaving the College, Sandham was gazetted to the 90th Light Infantry; and, the regiment being in India, joined the depôt, then at Preston. On the return of the 90th, at the end of 1869, he joined the head-quarters and proceeded to Edinburgh. In October, 1871, he obtained his lieutenancy (by selection), and in March, 1877, was appointed Instructor of Musketry to the regiment.

In January, 1878, the 90th, being one of the first regiments on the roster for foreign service, was ordered to the Cape in consequence of a sudden call for troops occasioned by the rising of the Gaika and Galeka Kaffirs. Throughout the campaign of that year Sandham had charge of a company, and was frequently entrusted with detached commands, on each occasion winning the approval of his commanding officer. On the 30th of April, he was present at the attack on the Tubin Doda, which the Kaffirs held with the courage of despair. In this engagement Lieutenant Saltmarshe of the 90th was killed, and Captain Stevens, of the same regiment, severely wounded.

On the termination of hostilities Sandham proceeded with the head-quarters and five companies of the regiment, which, together with Harness's battery, were placed under the command of Colonel Evelyn Wood, with orders to march overland to Natal. After six weeks' marching, broken by a halt of one month at Kokstad, East Griqualand, Wood's force reached Maritzburg. Here the 90th remained until the 20th of October, when it was ordered to concentrate at Utrecht, Transvaal, the future base of operations of Wood's Column; it was there encamped after its arrival, until the early days of 1879, when a general move was made towards the Zulu frontier.

Captain Sandham, who had recently obtained his company, took part in the subsequent advance of the column into the enemy's country, and served with it throughout its various operations during the earlier phases of the war. About the middle of March his health began to fail, and shortly afterwards he fell a victim to enteric fever, dying in camp at Kambula on the last day of March, 1879, two days after the gallant repulse of the enemy at that position by the column.

ARTHUR TYNDALL BRIGHT,

2nd Lieutenant, 90th Regiment (Light Infantry).

ARTHUR TYNDALL BRIGHT,

LIEUTENANT, 90TH LIGHT INFANTRY.

LIEUTENANT ARTHUR TYNDALL BRIGHT, who died in camp at Kambula on the 29th of March, 1879, from wounds received in action, was the third son of Tyndall Bright, Esquire, of Woodcote, Aigburth, Liverpool. He was born on the 14th of August, 1857, and commenced his education under the Rev. T. Browning, at Thorpe Mandeville; thence he went to Eton in 1870, entering Mr. E. C. Austin Leigh's house, and remained there until Christmas, 1875. His career at Eton was a bright one. "He seemed formed in nature for a public-school boy," wrote the head of his house after the receipt of the news of his death, "because his principles were high, his sense of honour unblemished, and his love for liberty that he knew was given him to use and not to abuse unbounded. . . . For two years a member of the eight, second to none as a foot-ball player, a keen and excellent volunteer officer, a most promising artist, —loved by all who knew him in the school, and better loved by those who knew him better in his house—Eton was as dear to him as he was to Eton." From Eton he proceeded to the Rev. E. Clayton's at Blackheath, to read for the Army Examination. Taking a high place in the list of successful candidates, he entered Sandhurst in February, 1877, from whence he passed out in the following December, taking honours in the final examination, and gaining a certificate of proficiency in Tactics, Fortification, Drill, Gymnastics, and Riding. The character he won for himself at Sandhurst is briefly epitomized by Major Williams, R.A., of the College, in the following words: "When Colonel, now General Sir Evelyn Wood asked me one day if I could name to him a lad for his regiment, then about to sail for the Cape, whose characteristics should be 'perfect gentleman and keen soldier,' I could and did without a moment's hesitation answer, 'Yes, Arthur Tyndall Bright.'" He was gazetted to the 90th Light Infantry, in January, 1878, and a month later embarked for the Cape, the regiment being at that time actively engaged in the prosecution of the campaign against the Gaikas.

On arriving in South Africa, Lieutenant Tyndall Bright joined his corps in the Perie bush, some twenty miles north of King William's Town, and on the termination of hostilities proceeded with the head-quarters and five companies, which, together with Harness's battery, were placed under the command of Colonel

Evelyn Wood, with orders to march overland to Natal. The force arrived at Maritzburg ten weeks later: here the 90th remained until the 20th of October, when it was ordered to concentrate at Utrecht, Transvaal, the future base of operations of Wood's column; there, after its arrival, it was encamped until the early days of 1879, when a general move was made towards the Zulu frontier.

During this time Bright had been steadily pursuing the daily duties and routine of a soldier's life, in which he displayed a special interest. He soon brought himself under the immediate notice of Colonel Wood by his talent as a draughtsman, substantial proof of which he gave in a carefully executed drawing of the Inhlazatye Mountain from details supplied by one who was familiar with its general situation. In the successful expedition undertaken by Colonel Wood into Zululand, for the purpose of affording protection to a tribe which had declared for British rule, Bright was selected to accompany his chief and sketch the Zlobane Mountain, that stronghold which was destined to be, a few weeks later, the scene of such stirring and tragic events. The attack of the column on the force which held its craggy precipices took place on the 28th March, and the enemy's attack on the camp at Kambula followed on the 29th. On the latter occasion Captain Maud of the 90th was called upon to temporarily fill the place of Ronald Campbell, Wood's gallant and valued staff officer, who had been slain on the previous day, and the command of the G Company devolved on Arthur Tyndall Bright. The enemy, flushed with their recent success, made the most determined onslaught, approaching again and again to within a few yards of the position held by the column. When for three long hours the defenders of the laager had stoutly resisted them, and dense masses still congregating in the valley beneath showed that a final effort would yet be made, Wood decided on making a counter attack. For this purpose two companies of the 90th were ordered to advance, and at the point of the bayonet force back the threatening impi. One of these two was the G Company, and those who knew Arthur Tyndall Bright can realize with what pride he placed himself in front of the advancing line. It was in this position, while gallantly leading and cheering on his men, that he received his death wound. Though he was tenderly watched and cared for by the medical attendants, and by his faithful servant, he only lingered for a few hours, his name being added, ere the day was quite spent, to the glorious roll of those who have rendered up their lives for Queen and country.

General Sir Evelyn Wood, writing upon the life of Arthur Bright, says:—"Arthur Tyndall Bright was a beautiful character, wrote a former comrade, when he heard that the brave young life had been given up on the very threshold of manhood. It was given up in the light of victory. He had sought the post of danger with honourable eagerness, and his unstained past fitted him to encounter sudden death, but it was hard for his surviving friends to realize that he was gone, for he was lively in the best sense of the word. His high spirit, ballasted as it was by a conscientious firmness of mind not common at his age, his cheery grace of manner, his vigour in manly sports, all combined to make him one of those foremost figures in life's groups that seem alike to impress and attract friends. He excelled, too, in the lighter accomplishments, and his sweet, clear voice was greatly appreciated by the soldiers, who used to take especial pleasure in hearing him sing such ballads as 'Nancy Lee' and 'Far Away,' for soldiers on active service delight in pathetic music, perhaps because there is a sense of impending farewell in times when no one knows what a day may bring forth. And when the day came that abruptly stilled the voice of the singer, everyone who had known, and therefore loved him, felt that the loss of Arthur Bright was not the loss only of his country, nor even of his personal friends, but that it was, too, a loss to everyone who had been brought into contact with him."

There is in some men an indescribable charm which attracts others towards them, which induces a linking of arms and a few moments' friendly chat even in the busiest times. This charm was in Arthur Tyndall Bright, and short as was his career there are many left behind who will cherish the recollection of him as that of an upright, noble, and affectionate comrade.

GEORGE CHARLES JEFFERYES JOHNSON,

LIEUTENANT, 99TH REGIMENT (DUKE OF EDINBURGH'S).

GEORGE CHARLES JEFFERYES JOHNSON,

LIEUTENANT, 99TH REGIMENT (DUKE OF EDINBURGH'S).

LIEUTENANT GEORGE CHARLES JEFFERYES JOHNSON, who was killed in action at Ginghilovo on the 2nd of April, 1879, was the second son of William Johnson, of Vosterberg, in the county of Cork, Esq., Deputy-Lieutenant of the county, High Sheriff in 1861, and a magistrate for both the city and county. He was born on the 25th of April, 1850, at Woodlands, near Cork, and was educated at Cheltenham College. Leaving Cheltenham in August, 1868, he proceeded to Northgrove House, Southsea, to read for the Army Examination, and subsequently taking a high place in the list of successful competitors, was appointed, in February, 1872, to the 97th Regiment. Proceeding at once to Sandhurst, he applied himself zealously to the prosecution of his studies, and, passing out from the college at the end of the year, obtained a first-class certificate. Joining the 99th Regiment—into which he had been exchanged while at Sandhurst—at Shorncliffe, he served with it at that station, at Fort George, at the Curragh, at Templemore, and at Chatham, passing most creditably, in the interval, through a course of garrison instruction, and coming out from the School of Musketry at Hythe with a first-class certificate. In February, 1874, he succeeded to his Lieutenancy, his commission being antedated in consequence of his success at Sandhurst. While at Chatham he was appointed Instructor of Musketry to the regiment—an appointment which he held till the time of his death.

In December, 1878, Lieutenant Johnson embarked with the regiment for Natal, and, arriving at Durban, immediately proceeded with it to the Lower Tugela Drift, to join the force then being concentrated there with a view to the impending breaking-out of hostilities with the Zulus. He took part in the advance of Colonel Pearson's column of the army of invasion, in January, 1879, into the enemy's country, and was present at the battle of Inyezane on the 22nd (when his colour-sergeant was shot by his side), and at the subsequent occupation of Etshowe. He returned to the Lower Tugela on the 29th, and being soon afterwards the senior officer present at Fort Pearson, commanded at that station for a period of six weeks, the garrison consisting of his own company of the 99th, a party of engineers, a detachment of artillery with two guns, and some native troops. His appearance was so extremely youthful as to attract the attention of Lord Chelmsford at this time, and to elicit an inquiry as to what service he might have seen.

On the formation of the Etshowe Relieving Column, Lieutenant Johnson was attached, with five companies of his regiment, to the 1st Brigade, and took part, in the last days of March, in the advance of the column to the Ginghilovo Stream. His captain having been promoted, he was in command of his company, which, on the night of the 1st of April, formed one of the outlying picquets, and which, being fired on by the enemy at earliest dawn on the morning of the 2nd, carried in to the column the intelligence that the Zulus were advancing to the attack. No sooner had the scouts and picquets entered the laager than the enemy commenced their desperate onslaught. Lieutenant Johnson, being a skilful marksman, had taken a rifle from the hand of one of the men for the purpose of firing at a concealed Zulu who was doing much mischief. An officer of the 99th Regiment, who was lying at his side, reports that "he was fighting manfully, as if he were at Rorke's Drift fighting for his life." He had fired the rifle several times, when, suddenly placing his hand to his breast, he exclaimed, "I am shot!" and, sinking to the ground, instantly became insensible. He was at once removed to the hospital tent, and there, after the lapse of some ten minutes, during which he remained, apparently, still unconscious, his young life passed away.

Lieutenant Johnson was the life and soul of his regiment, which, as one of his superior officers declared, could have better spared an older man. "The 99th are proud of him," wrote one of his comrades, interpreting the sentiment of all. In addition to his being a thorough soldier, he was an accomplished gentleman, a keen sportsman, and a very straight rider to hounds. The family to which he belonged is one of the oldest in Cork, having been located in the county for very many generations. One of his ancestors was Governor of Cork in the troubled period of the last century; and another, Lieutenant-Colonel Noble Johnson, of the 87th Royal Irish Fusiliers, was killed in action at Monte Video in 1805. It is intended to bring home Lieutenant Johnson's remains for interment in the old family vault in Cork Cathedral, where a tablet will be erected to his memory. The officers of the 99th Regiment have already erected one in Chatham Church, and also a monument of grey granite over the grave at Ginghilovo.

ARTHUR STEWART FIELDING DAVISON,

Lieutenant and Adjutant, 99th Regiment (Duke of Edinburgh's).

ARTHUR STEWART FIELDING DAVISON,

LIEUT. AND ADJUTANT, 99TH REGIMENT (DUKE OF EDINBURGH'S).

LIEUTENANT AND ADJUTANT ARTHUR STEWART FIELDING DAVISON, who died at Etshowe on the 27th March, 1879, was the third son of Captain Davison, of Sedgefield, Durham, and of South Stoneham House, Hampshire, by his marriage with Louisa, daughter of T. Chambers, Esq., of Sheerness, Kent. He was born on the 22nd of May, 1856, and was educated at Harrow; leaving the school in 1873, he proceeded to Captain Massy's, at Croydon, to read for the Army Examination. He entered Sandhurst in 1874, and, passing out with a first class certificate, was gazetted to a Lieutenancy in the 99th Foot; his commission being antedated a year in consequence of his success at the college. Joining the regiment at the Curragh, he served with it at that station, at Kilkenny, at Templemore, and at Chatham, passing most creditably, in the meantime, through a course of garrison instruction, and coming out from the School of Musketry at Hythe with a first-class certificate. In November, 1878, while at Chatham, he received the appointment of Adjutant.

In December, 1878, the 99th Regiment was ordered out to Natal, to join the force then being prepared to act against the Zulus in the event of their refusing to comply with the terms of Sir Bartle Frere's ultimatum. Disembarking at Durban, Lieutenant Davison proceeded with the regiment to the Lower Tugela Drift, and took part in the subsequent advance of Colonel Pearson's Column, in January, 1879, into the enemy's country. The last letter received from him by his family was one written in excellent spirits from Cape Town, bearing date 3rd of January. He was present at the battle of Inyezane on the morning of the 22nd, and at the subsequent occupation of Etshowe. In the protracted waiting-time which succeeded the arrival of the column at that position, throughout the wearisome routine which fell to the lot of the beleaguered force, he distinguished himself by the gaiety of his spirits and by his thoughtfulness for others. The constant exposure to which the garrison was subjected proved, however, too much for his strength, and early in March he was stricken with typhoid fever; from the first days of his illness he continued to grow weaker and weaker, and eventually died just a week before the besieged garrison was relieved.

In a letter to Captain Davison, bearing date April the 10th, 1879, Colonel Welman wrote: "In your son we have lost a brave and skilful officer. He was a general favourite in the regiment." The words are echoed in the hearts of all to whom Davison was known.

WILLIAM IRVINE D'ARCY,

2nd Lieutenant, 99th Regiment (Duke of Edinburgh's).

WILLIAM IRVINE D'ARCY,

2ND LIEUTENANT, 99TH REGIMENT (DUKE OF EDINBURGH'S).

SECOND LIEUTENANT WILLIAM IRVINE D'ARCY, who died in the Military Hospital at Durban on the 23rd of September, 1879, was the eldest son of William D'Arcy, Esquire, late Captain, 67th Regiment, of Castle Irvine, Fermanagh, Ireland, by his marriage with Louisa, daughter of John Cockburn, Esquire, Royal Horse Artillery. He was born on the 24th of April, 1859, at Dover, and was educated at Mr. R. H. Hammond's, at Ewell, near Dover. On the 9th of February, 1877, he was appointed Sub-Lieutenant in the Fermanagh Light Infantry Militia, and in the first training acquitted himself so creditably as to cause his being recommended for a line commission. "He is a very zealous and intelligent officer," wrote his Colonel, "and has conducted himself in a manner highly commendable." He was gazetted to the 99th Regiment on the 4th of December, 1878, and receiving orders to sail for the Cape, embarked, a month later, on board the "Nyanza" at Southampton. Arriving at Durban at the end of January, 1879, he was at once sent to the front to join the portion of his regiment which was stationed on the Lower Tugela—the head-quarters being at that time shut up in Etshowe.

Lieutenant D'Arcy served for two months on the Natal frontier. On the formation of the Etshowe relieving column, he was attached with the five companies of the 99th to its 1st Brigade, and took part in its advance, in the last days of May, into Zululand. He was present at the battle of Ginghilovo on the 3rd of April (within four months of his being gazetted), and subsequently accompanied the regiment in its march back to the frontier. A few weeks afterwards his health became slightly impaired, apparently from the violent alternations of temperature to which he had been exposed in so short a period, and in the last week in June he went into hospital at Fort Pearson. There he contracted typhoid fever, from which, however, under skilful treatment and tender nursing, he recovered sufficiently to enable his being removed to Durban. His letters from that town, written to his family, were of the most cheerful description, telling of his hopes, amongst others, of returning home on six months' leave. "I feel all right in my health, but cannot walk much," he wrote in a letter dated September the 15th, and borne home in the very packet which brought tidings of his death. Four days after penning the above words, in consequence of a sudden fall in the temperature, he contracted a slight cold, and within a week passed quietly away.

Sprung from a branch of the old family of the D'Arcy Irvines, of Castle Irvine, Fermanagh, Lieutenant D'Arcy was not the first of his name who has rendered up his life in the service of his country. By his comrades of the 99th—to whom, notwithstanding the shortness of his sojourn with them, he had greatly endeared himself—a monument to his memory has been erected over his grave in the military cemetery at Durban.

HENRY JOHN HARDY,

LIEUTENANT, RIFLE BRIGADE (PRINCE CONSORT'S OWN).

HENRY JOHN HARDY,

LIEUTENANT, RIFLE BRIGADE (PRINCE CONSORT'S OWN).

LIEUTENANT HENRY JOHN HARDY, who died at Landman's Drift, Natal, on the 4th of October, 1879, was the second son of Sir John Hardy, Baronet, of Dunstall Hall, Staffordshire, by his marriage with Laura, daughter of the late William Holbech, Esq., of Farnborough. He was born at Oldbury Hall, Warwickshire, on the 12th of December, 1850, and was educated at Eton. Entering the army in December, 1868, he was gazetted to an Ensigncy in the 1st Battalion of the Rifle Brigade, and in October, 1871, became Lieutenant. In 1873 he proceeded with his battalion to India, and, during the visit of the Prince of Wales to that dependency, was appointed Aide-de-Camp to Lord Northbrook. He returned to England with the Viceroy in 1876, and shortly afterwards exchanged into the 3rd Battalion of the Brigade.

At the latter end of May, 1879, Lieutenant Hardy was sent out on special service to Natal. Landing at Durban early in July, he joined the staff of Sir Garnet Wolseley, and was appointed orderly officer to General Colley, C.B. He accompanied the generals and staff in a tour to Fort Pearson and Umlatoosi (where Dabulamanzi, the king's brother, and minor chiefs, declared their submission); Pietermaritzburg, Rorke's Drift, and Isandhlwana were visited; and Ulundi was reached on the 10th of August. Patrols were immediately despatched in search of Cetchwayo; and Lieutenant Hardy, with others of the staff, accompanied Lord Gifford, and was in hot pursuit for five days and nights; in another patrol, under Major Nourse, he was out for six days, and assisted in driving in between two and three thousand cattle. The work was most severe, the food and water were bad and insufficient, and the exposure—in consequence of no tents being taken—was considerable. On the 30th of August Lieutenant Hardy was employed to escort Cetchwayo into Ulundi, and kept guard over his tent during the two hours the King remained there. On the 3rd of September Sir Garnet Wolseley and his staff left Ulundi for Prætoria.

Lord Gifford had been sent home with despatches, and Lieutenant Hardy was appointed Aide-de-Camp to Sir Garnet Wolseley in his place, as also Camp Commandant. The night march from Ulundi was a severe one, and a halt was not made until noon on the following day. On the 6th Captain Hardy was taken ill, at the Inhlazatye Mission Station, with a very severe attack of dysentery, and was conveyed in a waggon to Conference Hill; being too weak to continue the journey to Prætoria, he was placed in the hospital marquee, and remained there for three weeks. The weather during this period was most stormy and the dampness of the tent, caused by the heavy rain, brought on a severe relapse. As soon as it was possible to remove him, he was taken to a farm-house at Landman's Drift, and at first seemed a little better for the change; he was most carefully nursed by his friend, Captain Herbert Stewart, and by his faithful servant, Private Augustus Underwood, but never really rallied, and at length died on the 4th of October. His remains were taken to the cemetery at Ladysmith, and were there interred, with military honours, on the 7th.

In announcing Captain Hardy's death, Sir Garnet Wolseley wrote:—"He was a first-rate aide-de-camp, and a very good officer—in every way a man after my own heart, and I had looked forward to having him always with me in any further employment. The service has lost a first-rate soldier, and his death has cast a gloom over us all."

THE HON. STANDISH WILLIAM PRENDERGAST VEREKER.

THE HONOURABLE

STANDISH WILLIAM PRENDERGAST VEREKER.

STANDISH WILLIAM PRENDERGAST VEREKER, who was killed at Isandhlwana on the 22nd of January, 1879, was the third son of the present Viscount Gort, by his marriage with Caroline Harriet, daughter of Viscount Gage.

He was born on the 23rd of February, 1854, and was educated at Westminster School and Worcester College, Oxford. From Oxford he proceeded to the Royal Agricultural College at Cirencester, and subsequently spent two years studying agricultural work and collateral subjects under practical farmers, chiefly on Mr. Horner's estate at Athelhampton, near Dorchester.

On the 22nd of July, 1878, he embarked for South Africa, and a month later arrived at Cape Town. Finding the war with the independent tribes still in progress on the Transvaal frontier, he and some friends who had travelled with him (one of whom was Metcalfe Smith, the young militia officer, for saving whose life Major Leet received, subsequently, his Victoria Cross) proceeded by way of Natal to that district, and there joined the Frontier Light Horse, under Colonel Redvers Buller; with that force he served for the remaining weeks during which the operations against Sekukuni were continued.

On the reorganization of the army in view of the impending invasion of Zululand, Vereker received a commission in the 3rd, or Lonsdale's, Regiment of the Natal Native Contingent, a corps belonging to the Head-quarter Column, then in course of concentration on the Buffalo River. He subsequently took part in the advance of that force, in January, 1879, into the enemy's country, and was present at the storming of Sirayo's stronghold, in the Bashee Valley. He accompanied the column to Isandhlwana, and in the disastrous encounter with the enemy at that position on the 22nd—just six months from the day of his embarkation from England—closed the brief span of his life with an act of heroic and characteristic generosity. Captain Raw, of the Native Contingent, who was one of the few who survived the fatal day, and afterwards did good work against the Zulus, was fighting by his side until resistance was rendered hopeless by the slaughter of almost all our force, and the precipitous drift leading towards the Tugela offered mounted men the best chance of escape. Vereker had lost his horse, and his friend succeeded in catching one and bringing it to him. " He saw him a few seconds before the retreat," runs the brief record. " He got him a horse, which a native claimed, and which poor Vereker refused to deprive him of; he thus deprived himself of all chance of escape."

Four months afterwards Vereker's body was found on the field of battle by Captain Viscount Downe, still unstripped, and was easily identified. At his hands it received a soldier's sepulture.

THOMAS ALDERTON,

Assistant-Commissary, Commissariat and Transport Department.

THOMAS ALDERTON,

ASSISTANT COMMISSARY, COMMISSARIAT AND TRANSPORT DEPARTMENT.

ASSISTANT COMMISSARY THOMAS ALDERTON, Adjutant of the Army Service Corps, who was drowned in crossing a river in the Orange Free State, near Bethlehem, on the 5th of April, 1879, was a native of Hastings, Sussex; his father being in trade in that town at the time of his birth. He was born in the year 1833, and at an early age was apprenticed to a grocer in Lewes. He entered the army in the spring of 1854, enlisting in the Scots Fusilier Guards; was promoted Sergeant in a very short time; joined the regiment in the Crimea just after the fall of Sevastopol, and shared its perils and hardships through the severe winter which followed. At the expiration of the war he was transferred to the Military Train as pay-sergeant at the depôt; shortly afterwards he became Troop Sergeant-Major, and in 1860, Quartermaster Sergeant. In February, 1870, he obtained his commission in the Army Service Corps, and from that date until 1878 fulfilled his duties as an energetic officer at Portsmouth, Aldershot, and Dublin.

On the 3rd of October, 1878, Alderton left Dublin to embark for South Africa. Arriving at Natal, he was there attached to the Commissariat under General Strickland, as Adjutant, until February, 1879, when he was sent by the General to the Orange Free State to purchase horses for the force. He arrived at the Ihlotic Heights, Basutoland, on the evening of the 1st of April, and put up at the house of Dr. Taylor. On the following day he was occupied with his duties; he was then apparently in the enjoyment of good health, but during the night he became feverish, and, by the advice of his host, remained in bed throughout the succeeding day. On the 3rd he was considerably better, but at the doctor's request abstained from quitting the house, occupying himself with writing and with inspecting horses from the verandah of his room. Characteristically desirous to perform his duty at all hazards, he started off, contrary to the doctor's advice, on the morning of the 4th, on a ride of sixty miles, accompanied by two Europeans—his destination being the little town of Bethlehem, in the Orange Free State. About sundown he reached the house of a Dutch farmer, with whom Dr. Taylor had recommended him to put up, who advised him not to attempt to cross any of the streams, which were much swollen with rain, at night. In a letter writen to Mrs. Alderton, bearing date April the 11th, 1879, Dr. Taylor gives the following account of the manner in which he met his death:—

"He said he must get to Bethlehem that night, and rode away, having with him two white men who went about with him and collected the horses as he bought them. They came to the edge of the stream after dark, though the moon was up, and then one of the men told him the water was dangerous, and said they had better remain on the bank till the morning; but the Captain said he was anxious to get on, and they must go through.

"The man accordingly went through first, riding one horse and leading the others, and got safely up the opposite bank.

"The Captain and the other man now rode into the water together, and were crossing side by side when, suddenly, the Captain's horse started in front of his servant's, and he fell off the horse backwards into the water with a cry, and was gone. All the men saw of him was his two hands held out of the water above his head for an instant, and then he was hurried away by the current. They both jumped into the water, and dived and searched in all directions, but uselessly, the darkness hiding all objects from view. It is surmised that his spurs coming in contact with the horse's flanks made it start forward suddenly, and throw its rider off backwards. Such is the sad story of his sudden death, which has cast a gloom over all of us here."

The body was subsequently recovered and conveyed to St. Augustine's Vicarage, Bethlehem, where it received Christian burial, the British flag its pall.

"It will be a great source of comfort to you," continues Dr. Taylor's letter, "to know that your husband met his death in consequence of his anxiety to do his duty; the reason why he was in such haste being not from a desire to get into Bethlehem for his own personal convenience or comfort, but that he might pay off and discharge some men he had hired, in order that they should not be drawing pay from the Government after their services were no longer required."

Assistant Commissary Alderton was a zealous and energetic officer, popular not only in the corps, but beyond it. His capacity for work was great, his perseverance such as was well calculated to overcome the innumerable difficulties which beset the path of the officer in the department of the service to which he belonged. His loss is deeply mourned by all who knew him: his death has caused a void which will not readily be filled up.

STEPHEN THORNTON PHILLIMORE,
Deputy Commissary, Ordnance Store Department.

STEPHEN THORNTON PHILLIMORE,

DEPUTY COMMISSARY, ORDNANCE STORE DEPARTMENT.

DEPUTY COMMISSARY STEPHEN THORNTON PHILLIMORE, who died at Utrecht on the 7th of April, 1879, was the third surviving son of the Rev. George Phillimore, rector of Radnage, Bucks. He was born on the 15th of August, 1853, and was educated at Christ's College, Finchley. In April, 1872, he entered the Ordnance Store Department (called at that time the "Control"), taking fourth place in order of merit among forty successful candidates at the competitive examination. He served at home stations for a period of some five years, being quartered at Chatham, Woolwich, Devonport, and Edinburgh, until 1877; in the month of February of that year he embarked for South Africa.

He remained stationed at Cape Town from the date of his arrival till the following July, when, in consequence of the illness of one of his colleagues, he received orders to proceed to Natal. Arriving at Pietermaritzburg, he was appointed senior officer in charge, and discharged the arduous double duties of that post for a period of six months. In January, 1878, he was released from the appointment in order that he might return to his original station, Cape Town; owing, however, to the outbreak of the Kaffir war, he was detained at King William's Town, where there was a heavy strain on the Department; and eventually, in February, received orders from General Sir A. Cunynghame to proceed direct to Ibeka, in the Transkei. There he remained until July, having the entire charge of the ordnance stores, and the heavy responsibilities incident thereto, living under canvas, and seeing a good deal of the surrounding country in various expeditions on duty.

In July, 1878, in view of the impending invasion of Zululand, he returned to Natal and the Transvaal, and being attached to General Wood's column from the time of its formation, remained on active service as long as his strength lasted. On the 14th of January, 1879, the "temporary rank during the hostilities" of Deputy Commissary was conferred upon him, in recognition of his services. The difficulties in the way of transport inherent to the prosecution of the campaign rendered the strain on his department incessant and severe. Unsparing of self and devoted to his work, he suffered from the consequences, and early in March he was placed on the sick list at Utrecht. After several weeks of illness, through which he was attended with unceasing care by his friend Surgeon-Major Cuffe, C.B., and tenderly nursed by his soldier servant, Leece, of the 90th, he died at Utrecht, on the 7th of April, of the enteric fever with which he had been stricken while faithfully discharging his duty.

The following extracts from two out of many letters testifying to his worth will serve to show the estimation in which Phillimore was held by those with whom he came in contact :—"I desire," wrote General Wood, "to record my warm appreciation of this officer's devoted energy while under my command. Though he was most careful to guard against any unauthorized or unnecessary expenditure, he exerted every effort to supply all my demands, smoothing over difficulties to the best of his ability;" and Deputy Commissary-General Wright, in a letter to the Rev. G. Phillimore, bearing date 21st April, 1879, from Natal, wrote: "The feeling of regret for the loss of your son is universal in these parts. He had made himself a favourite with all whom he met, and I can personally, as his senior officer, vouch for his ability, zeal, and anxiety at all times in the performance of his duties."

Over his grave at Utrecht a headstone has been erected by his family, and a tablet has been placed by his brother officers to his memory in the parish church of Radnage, Bucks.

JOHN HARDWICK,

Assistant Paymaster, Army Pay Department.

JOHN HARDWICK,

ASSISTANT PAYMASTER, ARMY PAY DEPARTMENT.

LIEUTENANT JOHN HARDWICK, who died in London on the 1st of December, 1879, from consumption of the lungs brought on by exposure and fatigue during the Zulu war, was the only son of the late John Hardwick, Esquire, D.C.L., F.R.S., for thirty-five years Metropolitan Police Magistrate at Marlborough Street, his mother being Charlotte, daughter of Colonel in de Beton, of Sweden. He was born on the 1st of June, 1851, and was educated at Eton. Entering the army in November, 1875, he was stationed from that time at Manchester till July, 1878, when he was ordered to South Africa. He arrived at Cape Town a month later, and at once proceeded to Pietermaritzburg.

Throughout the period during which Lieutenant Hardwick was present in Natal, his duties, in consequence of the heavy pressure of work on his department, were of a very arduous character, and there are few places at which our troops were stationed over a very wide extent of territory that he was not obliged to visit. In September he was sent to Newcastle and Utrecht in charge of specie, and throughout the journey was obliged to pass his nights in the open air. In October he proceeded to organize and take charge of the Army Pay Department at Durban, Thring's Post, and the Lower Tugela—a duty which involved constant riding between the two latter positions—a distance of seventy miles. At the latter end of December he had an attack of intermittent fever. Four days later he was ordered to proceed at once to take charge of the department at Helpmakaar, a hundred and sixty miles distant. He made the journey in five days on horseback, under continuous rain, swimming rivers, and sleeping three nights in the open in damp clothes, with nothing but biscuits to eat and muddy water to drink. The consequence was that on arriving at Helpmakaar he was again attacked with fever, complicated with bronchitis and rheumatism. On the arrival of Surgeon-Major Shepherd he was pronounced unfit to advance with Glyn's column, to which he was attached, into Zululand, and was sent back to Pietermaritzburg to be placed on the sick list. On arriving there, however, he was ordered to proceed to Durban, and take charge of the department there. In February, 1879, he was sent to take charge of the pay duties of the advance column, Lower Tugela, Fort Tenedos, and St. Andrew's,

Zululand. This involved riding between the different stations in all weathers. He had intended proceeding with the relief column to Etshowe, but, in consequence of his bronchitis being still severe, he was unable to do so, and returned to Durban on the 5th of April. The fatigue and exposure to which he was subjected proved too much for his already enfeebled frame, and three days after his arrival he was again stricken with fever. He rallied sufficiently to admit of his being invalided home in the month of June, but reached England only to die. Gradually sinking from the hour of his arrival, he finally expired on the 1st of December. His remains were interred at Hove Church, Brighton, where those of his father had already found a last resting-place.

Lieutenant Hardwick, whose loss is deeply deplored by the wide circle of friends to whom his kindness of heart and geniality of manner had endeared him, had married, only in September, 1877, Agnes Alyne Georgiana, only daughter of the late Rev. Arthur Hyde Hulton, B.A., of Bardsley House, Lancashire, and niece of the Hon. and Right Rev. Henry Montague Villiers, D.D., late Bishop of Durham.

PETER SHEPHERD, M.B.,
Surgeon-Major

PETER SHEPHERD, M.B.,

SURGEON-MAJOR.

DR. PETER SHEPHERD, who was killed at Isandhlwana on the 22nd of January, 1879, was the second son of the late Peter Shepherd, farmer, of Craigmill, Leochel Cushnie, Aberdeenshire. He was born on the 25th of August, 1841, at Craigmill, and received the rudiments of his education at the local school, under Mr. William McRobert; from thence he passed, in 1860, to the Grammar School and University, Aberdeen. He graduated in April, 1863, and entered the army in the same year.

His first foreign service was at Durban, Natal, where he joined the 99th Foot as Assistant-Surgeon, and subsequently proceeded with it to Maritzburg and Graham's Town. He accompanied the regiment on its return to England in 1869, but shortly afterwards, in consequence of a desire to see more foreign service, exchanged from it and proceeded to India. He was next gazetted to the 4th Hussars, and continued with that regiment until 1873, when, on regimental appointments being abolished, he was transferred for duty to the 5th Lancers: in January, 1874, he returned with that regiment to England.

For the next four years Dr. Shepherd did duty at Woolwich; in September, 1876, he obtained his majority; early in 1878 he was detailed, by the War Office, Examiner to the Order of St. John of Jerusalem, with the ambulance classes of which he did much important work.

In November, 1878, Dr. Shepherd was again sent out to Natal: on arriving, he was attached to the 24th Regiment, and subsequently took part with it in the advance of Glyn's column, to which it belonged, into Zululand. In the disastrous encounter with the enemy which took place at Isandhlwana on the 22nd of January, 1879, he shared the fate of the eight hundred of his countrymen who fell. The following is the sad history of his death, as related by an eye-witness, Mr. Muirhead, of the Natal Carabineers:—

"As we were riding for our lives, the Zulus pursuing us, my companion, a trooper named Kelly, staggered in his saddle, evidently hit with an assegai. I stopped my horse to see what was the matter, and tried to support him, but could not, and had to lift him off on to the ground.

"At that moment Dr. Shepherd came galloping past. I called out to him, and he dismounted to examine poor Kelly. After carefully examining him, he said: 'Ah, poor fellow! too late, too late!' I had just mounted my horse, and Dr. Shepherd was in the act of putting his foot into the stirrup, when he was struck fatally with an assegai."

Dr. Shepherd was an officer devoted to his profession; distinguished for a skill and tenderness even in that branch of the service to which he belonged. His friends and brother officers have resolved to perpetuate his memory by presenting to the Senatus of the Aberdeen University a gold medal for Surgery, to be called the "Shepherd Memorial Medal," to be given annually at the graduation to the student who shall excel in the principles and practice of Surgery. A marble tablet has been already erected to his memory in the parish church of Leochel Cushnie. It is, perhaps, worthy of record that his last act prior to leaving England was to present to the Order of St. John, of which he was an honorary associate, the copyright of an ably written little handbook, compiled by him for the express use of the ambulance classes.

ARTHUR WILLIAM HALL,

Lieutenant of Orderlies, Army Hospital Corps.

ARTHUR WILLIAM HALL,

LIEUTENANT OF ORDERLIES, ARMY HOSPITAL CORPS.

LIEUTENANT OF ORDERLIES ARTHUR WILLIAM HALL was the second son of Mr. Joshua Hall, coachbuilder, of Norwich, and was born on the 20th of August, 1841. He was educated at the Blue-Coat School of his native town, and afterwards, for a time, served at his father's trade. He joined the ranks on the 18th of August, 1858, enlisting in the 34th Regiment—in which corps he did good and faithful service, at home and in India, for a period of fifteen years.

His character and position are well attested by the following record of promotions—viz., to Corporal on the 7th of June, 1860; to Sergeant on the 14th of April, 1864; and to Hospital Sergeant on the 31st of October, 1867; the latter most important appointment being held by him for a period of nearly six years, and up to the date of his transfer to the Army Hospital Corps, on the substitution of the present hospital system for that previously existing in the army.

Sergeant A. W. Hall was transferred to the Army Hospital Corps on the 13th of July, 1873, retaining his rank on transfer. He was subsequently promoted Colour-Sergeant on the 23rd of August, 1876, and was gazetted to Commissioned rank on the 8th of June, 1877. On the 1st of May, 1877, he was awarded the silver medal and gratuity for long service and meritorious conduct.

Lieutenant of Orderlies A. W. Hall continued to serve at the head-quarters of the Army Hospital Corps until the 30th of July, 1878, when he embarked for service in South Africa with a detachment of his regiment. On arrival at the Cape, he was without delay detailed for duty at the front, and served with Colonel Glyn's column, then concentrating at Helpmakaar. He accompanied that force on its advance into the enemy's country, sharing its perils and hardships, and rendering important service as officer in charge of stores and equipment; supervising the welfare, comfort, and safety of the soldier rendered helpless by sickness or wounds. He thus continued to perform his duties until the fatal day at Isandhlwana, where he died with other brave officers and soldiers—died vainly fighting for life, but not in vain for honour or for country.

JOHN ALFRED GISSING,

Lieutenant of Orderlies, Army Hospital Corps.

JOHN ALFRED GISSING,

LIEUTENANT OF ORDERLIES, ARMY HOSPITAL CORPS.

LIEUTENANT OF ORDERLIES JOHN ALFRED GISSING, who died on board the steam-ship "Roman," in Mossell Bay, South Africa, on the 3rd of January, 1879, was the son of Mr. F. J. Gissing, of the Wickham Skeith Abbey, Norfolk. He was born in 1841, and was educated in London. On the 9th of December, 1861, at the age of twenty years, he entered Her Majesty's service as a private, joining the depôt of the 30th Regiment at Parkhurst Barracks, Isle of Wight. He was promoted to the rank of Corporal in October, 1863; and to that of Sergeant in March, 1865. On the occasion of the arrival of the Prince of Wales at Cowes, after his marriage, Sergeant Gissing formed one of the guard of honour.

In 1865 he proceeded to Canada to join the head-quarters of the 30th, then at Montreal: he served with the regiment at that city; at Quebec (where he attended at the great fire in the Lower Town, in 1866); at Point Lewis; at Halifax, Nova Scotia; and at the little village of Camperdown, where he acted as Director of Signals. Shortly afterwards he was appointed Hospital Sergeant to the regiment—an appointment which he retained until, in 1874, he was transferred to the Army Hospital Corps.

Returning home with the regiment, he arrived in Ireland on the 1st of June, 1869, and served for two years at Waterford and Dublin. In 1871 he proceeded with the regiment to Jersey; from thence, in 1872, to Aldershot; and from thence, in 1873, to the forts on Portsdown Hills, near Portsmouth. Early in the following year he was transferred to the Army Hospital Corps. His comrades took advantage of the occasion of his leaving them to bestow on him some small token of their regard, and at a meeting of the mess, held in his honour, his brother sergeants testified, in many kindly phrases, to the high estimation in which they held him. He was ordered to the Hilsea Station Hospital, and there took over the duties of compounder, and, subsequently, those of ward master and steward; in the tenure of these appointments he acquitted himself so creditably as to win the approbation of all with whom he was thrown in contact, and on the 9th of June, 1877, his zeal and ability were rewarded by Commissioned rank being bestowed upon him. He was shortly afterwards ordered to Aldershot, where, on his arrival, he took over the duties of paymaster; proceeding, subsequently, to Preston, he was appointed officer in charge of the hospital, and district visiting officer.

In October, 1878, Lieutenant Gissing was ordered out to South Africa, in view of the impending hostilities with the Zulus. Passing through Aldershot, he proceeded, with a detachment of the corps, to Southampton; embarked with it at that port early in November, and arrived at Cape Town at the end of the month. His health, which for some time had been failing, now became seriously impaired, notwithstanding which, he begged earnestly to be allowed to proceed to the front. His request being complied with, he embarked for Natal, and landed at Durban on the 12th of December. The barracks lay two miles distant from the landing stage, and over a portion of the route he had to be supported in the arms of his comrades. No sooner had he arrived than his case was found to be so serious as to necessitate his being at once invalided home. He was accordingly taken back to Durban, and seen on board the steam-ship "Roman," by one of his friends, on the last day of the year: there, in spite of the strenuous efforts made on his behalf by Dr. Taylor, the surgeon of the vessel, and tender nursing on the part of the stewardess, he gradually sank, and finally expired on the fourth day after his arriving on board. His remains were carried on to Cape Town, and were there interred with military honours.

Lieutenant Gissing married, in 1865, Phœbe, youngest daughter of Mr. W. White, of Newport, Isle of Wight, and had issue of the marriage nine children, six of whom survive. He was a good husband and father, true-hearted as he was hard-working, and gentle as he was brave.

JEREMIAH TROY,
LIEUTENANT OF ORDERLIES, ARMY HOSPITAL CORPS.

JEREMIAH TROY,

LIEUTENANT OF ORDERLIES, ARMY HOSPITAL CORPS.

NO accurate account of this officer's antecedents prior to his entry into Her Majesty's service can at present be obtained. He joined the 8th Hussars as a private soldier on the 24th of August, 1855, and two years later landed with his regiment in Bombay. He was present at the siege and capture of Kotah on the 30th of March, 1858, and afterwards served in Benares and Kooshana, and other stations, until his regiment again returned to England. He was transferred to the Army Hospital Corps on the 1st of January, 1866, and served at the Royal Victoria Hospital, Netley; Herbert Hospital, Woolwich; and Head-Quarters of the Army Hospital Corps, London.

Promotion in his new corps, in the various non-commissioned grades, sufficiently indicates his career as being that of a well-conducted, intelligent soldier, whose services were utilized and appreciated accordingly. He attained the rank of Corporal on the 1st of April, 1866; that of Sergeant on the 9th of November, 1866; and that of Colour-Sergeant on the 9th of June, 1877.

From October, 1874, to March, 1878, he was posted for duty at Halifax, Nova Scotia. He was promoted to Her Majesty's Commission in the latter month, and after a brief period of service at home, embarked at Portsmouth on the 29th of May, 1879, *en route* for active service in South Africa, in charge of a detachment of his corps, together with stores and appliances intended for service of the troops in the field and hospital.

Lieutenant Troy's hitherto unassuming but valuable services, as above recorded, were now shortly to be brought to a close. Exposure to climate under trying circumstances rapidly told upon his health, and at Durban, on the 8th of October, 1879, he fell a victim to disease which terminated fatally, thus bringing to conclusion a service of twenty-four years.

This officer was in possession of the silver medal for long and meritorious service.

LEWIS CADWALLADER COKER,

Midshipman, Royal Navy.

LEWIS CADWALLADER COKER,

MIDSHIPMAN, ROYAL NAVY.

MIDSHIPMAN LEWIS CADWALLADER COKER, who died at Etshowe on the 16th of March, 1879, was the youngest son of the Rev. Cadwallader and Emily Harriet Coker. He was born on the 20th of May, 1860, at Shalstone Rectory, Bucks, and having commenced his education at Rugby (from whence he proceeded to Southsea), entered, in August, 1872, the training-ship "Britannia." His career on that vessel was a bright one: vigorous in health, popular among his comrades, applying the same ardent zeal to his work which he applied to his play, he passed through the various grades of school-office, and eventually attained the rank of chief captain on board. From the "Britannia," he proceeded, in 1874, to the "Invincible," in which he served during that year and the following; from the "Invincible" to the "Tourmaline," in which he served during 1875 and 1876; and from the "Tourmaline" to the "Active," in which he served from 1876 to the end of 1878. Early in the latter year the "Active" was ordered to African waters, and was cruising in St. Simon's Bay at the time of the massing of Lord Chelmsford's forces on the Natal and Transvaal frontiers preparatory to the impending invasion of Zululand.

Midshipman Coker was selected to form one of that gallant Naval Brigade which was landed at Durban in November, and placed at the General's disposition by Commodore Sullivan, the officer commanding on the station. He proceeded with it immediately to the front to join Colonel Pearson's column, then in course of formation on the Lower Tugela. Taking part in the subsequent advance of that force into Zululand, in January, 1879, he was present at the battle of Inyezane on the morning of the 22nd. During the advance of the column from camp he was in command of the Gatling gun, and in a despatch written after the engagement—the first, it is believed, ever penned by a midshipman as a commanding officer—he related how he brought it into action, paying his tribute at the end of the communication, in due course, to the steady behaviour of his men under fire. "Mr. L. Coker, midshipman, under considerable difficulties, brought his gun into action with promptitude, gallantry, and skill," wrote Commodore Sullivan from the "Active," in his official account of the affair, "and I learn from reliable sources did considerable execution with the Gatling under his charge." The enemy repulsed, he marched in charge of his gun with the column into Etshowe, and formed one of the beleaguered garrison which so tenaciously, and for so long, held that strategically important position. There is something touching, viewed in the light of after events, in the devotion he displayed, throughout the siege, to the object of his charge. "Coker thought that he should be always near his gun, and ready for action," wrote Captain Pelly Clarke, Brigade Major at Etshowe, telling of how it was the lad's habit to sleep through the night in the open air, for the sole reason that he might be close to it. The constant exposure proved too much, however, even for his hardy young frame, and in the early days of March he was stricken with dysentery: owing, to some extent, to the paucity of medical necessaries, and in spite of the tender care lavished on him by Dr. Norbury, of H.M.S. "Active," and his comrades, he gradually grew weaker, and when the month was barely half spent, breathed his last. "Humanly speaking, his life would have been spared had he not sacrificed himself to a sense of duty," wrote General Pearson; and Sir Evelyn Wood, speaking at a banquet given in his honour at Chelmsford, after his return home, used the following words with reference to him: "You have all heard of the hard work they did in bridging over the Tugela, and of their determined conduct at the Inyezane and at Etshowe," he said, in allusion to the services of the Naval Brigade, "but you have probably not heard of their patience in sickness, the brightest example, perhaps, of this English-like trait being Mr. Coker, who rests, alas! in the graveyard at Etshowe."

The character young Coker earned for himself in the gallant service to which he belonged is aptly summarized in the words of Commodore Sullivan, who, writing from the "Active" immediately after the receipt of the news of his death, paid the following tribute to his memory:—

"I can hardly express adequately my poignant regret at losing so fine and promising a young officer. His manly, generous, and open character won the affection and esteem of all on board, from myself down to the youngest boy in the ship. Ever ready for any work, his zeal, combined with marvellous sweetness of temper, entire devotion to his duty, and utter abnegation of self, commanded the love, respect, and admiration of all with whom he came in contact. I only express the general feeling when I say that his loss is deplored by every officer and man in the ship, and by none more than myself."

RECORDS OF SERVICE.

OFFICERS WHO WERE EMPLOYED ON SPECIAL SERVICE.

Rank.	Name.	Regt.	Services.
Lieut.-Gen.	Sir G. J. Wolseley, *G.C.M.G., G.C.B.*	Staff.	Was Commander-in-Chief of the Forces in South Africa, Governor of Natal and the Transvaal, and High Commissioner for Native and Foreign Affairs to the northward and eastward of those colonies in the last phase of the Zulu war, and throughout the Sekukuni campaign; reorganized the forces for the last invasion of Zululand, which resulted in the capture of the King and the pacification of the whole of the territory contiguous to the colony of Natal. (*G.C.B.*)
Major-Gen.	Lord Chelmsford, *G.C.B.*	Staff.	Held the appointment of Lieut.-Gen. Commanding the Forces in South Africa till the last phase of the war. Organized the forces and planned the operations for the first and second invasions of Zululand. Commanded in person the Etshowe Relief Column and the two northern columns in their several advances, and at the battle of Ginghilovo, the relief of Etshowe, and the battle of Ulundi respectively, as also in numerous minor operations. (*G.C.B.*)
Major-Gen.	Hon. Sir H. H. Clifford, *V.C., K.C.M.G., C.B.*	Staff.	Served as Inspector-General of Lines of Communication and Base throughout the war. Was charged with the defence of Natal on the second advance of the Field Force. Took a prominent part in the concluding operations of the war. (*C.M.G.*)
Major-Gen.	H. H. Crealock, *C.B., C.M.G.*		Commanded the 1st Divis. of the South African Field Force from the date of its formation in April, 1879, till it was broken up on the submission of the chiefs of the southern districts and the close of the campaign. (*C.M.G.*)
Major-Gen.	E. Newdigate, *C.B.*	Staff.	Proceeded to Natal in Feb., 1879, and commanded the 2nd Divis. of the Field Force from the date of its formation till the conclusion of its operations and the close of the campaign. Was mentioned by Lord Chelmsford in his concluding despatch as having specially assisted him during the recent operations. (*C.B.*)

Rank.	Name.	Regt.	Services.
Major-Gen.	F. Marshall, *C.M.G.*		Proceeded to Natal in Feb., 1879, and commanded Cavalry Brigade of the 2nd Divis. from the date of its formation till the conclusion of its numerous and varied operations and the close of the campaign. (*C.M.G.*)
Colonel.	H. Rowlands, *V.C.*, *C.B.*	Half-pay.	Col. Rowlands, who had commanded the forces throughout the first Sekukuni campaign, and had been present in every action under fire, commanded the No. 5 column of the Field Force in South Africa from the commencement of the Zulu war until the beginning of March, when that column was merged into No. 4 Column. Was present at the attack on the Zulus at the Taluka Mountain, and at Manyanyoba's caves. Carried out defensive measures at Prætoria to face 5,000 insurgent Boers, encamped within fifteen miles of the city. Was subsequently appointed Brigadier Commanding 1st Brigade 1st Divis., and served in that capacity until the close of the war.
Colonel.	Sir C. K. Pearson, *K.C.M.G.*, *C.B.*	Half-pay.	Commanded the 1st Column of the Field Force from the date of its formation till the reorganization of the forces subsequently to the relief of Etshowe: during the advance from the Tugela; at the battle of Inyezane, and throughout the ten weeks' blockade. (*K.C.M.G.*)
Colonel.	W. Bellairs, *C.B.*	Staff.	Served during the war as D.A. and Q.M.G. on the Hd.-Qrs. Staff. Commanded the force left in camp during the battle of Ulundi. Was one of the officers referred to by Lord Chelmsford in his concluding despatch as having specially assisted him during the recent operations.
Brig.-Gen.	Sir H. E. Wood, *V.C.*, *K.C.B.*	Staff.	Commanded the 4th Column, and subsequently the Flying Column, of the Field Force, throughout their numerous and varied operations during the war—including the action at the Zunguin Nek on the 24th Jan., the attack on the Zlobane, the battle of Kambula, and the battle of Ulundi. Was one of the officers referred to by Lord Chelmsford in his concluding despatch as having specially assisted him during the recent operations, and by Sir Garnet Wolseley as an officer to whose military genius their success was in a great measure attributable. (*K.C.B.*)
Colonel.	Sir G. P. Colley, *K.C.S.I.*, *C.B.*, *C.M.G.*	Staff.	Proceeded to South Africa with Sir G. Wolseley as Chief of Staff, and served in that capacity till the conclusion of the war. (Mentioned in despatches; *C.M.G.*)
Colonel.	S. P. Jarvis, *C.M.G.*	Half-pay.	Embarked for Natal in charge of drafts, and served with the Field Force in the last phase of the war.

Rank.	Name.	Regt.	Services.
Colonel.	R. H. Buller, *A.D.C.*, *V.C.*, *C.B.*, *C.M.G.*	Staff.	Commanded the mounted troops of Wood's Column in the whole of their numerous and varied operations during the war—including the action at the Zunguin Nek on the 24th Jan., the attack on the Zlobane, the battle of Kambula, and the battle of Ulundi, as also in the incessant raiding into the enemy's country in the interval between the 1st and 2nd invasions. Was decorated with the Victoria Cross for gallantry displayed in the reconnaissance of the 3rd July. (Repeatedly mentioned in despatches; *A.D.C.*, *C.M.G.*)
Colonel.	C. M. Clarke, *C.B.*	Half-pay.	Commanded the 57th Regt. during the advance of the Etshowe Relief Column, including the battle of Ginghilovo. Subsequently commanded the 2nd Brigade 1st Divis. of the Field Force. Commanded the column which marched to Ulundi and back viâ Middle Drift. (Mentioned in despatches; *C.B.*)
Bt. Col.	East, C. J.	Staff.	Joined Lord Chelmsford as D.Q.M.G. to the Forces in South Africa on the 22nd June, 1879; was present as senior staff officer at the battle of Ulundi, and remained with Lord Chelmsford until he resigned the command. Remained in the same capacity on the staff with Sir Garnet Wolseley, and was present with him during the subsequent operations for the final pacification in Zululand; proceeded with him to Victoria, and returned thence to England to resume the appointment of A.Q.M.G., Intelligence Department.
Lieut.-Col.	Hale, L. A.	Half-pay.	Landed at Durban on the 24th July, 1879, and proceeded next day to Port Durnford to act there as A.A. and A.Q.M.G., and overseer of line of communications and base, on the staff of Major-Gen. Clifford. Commanded the station from the date of the departure of Brig.-Genl. Rowlands (6th Aug.) until it was evacuated on the 22nd, 1879. Embarked Cetchwayo from Port Durnford.
Bt. Lt.-Col.	Clery, C. F.	Half-pay.	Served with the Field Force throughout the war first as principal staff officer in Glyn's Column, subsequently as A.A.G. in the Flying Column (Mentioned in despatches; Brevet of Lieut. Col.)
Major.	Wood, Hon. H. J. L.	Half-pay.	Embarked for Natal in charge of drafts, and served with the Field Force in the last phase of the war.
Major.	W. F. Butler, *C.B.*	Half-pay.	Served during the war as A.A. and Q.M.G. on lines of communication and at base.
Major.	Byng.	Half-pay	Served as extra A.D.C. to Gen. Crealock throughout the operations of the 1st Divis.
Captain.	Talbot, Hon. R. A. J.	1st Life Gs.	Embarked for Natal with cavalry drafts. Served in the latter part of the war on the staff of Baker Russell's column.

RANK.	NAME.	REGT.	SERVICES.
Bt. Major.	Viscount Downe.	2nd Life Gs.	Served as A.D.C. to Gen. Marshall throughout the whole of the operations of the Cavalry Brigade. Mentioned by the Gen. as rendering invaluable service.
Captain.	Doyle, F. G.	2nd Dn. Gs.	Accompanied Sir Garnet Wolseley to South Africa in May, and was employed on special service till the conclusion of the campaign in Zululand as Commandant at Hd.-Qrs. of the army.
Captain.	Gould, A. L. G.	2nd Dn. Gs.	Embarked for Natal with cavalry drafts, and served with the Field Force in the later phases of the war.
Bt. Major.	Stewart, H.	3rd Dn. Gs.	Served as Brigade Major in the Cavalry Brigade from the date of its formation till the conclusion of its operations. Mentioned by Gen. Marshall as "a Brigade Major second to none in the service."
Lieutenant.	Wilson, B. R.	4th Dn. Gs.	Embarked for Natal with cavalry drafts, and served with the Field Force in the later phases of the war.
Captain.	Dickson, J. B. B.	1st Dns.	Served in the latter part of the war with the Native Carrier Corps.
Lieutenant.	Amyatt-Burney, H. A.	Late1stDns.	Embarked for Natal with the K. D. Gs. in Feb., and served with the regiment during the war. Took part, in Major Marter's squadron, in the capture of the King.
Lieutenant.	James, W. C.	2nd Dns.	Served with the 17th Lancers during the whole of the advance of that regt. in Zululand with the 2nd Divis. Was present at the cavalry affair at Erzungayan, and at the battle of Ulundi. Was wounded during the latter engagement, in the pursuit, with an assegai, and had horse also wounded with a bullet. Returned with the regt. to Pinetown, and embarked on the 27th Aug.
Lieut. and Adjt.	Hippisley, W. H.	2nd Dns.	Embarked for the Cape, Feb. 27th, with the reinforcements. Was attached as a volunteer to the K. D. Gs. Was present at the cavalry affair at Erzungayan. Subsequently did duty at Fort Newdigate with the squadron under Major Marter, of the K. D. Gs.
Lieutenant.	Morland, H. C.	5th Lcrs.	Embarked for Natal with cavalry drafts in May, and served with the Field Force in the last phase of the war.
Lieutenant.	Pennefather, E. G.	6th Dns.	Served with the K. D. Gs. during the war. Was present at the cavalry affair at Erzungayan. Served subsequently in Baker Russell's Flying Column.
Bt. Major.	McCalmont, H.	7th Hrs.	Proceeded to Natal as A. D. C. to Sir Garnet Wolseley, and served in that capacity in the last phase of the war.

Rank.	Name.	Regt.	Services.
Bt. Major.	Viscount St. Vincent.	7th Hrs.	Was attached to the 17th Lancers, proceeding with them to the Cape. On arrival there was placed on the Staff as extra A. D. C. to Gen. Marshall, and acted in that capacity till the advance of the divisions into Zululand. Again joined 17th Lancers, and was present with that regt. at the cavalry affair at Erzungayan, battle of Ulundi, and other minor engagements. Was present at the finding of the body of the Prince Imperial.
Lieutenant.	Byng, Hon. A. J. G.	7th Hrs.	Embarked with cavalry drafts in May, and served during the war with the Field Force in Natal and the Transvaal.
Lieutenant.	Jervis, Hon. J.	Late 7th Hrs.	Embarked for Natal with the K. D. Gs., and served with that regt. throughout its various operations during the war.
Bt. Lt.-Col.	Bushman, H. A.	9th Lcrs.	Accompanied Sir G. Wolseley to South Africa in May, and served on his personal Staff till the conclusion of the war.
Captain.	Beresford, Lord W. A. de la P.	9th Lcrs.	Served in the latter part of the war as Staff Officer to Col. Buller; was present at the battle of Ulundi. (Mentioned in despatches; received *V. C.* for gallantry displayed in Buller's reconnaissance of the 3rd July.)
Captain.	Watson, H. J.	11th Hrs.	Served with the K. D. Gs. during the war. Was Staff Officer at Conference Hill from the 13th June to the 3rd Aug. Served subsequently in Baker Russell's Flying Column.
Captain.	Russell, J. C.	12th Lcrs.	Commanded No. 1 squadron Mounted Infantry (with local rank of Lieut.-Col.), during the war; was present throughout the operations of Glyn's Column, and, subsequently, throughout those of Newdigate's Divis. (Mentioned in despatches; Brevet of Lieut.-Col.)
Bt. Colonel.	Sir Baker-Russell, *K.C.M.G.*, *C.B.*	13th Hrs.	Accompanied Sir G. Wolseley to South Africa, and served on his Staff till the conclusion of the war. Commanded the forces in the operations against Sekukuni, resulting in the storming of the stronghold and subjugation of the tribe. (Mentioned in despatches; *K.C.M.G.*)
Bt. Major.	Russell, F. S.	14th Hrs.	Served in latter phase of Zulu war as D. A. A. G., 2nd Divis. Was present at the battle of Ulundi. Was specially recommended as "having on that occasion displayed great qualifications as a staff officer in the field." Subsequently served as Commandant of Ladysmith.
Bt. Major.	Gardner, A. C.	14th Hrs.	Served with the Field Force throughout the war, first as Staff Officer in Glyn's Column, in which capacity he was present at the battle of Isandhlwana (mentioned in despatches; Brevet of Major); subsequently as Staff Officer in the Flying Column.

Rank.	Name.	Regt.	Services.
Major.	Salis-Schwabe, G.	16th Lcrs.	Embarked for Natal with cavalry drafts. Served in the latter part of the war in command of the Native Carrier Corps (2,000 strong) which he organized.
Captain.	Taaffe, C. R.	16th Lcrs.	Embarked for Natal with the K. D. Gs., and served with the regt. throughout the war; subsequently in Baker Russell's Flying Column.
Lieutenant.	Howard, H. R. L.	16th Lcrs.	Embarked for Natal with cavalry drafts in May, and served with the Field Force in the later phases of the war.
Major.	P. H. S. Barrow, *C.M.G.*	19th Hrs.	Served throughout the war in command of a squadron of mounted infantry and some irregular mounted troops. Was present at the battles of Inyezane and Ginghilovo, being in command of the Divisional Troops at the latter engagement, in which he was wounded. (Mentioned in despatches; Brevet of Major, *C.M.G.*)
Lieutenant.	Courtenay, E. R.	20th Hrs.	Served throughout the war as Staff Officer of the mounted troops of the Lower Tugela Column. Was present at the battles of Inyezane and Ginghilovo, and the relief of Etshowe (mentioned in despatches).
Lieutenant.	Wyndham, W. G. C.	21st Hrs.	Embarked for Natal with the K. D. Gs. in Feb., 1879, and served with the regt. during the war; subsequently in Baker Russell's Flying Column.
Colonel.	W. E. M. Reilly, *C.B.*	R.A.	Commanded the Royal Artillery in South Africa, and was present in the field with the army during the latter part of the war.
Lieut.-Col.	J. T. B. Brown, *C.B.*	R.A.	Landed at Durban (22nd March) in command of reinforcements, and proceeded to join Wood's Column, then at Kambula. Was detained a short time in temporary command at Utrecht, and while there was appointed to command the Artillery, 2nd Divis., consisting of Harness's, Le Grice's, Owen's, and Tremlett's batteries, and Alexander's Ammunition Column, attached to Gen. Wood's force. Joined Newdigate's Divis. at Landman's Drift, 9th May, and marched with it in command of the Artillery to Ulundi and back, being present at the action on the 4th July. (*C.B.*)
Lieut.-Col.	F. T. A. Law, *C.B.*	R.A.	While commanding the R. A. in South Africa was appointed Commandant of the Lower Tugela District, in Natal. Prepared the column for the relief of Etshowe, one of the two divisions of which he commanded in its subsequent operations. Was present at the battle of Ginghilovo. (Mentioned in despatches; *C.B.*)
Bt. Lieut.-Col.	H. Brackenbury, *C.B.*	R.A.	Proceeded to South Africa with Sir Garnet Wolseley, and served on his Staff, and as Military Secretary till the conclusion of the war. (Brevet. of Lieut.-Col.)

Rank.	Name.	Regt.	Services.
Major.	Alexander, R.	R.A.	Commanded the Ammunition Column in the advance of the 2nd Divis., including the battle of Ulundi.
Captain.	Yeatman-Biggs, A. G.	R.A.	Served on the personal Staff of Sir Garnet Wolseley in the last phase of the war. Commanded in Aug. the expeditionary force of mounted gunners which went in search of the King, and patrolled the St. Lucia Bay district.
Captain.	Poole, J. R.	R.A.	Served with the Field Force during the war.
Bt. Major.	Maurice, J. F.	R.A.	Accompanied Sir G. Wolseley to South Africa, and served on his personal Staff till the conclusion of the war. Took part, in Major Barrow's Force, in the pursuit of the King.
Bt. Major.	Alleyne, J.	R.A.	Served as Adjt. to Lieut.-Col. Tatton Brown throughout the war. Was present, in that capacity at the battle of Ulundi. (Mentioned in despatches; Brevet of Major.)
Bt. Major.	M. J. Clarke, *C.M.G.*	R.A.	Served with the Field Force during the war.
Bt. Major.	Fox, W. R.	R.A.	Served on the personal Staff of Gen. Clifford as D.A.A.G. during the war.
Bt. Major.	Vaughan, H.	R.A.	Served as Director of Transport to Wood's Column from Jan. to April. Was present at the action on the Zlobane (mentioned in despatches), and at the battle of Ulundi. (Mentioned in despatches; Brevet of Major).
Captain.	Bouwens, L. H.	R.A.	Served with the Field Force during the war.
Bt. Major.	Knox, W. G.	R.A.	Landed 15th May, 1879, at Durban, on passage from Afghanistan, and was first posted for duty with Crealock's Divis. Was subsequently selected by Lord Chelmsford to raise and organize an Irregular Artillery Corps in the Transvaal to act against Sekukuni. Raised, organized, and commanded Knox's Transvaal Artillery. Organized, in addition, a small-arm ammunition train for 7,000 men. Was present at the several reconnaissances into the enemy's country, and commanded the artillery at the storming and capture of the Fighting Koppie. Received Brevet of Major for services in South Africa.
Bt. Major.	Brackenbury, E. F.	R.A.	Served in the Gatling Battery R.A. in Zululand with Wood's Flying Column, and subsequently with Clarke's Column at the occupation of Ulundi. Commanded the Mountain Battery of the Transvaal Artillery during the Sekukuni campaign. Was present at the storming and capture of the chief's stronghold on the 28th Nov.
Lieutenant.	Creagh, A. G.	R.A.	Served as A.D.C. to Sir G. Wolseley in the last phase of the Zulu war, including the pursuit of Cetchwayo (with Capt. Lord Gifford's party). Served as A.D.C. to Sir G. Wolseley in the campaign against Sekukuni. Was present at the capture of the chief's town and stronghold. (Mentioned in despatches.)

Rank.	Name.	Regt.	Services.
Lieutenant	Williams, W. H.	R.A.	Served with the Field Force during the war.
Vet. Surg.	Burt, W.	R.A.	Proceeded, in March, 1879, to New York, for the purpose of purchasing mules for shipment to Natal. Arrived at Durban 21st April, and proceeded thence to the Lower Tugela to take charge of sick horse depôt. Transferred depôt, subsequently, to Nonote, and from thence to Durban. Afterwards served on line of communications between Lower Tugela and St. Paul's. At end of Nov. took over duties of Principal Vet. Surg., and continued to perform them until departure from Natal.
Vet. Surg.	Phillips, C.	R.A.	Served with the Field Force during the war.
Lieut.-Col.	Webber, C. E.	R.E.	Accompanied Sir G. Wolseley to Natal in May, 1879. Was appointed A.A.G. and A.Q.M.G. of lines of communications under Major.-Gen. Clifford on 28th June. Was Senior Staff Officer for the lines from Natal through Western Zululand from that date until the final evacuations in Sept., including the superintendence and local direction of the execution of the orders for the breaking up of the 1st Divis. and the formation of new columns, followed by the final evacuations and removal of the army and all its material from the forts and positions of Zululand and on the frontier of Natal. In the same position was the executive officer of the Inspector-Gen. for the lines of communications in the operations against Sekukuni, superintending and directing the removal of the vast accumulations of stores and transport from Zululand and the Utrecht district to the N.E. of the Transvaal; and finally, under the orders of the Inspector-Gen., carried out the instructions of the General Officer Commanding, so that all available troops distributed over the Utrecht district were concentrated on the 12th Dec., 1879, with three months' provisions and stores at Prætoria, to meet the General Officer Commanding on his return from the Sekukuni expedition, with a view to precautionary measures in consequence of the disturbed state of the Transvaal.
Bt. Colonel.	R. Harrison, *C.B.*	R.E.	Proceeded to the Cape in command of a field co. R.Es. in Feb., 1879. On landing at Durban was appointed R.E. officer at Army Hd.-Qrs. On 8th May was appointed A.Q.M.G. at Hd.-Qrs., and in that capacity was in charge of the Q.M.G's. Depart. of the Army during the advance of the columns into Zululand. Was present at various small engagements, and at the battle of Ulundi. Mentioned in Lord Chelmsford's despatch as one of the "officers who have specially assisted me during the recent operations in

Rank.	Name.	Regt.	Services.
			Zululand." Made a *C.B.* When Brig.-Gen. Wood was invalided to England, Col. Harrison was appointed by Sir G. Wolseley to the command of the Flying Column, on the breaking up of which he was sent on special service to Sekukuni's country. On completion of that duty he was appointed to the command of the troops in the Transvaal, which position he held during the operations against Sekukuni, and the movements rendered necessary by the threatened rising of the Boers in the autumn and winter of 1879. Was specially mentioned by Sir G. Wolseley in his final despatch as having rendered "most valuable services during the Sekukuni campaign," and also for the way in which he acted during "the agitations set on foot by a section of the Boer community."
Bt. Lieut.-Colonel.	Moysey, C. J.	R.E.	Was R.E. officer in charge of the Transvaal before the campaign. Accompanied Brig.-Gen. Wood's Flying Column throughout the war. Present at the battle of Ulundi. (Mentioned in despatches; Brevet of Lieut.-Col.).
Bt. Major.	Blood, B.	R.E.	Proceeded to the Cape as Capt. of the 30th co. Was made C. R.E. to Crealock's Divis., and served with it throughout the campaign. (Brevet of Major.)
Captain.	Heneage, F. W.	R.E.	Went to the Cape as A.D.C. to Major-Gen. Marshall, commanding the cavalry, and accompanied that officer during the campaign. Subsequently employed on the lines of communication.
Captain.	James, W. H.	R.E.	Proceeded to the Cape in May, 1879. Served on the Staff of Lord Chelmsford as D.A.Q.M.G., and was present at the battle of Ulundi. (Medal and clasp.)
Colonel.	Davies, H. F.	Gren. Gds.	Proceeded to the Cape in March, 1879, in command of drafts for the 24th Regt. Served in Newdigate's Divis. during the war, commanding the garrison at Landman's Drift in May.
Colonel.	Needham, Hon. R.	Late Gren. Gds.	Served during the war as Orderly Officer to Brig.-Gen. Wood. (Mentioned in despatches.)
Lieut.-Col.	Thynne, R. T.	Gren. Gds.	Embarked for Natal in May, 1879, in charge of drafts. Served with Newdigate's Divis. during the war. Was in command at Kwamagwasa.
Lieut.-Col.	Villiers, Hon. G. P. H.	Gren. Gds.	Served in the last phase of the war. Was appointed by Sir Garnet Wolseley Special Commissioner to Oham's Armed Forces, and materially assisted Sir Baker Russell in his campaign in the north-west of Zululand.
Lieutenant. Lieutenant. Lieutenant. Captain.	Carington, Hon. R. C. G. Farrer, W. D. M. C. P. Colville, Hon. C. R. W. (Master of Colville). Bertie, Hon. G. A. V.	Gren. Gds. Gren. Gds. Gren. Gds. Cold. Gds.	Proceeded to the Cape in March, 1879, with drafts, and took part in the advance of Newdigate's Divis., Capt. Bertie and Lieuts. Carington and Colville being present at the battle of Ulundi.

Rank.	Name.	Regt.	Services.
Bt. Colonel.	F. W. E. F. Walker, *C.B.*	Scots Gds.	Served as A.A.G. to Pearson's Column. Was present at the battle of Inyezane and the occupation of Etshowe during its two months' investment. (Mentioned in despatches.) Served, subsequently, as Commandant of the Lower Tugela. (*C.B.*)
Captain and Lieut.-Col.	Montgomery, W. E.	Scots Gds.	Served during the war as A.Q.M.G. to Newdigate's Divis. Was present at the battle of Ulundi. (Mentioned in despatches.)
Lieut. and Captain.	Gordon-Cumming, Sir W. G.	Scots Gds.	Embarked, on the 1st March, 1879, in the "Clyde" as a volunteer for the 24th, and was in her when she was wrecked off Dyer's Island. Accompanied the drafts for the 24th under Col. Davies up country as far as Landman's Drift, and served during the remainder of the campaign on the Staff of Gen. Newdigate. Was present at the battle of Ulundi.
Lieut. and Captain.	Cotton, Hon. R. S. G. S.	Scots Gds.	Proceeded to the Cape in March, 1879, in charge of drafts, and took part in the advance of Newdigate's Divis. Acted as Orderly Officer at the battle of Ulundi, at which engagement he was wounded.
Lieutenant.	Knight, H. R.	3rd Foot.	Served as Staff Orderly Officer, and A.D.C. to Col. Pearson, throughout the operations of the 1st Column; and subsequently in Crealock's Divis.
Bt. Major.	Woodgate, E. R. P.	4th Foot.	Served in Wood's Column through the whole of its operations during the war, first as General Staff Officer, and, on the death of Capt. Campbell, as Principal Staff Officer; and subsequently as A.A.G. in the Flying Column. (Mentioned in despatches; Brevet of Major.)
Bt. Major.	Barton, G.	7th Foot.	Served throughout the war, first as Staff Officer to Durnford's Column, and, subsequently, in command of the 4th Batt. N.N.C., till the end of the war, taking part in the battle of Ginghilovo; and afterwards in the operations of Clarke's Column. (Mentioned in despatches; Brevet of Major.)
Lieutenant.	Heron-Maxwell, W. H. S.	7th Foot.	Proceeded to Natal with drafts, and served in that colony and the Transvaal during the latter part of the war.
Lieutenant.	Nicholson, G. S.	7th Foot.	Proceeded to the Cape in charge of drafts, and served as Adjt. of the 4th Batt. N.N.C. throughout the operations of Clarke's Column. Had military command of the boats for landing the troops when the "Clyde" transport was wrecked off the Cape.
Captain.	Jocelyn, R. J. O.	8th Foot.	Embarked for the Cape with drafts. Served during the latter part of the war with the Native Carrier Corps.
Captain.	Wavell, A. G.	9th Foot.	Served with the Field Force during the war.

Rank.	Name.	Regt.	Services.
Bt. Major.	Huntley, H. C.	10th Foot.	Proceeded on transport service to South Africa in Nov., 1878, and served throughout the war, first as Transport Officer to the 2nd Divis. in its advance to Ulundi, and afterwards as Senior Transport Officer with Baker Russell's Column. (Brevet of Major.)
Captain.	Ballantyne, J. G.	11th Foot.	Proceeded to the Cape with drafts, and served with the Field Force during the later phases of the war.
Captain.	Paterson, A. M.	16th Foot.	Served with the Field Force during the war.
Captain.	Laurence, W. W.	18th Foot.	Proceeded to the Cape on transport service, and served on the lines of communication and at the base during the war.
Captain.	Oakes, G.	19th Foot.	Proceeded to the Cape with drafts, and served with the Field Force during the later phases of the war.
Bt. Major.	Molyneux, W. C. F.	22nd Foot.	Served as Senior A.D.C. to Lord Chelmsford during the war. Was one of the officers referred to by the General in his concluding despatch as having specially assisted him during the recent operations. (Brevet of Major.)
Lieutenant.	Evans, E. R.	23rd Foot.	Proceeded to the Cape with drafts, and served with the Field Force in the later phases of the war.
Bt. Major.	Brunker, H. M. E.	26th Foot.	Served with Frontier Light Horse under Col. Buller in Wood's Column, from date of crossing the Blood River till end of March. Present at action of Zunguin Nek, at the action on the Zlobane, and other minor affairs. Was appointed D.A.Q.M.G. on lines of communications at Durban to land reinforcements from England. Accompanied expedition in June to land stores, &c. on the Zulu coast at Port Durnford. (Brevet of Major.)
Lieutenant.	Bayly, J. C.	27th Foot.	Served throughout the war, first in the Transport Service, and subsequently in the Remount Establishment.
Captain.	Macgregor, H. G.	29th Foot.	Proceeded to the Cape in Nov., 1878, and served in the war, first as 2nd Staff Officer to Pearson's Column, in which capacity he was present at the battle of Inyezane and throughout the blockade of Etshowe; and afterwards as Brigade-Major of the 1st Brigade 1st Divis. (Mentioned in despatches; Brevet of Major.)
Captain.	Spratt, E. J. H.	29th Foot.	Proceeded on Transport Service to South Africa in Nov., 1878, and served on the lines of communications and at the base during the war.
Lieutenant.	Watson, A. G.	30th Foot.	Proceeded to Natal on Transport Service, and served on the lines of communications and at base.
Major.	Bayley, G.	31st Foot.	Served with the Field Force during the war.

Rank.	Name.	Regt.	Services.
Bt. Major.	Hart, A. F.	31st Foot.	Proceeded to South Africa in Nov., 1878, and served throughout the war; first as Staff Officer of the 2nd Regt. N.N.C. (two batts.), taking part with Pearson's Column in the battle of Inyezane (mentioned in report); then, as Staff Officer on the Etshowe Relieving Column, being present at the battle of Ginghilovo (mentioned in despatches); afterwards, as Brigade-Major of the 2nd Brigade 1st Divis.; and, finally, as Principal Staff Officer of Clarke's Column. (Brevet of Major.)
Lieutenant.	Reynolds, A. S.	31st Foot.	Was employed on special service with the Zulu Native Carrier Corps. Specially appointed for this duty by Sir G. Wolseley. (Medal with clasp.)
Major.	Stabb, H. S.	32nd Foot.	Proceeded to Natal in May, 1879. Was present at the battle of Ulundi. Was for some time attached as D.A.Q.M.G. to the 2nd Divis., and then as Staff Officer to the convoy under Col. Whitehead. Was afterwards Commandant of Fort Victoria till after the capture of Cetchwayo. Subsequently was employed as president of a board for the investigation and settlement of all claims preferred by colonists and others for losses received by them during the war. Was sent in charge of the expedition to erect the Queen's memorial cross which Her Majesty desired should mark the spot where the late Prince Imperial of France was killed.
Bt. Major.	Cherry, C. E. M.	32nd Foot.	Commanded 3rd Batt. 1st Regt. N.N.C. during the war. Was present throughout the whole of the operations of Pearson's Column.
Lieutenant.	Cochrane, W. F. B.	32nd Foot.	Served in the war, first, as Orderly Officer to Col. Durnford, being present in that capacity at the battle of Isandhlwana; subsequently with Wood's Column in command of the Natal Native Horse, taking part in the engagements on the Zlobane, at Kambula, and Ulundi.
Lieutenant.	Dunnington Jefferson, M.	33rd Foot.	Proceeded to the Cape on Transport Service, and was employed on the lines of communication and at base.
Major.	Barnes, E. R. B.	35th Foot.	Proceeded to the Cape with drafts, and served with the Field Force in the later phases of the war.
Bt. Major.	Grattan, H.	35th Foot.	Was employed on the Natal frontier and in Zululand in the early part of 1879.
Captain. Lieutenant.	Crofton, M. S. St. George, A. G.	38th Foot. 38th Foot.	Proceeded to the Cape with drafts, and served with the Field Force in the later phases of the war.
Bt. Lieut.-Colonel.	Wavell, A. H.	41st Foot.	Served with the Field Force during the war.

RANK.	NAME.	REGT.	SERVICES.
Lieutenant. Captain. Lieutenant.	Heldane, H. E. Boyle, C. J. Odell, W. H.	49th Foot. 52nd Foot. 52nd Foot.	Proceeded to Natal on Transport Service, and were employed during the war on the lines of communication and at the base.
Lieutenant.	Hutton, C. M.	52nd Foot.	Proceeded to the Cape with drafts, and served with the Field Force in the later phases of the war.
Lieutenant.	White, L. A.	53rd Foot.	Proceeded to Natal on Transport Service, and was employed during the war on the lines of communication and at the base.
Lieut.-Col.	Gosset, M. W. E.	54th Foot.	Served in the first advance into Zululand as A.D.C. to Lord Chelmsford, and was present in the actions fought by the Centre Column up to the 22nd Jan. Was afterwards A.Q.M.G. to the 2nd Divis. in the second advance, and was present at the battle of Ulundi. (Mentioned in despatches; Brevet of Lieut.-Col.)
Lieut.-Col.	Huskisson, J. W.	56th Foot.	Was appointed, at the commencement of the war, Commandant of Durban and A.Q.M.G. at the base, and Colonial Commandant of Durban and of the adjoining districts of Pinetown and Isipingo. Superintended the disembarkation of the greater portion of the troops sent to Natal, and made arrangements for encamping and equipping them previous to their advance. It was owing to his conduct during that interval of excitement among the inhabitants which followed the disaster at Isandhlwana that the commerce of the only seaport of the colony was not seriously obstructed. Pending the arrival of help, the volunteers of Durban were embodied under Major Huskisson's orders, and it was at his suggestion that a small corps of Indian immigrants was raised for the purpose of assisting in the heavy garrison and fatigue duties which had to be performed at the base of operations. Major Huskisson remained at his post until after the termination of the Zulu war. (Mentioned in the despatches of Lord Chelmsford and Admiral Sir F. Sullivan.)
Bt. Major.	Lord Gifford, *V.C.*	57th Foot.	Served in the latter part of the war, first with the 57th Regt., afterwards with the M.I., and finally as A.D.C. to Sir G. Wolseley. Lord Gifford took a leading part in the capture of the King, after which he was sent home with despatches.
Lieutenant.	Michel, C. B. D.	57th Foot.	Served throughout the war, first in the Transport Service, and afterwards in the Remount Establishment.
Bt. Lieut.-Colonel.	Grenfell, F. W.	60th Rifles.	Served in the war as D.A.A.G. at Hd.-Qrs., and was present at the battle of Ulundi. Was one of the officers referred to by Lord Chelmsford in his concluding despatch as having specially assisted him during the recent operations. (Brevet of Lieut.-Col.)

RANK.	NAME.	REGT.	SERVICES.
Bt. Major.	Fraser, E. L.	60th Rifles.	Served with the Field Force during the war.
Lieutenant. Lieutenant. 2nd Lieut.	Wells, G. H. Herbert, E. W. Garrett, J. R.	60th Rifles. 60th Rifles. 60th Rifles.	Proceeded to the Cape with drafts, and served with the 3rd Batt. 60th Rifles in the latter part of the war.
Bt. Major.	Murray, C. W.	61st Foot.	Proceeded to Zululand as A.D.C. to Maj.-Gen. Crealock in March, 1879. In May was appointed D.A.Q.M.G. to the 1st Divis. Made surveys of the routes to be taken by the Column; selected camping-grounds, &c. On the breaking up of the Divis. was appointed reconnoitring officer, with rank of D.A.Q.M.G., to Clarke's Flying Column, and was then attached to the M. I. under Major Barrow. Surveyed and reported on the whole route followed by the Column to the Black Umvolosi, beyond Ulundi. Was present during the search for the King. Selected the route to be followed by the Column to the Middle Drift.
Bt. Major.	Harvey, C. L.	71st L. I.	Major Harvey, who had served as principal Staff Officer throughout the first Sekukuni campaign, and was present in every action under fire, served as principal Staff Officer of No. 5 Column of Field Force in South Africa from the commencement of the Zulu war until the beginning of March, when that Column was merged into No. 2 Column. Was present at the attack of the Zulus at the Taluka Mountain and at Manyanyoba's caves. Commanded the force which advanced into the enemy's country, and stormed and captured the Eloya Mountain. As principal Staff Officer of the Transvaal carried out defensive measures at Prætoria. Served as Brigade Major of 1st Brigade 1st Divis. in the advance from Tugela River to Amitikulu River, Zululand. Subsequently appointed D.A.Q.M.G. to 1st Divis., and served in that capacity until the close of the war.
Captain.	Braithwaite, E. L.	71st L. I.	Left England with Sir G. Wolseley, and accompanied him until he arrived at Prætoria. Was shortly afterwards invalided home.
Bt. Major.	Essex, E.	75th Foot.	Proceeded to Natal in Nov., 1878. Was appointed Transport Officer to Glyn's Column. Was present throughout the battle of Isandhlwana, and witnessed the loss of the camp, escaping with a remnant of the force engaged, by the "Fugitives' Drift," through that portion of the Zulu army which had surrounded the rear of the camp. Accompanied the second advance as Director of Transport to Newdigate's Divis., and was present at the battle of Ulundi. Promoted Major for services during the campaign.

Rank.	Name.	Regt.	Services.
Lieutenant.	Baynes, D. L.	75th Foot.	Proceeded to Natal on Transport Service, and was employed during the war on the lines of communication and at the base.
Bt. Lieut.-Colonel.	Bengough, H. M.	77th Foot.	Arrived in Natal in Dec., 1878. Was placed in command of the 2nd Batt. N. N. C., which formed part of Durnford's Column, and which was left to protect the frontier at Kranz Kop on the departure of that force to join Glyn's Column. Crossed the Buffalo in command of the batt. on the 22nd Jan. On receipt of the news of the disaster at Isandhlwana, hastened towards Rorke's Drift, with the view of joining the General's force, but received orders *en route* to proceed to Helpmakaar. Was ordered from thence to Umsinga, where, in the face of the desertion of large numbers of his men, he constructed Fort Bengough. Joined, in command of the Batt. (which was then greatly increased in numbers and improved in discipline), Newdigate's Divis. in May, and took part in its advance into Zululand. Commanded the Hd.-Qrs. and three cos. which were present at the battle of Ulundi. Gen. Newdigate bore testimony to the good service rendered by the batt. in scouting and outpost duties in his despatch written after the action. Served in command of the batt. in Russell's Column until the capture of the King, when it was disbanded. (Mentioned in despatches; Brevet of Lieut.-Colonel.)
Captain.	Marryatt, H. Fz. R.	77th Foot.	Proceeded to the Cape with drafts, and served with the Field Force in the later phases of the war.
Lieutenant.	Westmacott, R. F.	77th Foot.	Served during the war as A.D.C. to Gen. Clifford.
Lieutenant.	Law, R. T. H.	77th Foot.	Proceeded to the Cape with drafts, and served with the Field Force in the later phases of the war.
Bt. Major.	Cardew, F.	82nd Foot.	Served during the war as D.A.Q.M.G. to Crealock's Divis. (Mentioned in despatches; Brevet of Major.)
Captain.	Martin, E. C.	87th Foot.	Proceeded to Natal on transport service, and was employed during the war on the lines of communication and at the base.
Captain.	Elliott, Hon. W. F.	93rd Foot.	Proceeded to Zululand in May, 1879. Was appointed Staff Officer to Major Barrow's force of mounted troops in June, and served in that capacity till the end of the war. Was present during the advance of the 1st Divis. from Fort Chelmsford to Port Durnford, and at the raids made by the mounted troops on the Mangwane and Undine kraals. Was present with Clarke's Column during its advance on Ulundi, and with Major Brown's force during the pursuit of the King.

Rank.	Name.	Regt.	Services.
Captain.	Hannay, O. C.	93rd Foot.	Proceeded to the Cape with drafts, and served with the Field Force during the later phases of the war.
Lieut.-Col.	J. N. Crealock, *C.B.*	95th Foot.	Was Military Secretary to Lord Chelmsford throughout the war. Acted as Senior Staff Officer to the force which, under the personal command of Lord Chelmsford, relieved Etshowe, and defeated the Zulus at the battle of Ginghilovo. Was slightly wounded at the latter engagement. Returned to England with Lord Chelmsford. (Repeatedly mentioned in despatches; *C.B.*)
Lieut.	Smith-Dorrien, H. L.	95th Foot.	Proceeded to South Africa as a volunteer. Was at first employed in the organization of the Transport Service. On the 21st Jan., 1879, was left at Rorke's Drift, but was ordered out to the camp at Isandhlwana on the night of the 21st. On the morning of the 22nd carried Lord Chelmsford's despatch to Col. Durnford, and then rode back to Isandhlwana camp. Was present throughout the engagement which ensued, and was the only man who escaped on foot and got into Helpmakaar, twenty miles distant, that night. Was subsequently employed on the lines of communication at Ladysmith, Helpmakaar, and Dundee. Took part in the advance of the 2nd Divis., and was in laager on the Umvolosi during the battle of Ulundi. Was then sent in charge of the convoy of sick and wounded to Ladysmith, and was in charge of the transport at Dundee until the conclusion of the war.
Captain.	Carey, J. B.	98th Foot.	Proceeded to the Cape in charge of drafts, and served as D.A.Q.M.G. to Newdigate's Divis. during the first part of its advance.
Bt. Lt.-Col.	Walker, A. L.	99th Foot.	Proceeded on Transport Service to South Africa in Nov. 1878. Was Officer Commanding at Stanger on line of communications during the first phase of the war. Subsequently served as D.A.G. in the 1st Divis. from the date of its formation till the conclusion of its operations. (Mentioned in despatches; Brevet of Lieut.-Col.)
Lieutenant.	Harford, H. C.	99th Foot.	Proceeded on Transport Service to South Africa in Nov., 1878. Served with Lonsdale's N.N.C. through the whole of its operations in the war as principal Staff Officer.
Bt. Major.	Pelly Clarke, E.	103rd Foot.	Arrived in Natal on two months' privilege leave from Mauritius in Oct., 1878. Though in a bad state of health at the time, he gave up his leave and was temporarily appointed by Lord Chelmsford Staff Officer to Col. Pearson's Column. Towards the end of Dec. he was relieved by an officer sent out from England, and was appointed Director of Transport to the column, and in that capacity superintended

Rank.	Name.	Regt.	Services.
			the crossing of the Tugela of the transport; accompanied the column to Etshowe; was present at the battle of Inyezane, and was with the column throughout the siege. On arriving in Natal was directed to return to Mauritius to take up his appointment there. (Mentioned in despatches.)
Bt. Major.	Dick, J. R.	103rd Foot.	Proceeded to Natal on Transport Service, and was employed during the war on the lines of communication and at the base.
Bt. Major.	Spalding, H.	104th Foot.	Served as D.A.A. and Q.M.G. on the Hd.-Qrs. Staff. Was in temporary command of the lines of communication at Rorke's Drift on the departure of Glyn's Column from its camp on the Buffalo. Received news from the Isandhlwana camp, on the 22nd Jan., of bodies of the enemy having been descried. Considering the ponts across the river to be insufficiently protected, proceeded to Helpmakaar for aid. On returning towards the Drift, was met by Major Upcher, in command of two cos. of the 24th, bearing news of the disaster at Isandhlwana. Pushed on with the cos. for Rorke's Drift, but came across a strong outpost of the enemy, and was met by fugitives who stated that the post had been taken and the garrison slain—tidings which appeared to be confirmed by the fact that flames were to be seen issuing from the building. Hastened back with the cos., menaced by the enemy, to Helpmakaar (which was devoid of garrison), with the object of protecting the ammunition and supplies there amassed, and formed a waggon laager round the commissariat store—the command of the detachment having been, in the meantime, taken over by Col. Hassard, R. E. Performed transport duty throughout the remainder of the war.
Captain.	Liptrott, J.	104th Foot.	Proceeded to Natal on Transport Service, and was employed during the war on the lines of communication and at the base.
Captain.	Cavaye, W. F.	107th Foot.	Was sent out to Natal in May, 1879, with drafts, and landed at Durban at the latter end of June. Was sent up country in command of a detachment about 300 strong, to join the 24th Regt. at Landman's Drift. Remained attached for duty with that regt., acting as District-Adjt., until appointed Commandant at Ladysmith. Served in that capacity until ordered to join Villiers's force in Zululand, which was shortly afterwards disbanded.
Captain.	Justice, P.	108th Foot.	Served with the Field Force during the war.
Captain.	Vaurenen, E.	109th Foot.	Proceeded to the Cape with drafts, and served with the Field Force in the later phases of the war.

Rank.	Name.	Regt.	Services.
Bt. Major.	Fryer, E. J.	Rifle Bde.	Served with the Field Force during the war.
Bt. Major.	Buller, E. H.	Rifle Bde.	Served during the war as A.D.C. to Lord Chelmsford and Commandant at Hd.-Qrs. Acted as Staff Officer to the 2nd Brigade, Etshowe Relief Column, and was present in that capacity at the battle of Ginghilovo. Was one of the officers referred to by Lord Chelmsford in his concluding despatch as having specially assisted him during the recent operations. (Brevet of Major.)
Bt. Major.	Somerset, A. H. T. H.	Rifle Bde.	Served during the war, first as Staff Officer at the Durban base of operations, and afterwards as Commandant at Ladysmith on the lines of communication. (Brevet of Major.)
Bt. Lt.-Col.	Robinson, C. W.	Rifle Bde.	Served as A.A.G. to the 2nd Divis. of the Field Force, from its formation in April, 1879, to the conclusion of its operations, including the battle of Ulundi. (Mentioned in despatches; Brevet of Lieut.-Col.)
Bt. Major.	Lane, R. B.	Rifle Bde.	Embarked for Natal in Feb., 1879, as A.D.C. to Gen. Newdigate, and served in that capacity through the whole of the operations of the 2nd Divis. of the Field Force. (Mentioned in despatches; Brevet of Major.)

KING'S DRAGOON GUARDS.

WHEN stationed at Aldershot, the regt. received, on the 12th Feb., 1879, a sudden order for service in South Africa. With the least practicable delay it was made up to war strength by volunteers from other corps, horses also being transferred; and on the 27th Feb. the left wing embarked at Southampton, under the command of Major Marter, in the hired transport "Spain;" the right wing, with Hd.-Qrs., following next day, under Col. Alexander, in the "Egypt." Both ships reached Durban on the 8th April, and each wing disembarked in order of arrival. The regt. marched to Pietermaritzburg by wings, the left arriving on the 18th and the Hd.-Qrs. on the following day. The regt. thus united left Pietermaritzburg on the 28th April, and proceeded to Dundee, where it was shortly afterwards joined by the 17th Lancers. On the 19th May both regts.—the brigade being under Gen. Marshall—marched to Rorke's Drift, bivouacking *en route*, and near the Drift.

Before daylight on the 21st the brigade crossed the Buffalo River, and advanced with such speed as due precaution would allow to the battle-ground of Isandhlwana. Many bodies were recognized and buried, and thirty-nine waggons and a rocket-cart were brought away, every available horse of the transport service having been taken for the purpose.

The regt., after a day's rest, set out for Landman's Drift, and proceeded thence to Koppie Allein, on the Blood River, where it arrived on the 26th May. On the 27th two squadrons under Major Marter made a lengthened reconnaissance into Zululand, in order that the line of advance for the 2nd Divis., then assembling at Koppie Allein, might be determined.

On the 1st June about 174 of all ranks, under Major Marter, marched into Zululand with the 2nd Divis., forming two strong field squadrons in single rank. The Hd.-Qrs. and four troops marched to Conference Hill, there to be stationed, and two troops, under Capt. Willan, set out for Rorke's Drift, to hold that post. The detachment under Major Marter formed part of the cavalry force which went out of the camp at Itelezi Hill, under Gen. Marshall, on the 2nd June, to search for the Prince Imperial's body, one troop, with a troop of the 17th Lancers, forming the escort on the way in.

On the 6th June Major Marter's two squadrons took part in the reconnaissance made by Gen. Marshall in the neighbourhood of the Upoko River. Some of Col. Buller's men from Wood's column joined the force *en route*. The Zulus were found strongly posted in a wood at Erzungayan, which was intersected with dongas, and in front of which was a line of four large kraals. Buller's men managed to fire the kraals, but a heavy fusillade was poured upon them from the wood, and several of their horses being killed and their men wounded, they retired. Col. Lowe then took the 17th Lancers to within 150 yards of the wood, and, dismounting some men, opened fire. Seeing this, and fearing the Zulus might rush out upon the horses, the K. D. Gs. formed up on the flank and right rear of the 17th; the Zulus, however, remained completely concealed in the wood. After a time the troops retired by Gen. Marshall's order, the enemy following in skirmishing order and round by their dongas on either flank. The Dragoons had barely crossed the Upoko, in which were quicksands, when a brisk fire was opened upon them from the further bank. On the 8th June Major Marter's detachment took part in a reconnaissance in force round the hills where the cavalry affair had taken place on the 6th. Some hundreds of Zulus were seen, and about twelve kraals were shelled and burnt.

The detachment left the 2nd Divis. on the 17th June, being ordered to proceed to Fort Newdigate in order to reconnoitre the country towards Ulundi by the Inhlazatye Mountain, and assist in escorting convoys towards the front. Major Marter took command of the fort, the garrison consisting of (besides the Dragoons) two cos. 21st Fusiliers, one co. Bengough's Native Contingent, two Gatling guns with detachment R.A., and sixty mounted natives. On the 21st Col. Davies, Grenadier Guards, arrived, and assumed command as senior officer.

From date of reaching Fort Newdigate (17th June) until 26th July the detachment was employed almost without intermission in reconnoitring distant parts of the country, being generally in the saddle from before daylight till after dark. In these raids some scores of native villages were destroyed. From the same date all stores for the front were escorted up by the detachment alone as far as Fort Newdigate or Fort Marshall, for which purpose it had very frequently to proceed to Koppie Allein (twenty-five miles distant), bivouac, and return with its charge next day.

Whilst the detachment was at Fort Newdigate, Major Marter and three of his men, at the suggestion of Col. Davies, built a monument over the spot on which the Prince Imperial's body was found.

On the 26th July Sir Garnet Wolseley having broken up the previously existing constitution of the forces, and reorganized them in columns, with one of which (Clarke's) he intended to proceed to Ulundi, the detachment took part in the advance as the cavalry portion of an escort to about 150 ox-waggons laden with stores for the front.

On the 7th Aug. the detachment marched to Emptonjaneni, twelve miles distant from Ulundi. In the night occurred a fearful storm of wind and rain, which began before the tents were well fixed at dusk, and continued till about 11 a.m. next day. At its termination 360 transport bullocks lay dead in the camp, about ninety more being afterwards found in the bushes around.

On the 9th Aug. one troop (Capt. Gibbings') was detailed, with the Mounted Infantry and natives of Clarke's column under Major Barrow, to make a reconnaissance of the Ulundi plain. On the 13th the detachment marched to Ulundi, and joined Sir Garnet Wolseley's camp. On the 14th it marched out from Ulundi at 7.30 a.m. under the following verbal orders, viz.: 1st. To endeavour to trace out the reputed old waggon-road from Ulundi to Conference Hill, and report as to its practicability for wheeled transport; 2nd. To find and communicate with Baker Russell's column, supposed to be near the Intabinkulu Mountains, about fifty miles off; 3rd. To return by another route past the Ishlalo Mountain, taking notes of the ground, and reporting as to whether it would be practicable in case of the King being captured to march the army out of the country by that line. These orders were completely carried out; the report furnished was accepted by Sir Garnet as satisfactory, and the army was eventually marched out of the country by the route indicated. On the 18th Aug. Major Marter marched with a squadron K. D. Gs. under orders to establish a chain of outposts to St. Paul's (forty miles distant), and to keep up the communication throughout the line by patrolling day and night, in order to prevent the King from breaking across. The detachment then proceeded by a forced march to Fort Victoria, and subsequently joined Clarke's column. On 27th Aug. the expedition was commenced which resulted in the capture of the King.

SERVICES OF OFFICERS OF THE KING'S DRAGOON GUARDS.

Rank.	Name.	Services.
Colonel.	Alexander, H.	Embarked at Southampton in transport "Egypt" 28th Feb., 1879, in command of Hd.-Qrs. and right wing. Marched with the regt. from Durban to Koppie Allein on the Blood River. When the 2nd Divis. crossed into Zululand on 1st June, proceeded with Regimental Hd.-Qrs. and four troops to Conference Hill, where he remained till Aug., moving then to Utrecht, and later to Wesselstroom. Commanded Utrecht District for several months.
Bt. Lieut.-Col.	Marter, J. C.	Commanded left wing on voyage out. Served with regt. from 9th April, and commanded a detached squadron in the field from 1st June until conclusion of campaign, including cavalry affair at Erzungayan. Captured the Zulu King in the Ngome Forest, and brought him to Ulundi, having under his command at the time a squadron K. D. Gs., a co. Natal Native Contingent, and an officer and ten men irregular mounted troops. (Mentioned in despatches and promoted Bt. Lieut.-Colonel.)
Captain.	Benthall, J. M.	Served at Conference Hill during the war, until employed at sick horse depôt at Landman's Drift.
Captain.	Gibbings, A.	Served under Major Marter from 1st June to 9th Sept., including capture of King. Present at the cavalry affair at Erzungayan.
Captain.	Thompson, W. H.	Served under Major Marter from 1st June to 26th July. Present at Erzungayan.

Rank.	Name.	Services.
Bt. Major.	Brownlow, W. V.	Served as Asst. Transport Officer with 2nd Divis., and as extra A.D.C. to Col. Lowe at battle of Ulundi. Afterwards commanded a squadron with Baker Russell's column.
Captain.	Becher, C. A. G.	Marched up country with the regt. Proceeded to Transvaal to purchase horses, and subsequently returned to Conference Hill.
Captain.	Godson, R. G.	(Exchanged into 3rd Hussars.) Served at Conference Hill until 25th Aug., when, with his troop, he joined the detachment under Major Marter at Fort Newdigate, relieving Capt. Thompson's troop. Took part in its subsequent services, including capture of the King.
Captain.	Douglas-Willan, H. P.	Commanded a squadron at Rorke's Drift, making frequent raids into Zululand, until the arrival of Sir Garnet Wolseley. Marched to Ulundi with Sir Garnet, his troop forming the personal escort of the General from the time he entered until he quitted Zululand, and afterwards as far as Prætoria. Took part in several expeditions after the King.
Captain.	Watson, H. J.	(Exchanged into 11th Hussars.) Was Staff Officer at Conference Hill from 13th June to 3rd Aug., and served afterwards with the squadron of the regt. in Baker Russell's Column.
Lieutenant.	Sadlier, N.	Served with the K. D. Gs. in Major Marter's squadron. Was present at the cavalry affair at Erzungayan.
Lieutenant.	Marrow, P.	Served with the K. D. Gs. in Major Marter's squadron. Was present at the cavalry affair at Erzungayan. Acted as Adjt. and Qr.-Mr. to the squadron, and subsequently as Staff Officer at Fort Newdigate.
Lieutenant.	French-Brewster, R. A. B.	Served in the campaign as Deputy Provost-Marshal of the 2nd Divis., and was present at the battle of Ulundi. Served afterwards with the squadron K. D. Gs. in Baker Russell's Column.
Lieutenant.	Alexander, J.	Served with the K. D. Gs. in the squadron under Major Marter from 1st June to conclusion of war. Was present at the cavalry affair at Erzungayan, and the capture of the King.
Lieut. and Adjt.	Nicholas, R. G.	Served at Conference Hill during the war.
Lieutenant.	Dewar, J. C.	Served at Conference Hill during the war. Served with Mounted Infantry of Russell's Column as a volunteer throughout the operations against Sekukuni, and was present at the attack and capture of the stronghold, 28th Nov., 1879 (severely wounded).
Lieutenant.	Lowry, R. T. G.	Served at Conference Hill during the war.
Sub-Lieutenant.	Harkness, W. H.	Served at Conference Hill during the war.
2nd Lieutenant.	Goold-Adams, W. R.	Served at Rorke's Drift during earlier phases of the war. Served in Capt. Willan's troop whilst it formed Sir Garnet's escort, and during its pursuit of the King.
2nd Lieutenant.	Willett, J. S.	Embarked in June, and joined regt. at Utrecht.
2nd Lieutenant.	Wright, E. L.	Embarked in June, and joined regt. at Utrecht. Served as a volunteer with the Mounted Infantry in the attack on Sekukuni.

Rank.	Name.	Services.
Paymaster (*ret. Major*).	Balders, C. M.	(3rd Hussars.) Proceeded to South Africa with the regt., and served at Pietermaritzburg during the war.
Quartermaster.	Murphy, H.	Served at Conference Hill during the war, and accompanied the regt. to the Transvaal.
Vet.-Surgeon.	Longhurst, S.	Accompanied Capt. Becher to the Transvaal to purchase horses, and served subsequently at Conference Hill.
Vet.-Surgeon.	Moore.	Served at Conference Hill and Landman's Drift, and with Sir Garnet's escort throughout.

17th (DUKE OF CAMBRIDGE'S OWN) LANCERS.

THIS regt. was stationed at Hounslow and Hampton Court, when, in Feb., 1879, an order arrived for it to hold itself in readiness to proceed to Natal. Officers and men on leave were ordered to rejoin at once, and 75 volunteers arrived from the 5th and 16th Lancers. On the 24th Feb. the left wing, under Major Boulderson, embarked in the "France" at Southampton, and the right wing with Hd.-Qrs., under Col. Drury Lowe (who had rejoined the regt. in order to take command, Col. Gonne having unfortunately met with a serious accident whilst at revolver practice a few days previously), followed two days afterwards in the "England." On board this vessel, also, was Gen. Marshall and his Staff. The "England" arrived at Durban on the 7th April, and the "France" on the 12th. The regt. marched in wings by Pietermaritzburg to Landman's Drift and Dundee, arriving about the 8th of May. On the 19th both wings, forming part of the cavalry brigade under Gen. Marshall, took part in the reconnaissance to the battle-ground of Isandhlwana. After this the whole cavalry brigade moved to Landman's Drift, and, crossing the Buffalo, proceeded to Koppie Allein.

The regt. took part in the advance of the 2nd Divis. into the enemy's country, performing much arduous and important work. On the 2nd June it formed part of the cavalry force which, under Gen. Marshall, went out from the camp at Itelezi Hill to search for the Prince Imperial's body; one troop, with a troop of the K. D. Gs., forming the escort on the way in. On the 6th it took part in the reconnaissance made by Gen. Marshall in the neighbourhood of the Upoko River. The advanced guard, consisting of Wood's Irregular Horse, engaged the enemy at Erzungayan. Hearing the firing, the cavalry pushed on, and, getting into broken ground, halted. Two squadrons (Capts. Clark and Bouverie's) were taken on by Col. Lowe, and charged through a mealie-field. The Zulus, however, had taken to the hill, at the commencement of which there was a steep ridge, and poured a heavy fire upon the troops. Here Lieut. and Adjt. Frith was shot. After firing a couple of volleys the Lancers at length retired, Capt. Bouverie and two men carrying Frith's body, Capt. Clark's squadron protecting the retirement, which, though under a brisk fire, was of necessity carried on at a walk. During this time the squadron of the K. D. Gs. under Major Marter had formed up on the flank and right rear of the Lancers. After recrossing the river the force returned to Fort Newdigate.

The next day the 2nd Divis. moved up to the Upoko. While there, Wood's Column, with a wing of the 17th Lancers and a troop of the K. D. Gs. attached to it, under the command of Capt. Clark, were detailed to return to Landman's Drift and convoy up to the encampment a large supply of provisions on which the advance of the whole force depended. This service was successfully performed by Gen. Wood in about ten days. It was then decided that the whole of the K. D. Gs. should keep the lower line of communication up to Fort Marshall, from which place two troops of the 17th Lancers, under Capt. Clark (with the squadron were Capt. Alexander, Lieuts. Russell, Steele, H. Fortescue, and St. Quintin), should continue them to Ulundi; the whole under the command of Gen. Marshall, who now returned to the base at Landman's Drift. While escorting Gen. Marshall from the Upoko, Capt. Clark met with a severe accident, his leg and ankle being broken by his horse falling; this necessitated his removal to Fort Newdigate, and eventually his being invalided home, Capt. Alexander being left in command of the squadron employed on the line of communication.

On the 28th June the regt. took part in the reconnaissance in the Umvolosi Valley, where three military kraals were burnt. By the 2nd July the right bank of the Umvolosi was reached by the 2nd

Divis. and the Flying Column. The next morning at daybreak the force moved across the river, and reached the Nodwengo kraal without interruption, the Lancers forming the rear-guard. During the action on the 4th, the regt., with the Light Horse and Mounted Basutos, were dismounted inside the square. On the Zulus being turned, the 17th Lancers mounted and charged, and completed their rout. During the action, whilst in the square, Lieut. Jenkins was wounded by a bullet striking him on the jaw, which rendered him insensible. During the charge, Capt. Wyatt-Edgell was killed; Lieut. James, Scots Greys, was wounded on the breast by an assegai; one sergeant and a man were also killed, and several wounded. After the action the regt. proceeded to the King's kraal, which was burnt. Shortly afterwards Newdigate's Divis. was broken up, and the 17th Lancers returned to Natal and Koppie Allein. The regt., later, marched down to Pinetown, near Durban, where it remained six weeks until transports arrived; it then embarked for Mhow, India.

SERVICES OF OFFICERS OF THE 17TH (DUKE OF CAMBRIDGE'S OWN) LANCERS.

RANK.	NAME.	SERVICES.
Colonel.	D. C. Drury-Lowe, *C.B.*	(Late 17th Lancers.) Commanded the regt. throughout its operations in the campaign, including the cavalry affair at Erzungayan, and the battle of Ulundi.
Bt. Lieut.-Col.	Boulderson, S.	Served with the regt. throughout its operations in the campaign. Was present at the battle of Ulundi. (Mentioned in despatches, Brevet of Lieut.-Colonel.)
Captain.	Clark, S. Y.	Served with the regt. in the campaign until the end of June. Was present at the cavalry affair at Erzungayan. Commanded a wing of the Lancers and a troop of the K. D. Gs. attached to the Flying Column.
Captain. Captain. Captain. Captain. Captain. Captain. Captain.	Duke, J. C. Cooke, T. A. Belford, E. A. Alexander, J. F. (late 17th Lancers). Pleydell-Bouverie, *Hon.* J. Kevill-Davies, W. T. S. Swaine, C. E. (exchanged into the 11th Hussars).	Served with the regt. throughout its operations in the campaign, and were present at the battle of Ulundi. Capt. Alexander succeeded Capt. Clark in command of the squadron employed on the line of communications between Fort Marshall and Ulundi. Capts. Pleydell-Bouverie and Swaine were also present at the cavalry affair at Erzungayan.
Lieutenant. Lieutenant. Lieutenant. Lieutenant. Lieutenant. Lieutenant. Lieutenant. Lieutenant. Lieut. and Adjt. 2nd Lieutenant. 2nd Lieutenant. 2nd Lieutenant.	Russell, J. M. Wood, W. A. Neeld, M. G. Jenkins, H. C. Purvis, H. Fortescue, H. Steele, T. A. Herbert, E. B. Fortescue, *Hon.* L. H. D. Anstruther-Thomson, C. J. Butler, C. H. St. Quintin, F. D. H.	Served with the regt. throughout its operations in the campaign. Lieut. Russell was present at the cavalry affair at Erzungayan, and was employed on the line of communications to Ulundi. Lieuts. Wood, Neeld, Jenkins, Purvis, Herbert, Fortescue, Anstruther-Thomson, and Butler were present at the battle of Ulundi, Lieut. Neeld acting as Orderly Officer to Col. Lowe, and Lieut. Jenkins as Adjt. of the regt. The latter was severely wounded in the engagement. Lieut. Purvis served as Transport Officer during the war; Lieuts. Steele, H. Fortescue, and St. Quintin on the line of communications to Ulundi. The latter officer was also present at the cavalry affair at Erzungayan.
Paymaster.	Brown, J.	Capt. Brown proceeded with the regt. to South Africa, and was employed at Pietermaritzburg during the campaign.
Quartermaster. Vet.-Surgeon. Vet.-Surgeon.	J. Berryman, *V.C.* Lambert, J. Raymond.	Served with the regt. throughout its operations in the campaign. Were present at the battle of Ulundi.

ROYAL ARTILLERY.

N BATTERY, 5TH BRIGADE.

AT the latter end of 1878 Harness's Battery, which was encamped at Maritzburg, was employed in preparing for the impending campaign in Zululand. Marching for Helpmakaar, it remained under canvas at Greytown, *en route*, until after Christmas, and arrived at its destination on the 7th Jan., 1879.

The battery formed part of Glyn's Column of the army of invasion, and consisted, at the time of its entry into Zululand, of 130 of all ranks, with six guns, 73 horses, 36 mules, and six mule-carts, with transport waggons. In the disastrous encounter with the enemy at Isandhlwana, the battery lost Bt. Major Stuart Smith, 61 non-com. officers and men, two guns, 24 horses, 30 mules, and 534 rounds of ammunition, besides the whole of the camp equipment.

The battery recrossed the Buffalo River with the remains of the Column on the 23rd Jan., remained at Rorke's Drift post until the 25th, and then proceeded to Helpmakaar, where it remained until the 17th April; during this time much sickness prevailed.

Proceeding to Dundee on the 17th April, the battery formed part of Newdigate's Divis., and, reinforced by two guns under Capt. Vibart, took part in the advance of that force into the enemy's country. At Fort Newdigate two guns under Capt. Vibart, with Lieut. Curling, were detailed to form part of the garrison, and, subsequently, two guns under Lieut. Fowler were detailed to remain at Fort Evelyn. Remaining guns, with Lieut.-Col. Harness and Lieut. Parsons, continued with the 2nd Divis., and took part in the battle of Ulundi. The battery then returned with the Divis. as far as Fort Newdigate, where orders were received for it to await the arrival of Baker Russell's Column. On the 5th August it joined that force. Arriving at Enhlongana, it took part in the erection of Fort George. Leaving the guns under an officer, with the dismounted men, at this post, Col. Harness, with about 35 mounted men and officers, took part with Col. Baker Russell's patrol in the search for the King. The Column was shortly afterwards broken up, and the battery proceeded to the Transvaal.

SERVICES OF THE OFFICERS OF THE N BATTERY, 5TH BRIGADE.

RANK.	NAME.	SERVICES.
Bt. Lieut.-Colonel.	A. Harness, *C.B.*	Commanded the battery throughout the war, including the battle of Ulundi (mentioned in despatches; *C.B.*). Lieut.-Col. Harness had also commanded the battery during the long and difficult march of about 500 miles from Cape Colony to Natal.
Captain.	Vibart, F. M. E.	Served during the second phase of the Zulu war. Horsed and equipped the two guns which took the place of those lost at Isandhlwana. Commanded the R. A. at Forts Marshall and Evelyn on the line of communications. Commanded the R. A. of Baker Russell's Column in the north of Zululand.
Captain.	Curling, H. T.	Served throughout the war with the exception of a few weeks spent on sick leave whilst the battery was at Helpmakaar. Was on detachment at Fort Newdigate from the date of its establishment. Subsequently served in Baker Russell's Column.
Captain.	Fowler, W. J.	Served throughout the war. Commanded the two guns left on detachment at Fort Evelyn.

Rank.	Name.	Services.
Lieutenant.	Parsons, C. S. B.	Served throughout the war. Was with the main body of Glyn's Column on its departure from Isandhlwana, and subsequent re-occupation of the camp on the 22nd Jan. Accompanied the battery again into Zululand in May. Commanded two guns at the battle of Ulundi. Subsequently served in Baker Russell's Column.
Vet. Surgeon.	Duck, F.	Served throughout the war in veterinary charge of Wood's Column. Present at the action on the Zlobane; specially reported by Col. Buller for "gallantry displayed during the retreat."
Vet. Surgeon.	Glover, B. L.	Served throughout the war. Was with the main body of Glyn's Column on its departure from Isandhlwana, and subsequent re-occupation of the camp on the 22nd Jan. Established a sick horse depôt at Fort Pearson. Proceeded to the Transvaal to assist in obtaining remounts, and was subsequently employed in inspecting animals at Newcastle, Utrecht, Ladysmith, Rorke's Drift, Koppie Allein, Conference Hill, Landman's Drift, and Dundee.

M BATTERY, 6TH BRIGADE.

MAJOR SANDHAM'S battery arrived at Durban, from England, on the 22nd March, 1879. For about a month it was encamped at Cato's Manor, during which time the Prince Imperial was attached to it. On the 26th April it joined Crealock's Divis. at Fort Tenedos, where it was encamped till the 19th June; it then proceeded with the Divis. in its advance, taking part in its various expeditions, and assisting in the opening of Port Durnford, and in the burning of the Ondine kraal. On the 17th August a portion of the battery, consisting of mounted non-com. officers and men under Lieut. Thompson, took part in Capt. Yeatman-Biggs' expedition in search of the King. It proceeded up the coast as far as St. Lucia Bay, which it crossed. Gleaning no tidings of the object of its pursuit, it made its way to Ulundi, which it reached on the 29th. It would appear that had the coast not been thus patrolled, the King would have made for the thick forests in the neighbourhood of St. Lucia, as he had, in fact, proceeded a considerable distance down the Umvolosi when he heard of the approach of the party. The battery, subsequently, on the return of the forces to Natal, made its way back to Durban, where it arrived on the 14th Sept.

SERVICES OF THE OFFICERS OF THE M BATTERY, 6TH BRIGADE.

Rank.	Name.	Services.
Major.	Sandham, W. H.	Served in command of the battery through the whole of its operations during the war. (Mentioned in despatches.)
Captain.	Legard, J. D.	Served on Staff of Crealock's Divis. as D.A.Q.M.G., Intelligence Branch, from 26th April to 7th July, when invalided to base. Thanked by the General Commanding in his despatches. Received, also, thanks of H.R.H. the Commander-in-Chief for reconnaissances executed in Zululand.
Lieutenant. Lieutenant.	Shiffner, J. Jervis-White-Jervis, J. H.	Lieuts. Shiffner and Jervis-White-Jervis served with the battery during its various operations in the war.

RANK.	NAME.	SERVICES.
Lieutenant.	Thompson, J. H.	Served with the Field Force from the date of the arrival of the battery till the conclusion of the war. Was in command of the mounted gunners in Capt. Yeatman-Biggs' expedition in search of the King.
Vet. Surgeon.	Healy, M. F.	Was attached to Hd.-Qrs. and in veterinary charge of Crealock's Divis. from the end of March, 1879, to its break-up at the end of Sept., 1879. During the last three months the other officers of his department being invalided, Vet.-Surg. Healy was in sole charge.

N BATTERY, 6TH BRIGADE.

ON the 24th Feb., 1879, Major Le Grice's battery (strength, 173 non-com. officers and men, and 132 horses), embarked for Natal at Southampton, and on the 31st March arrived at Durban. After landing, it made its way, *viâ* Helpmakaar, to Landman's Drift, where, arriving on the 12th May, it formed part of Newdigate's Divis. It took part in the subsequent advance of that force into the enemy's country. At the battle of Ulundi on the 4th July it fired 68 rounds, doing considerable execution amongst the retreating enemy; its casualties during the engagement were one driver wounded, and two horses killed and two wounded.

After the battle two guns, under Capt. Crookenden and Lieut. Woodehouse, were detached, and, joining Wood's Column, proceeded with it to Quamagwasa. Capt. Crookenden then marched his guns back to Ulundi, and, after being stationed there about a month, returned to Maritzburg, where he awaited the Hd.-Qrs. of the battery.

The Hd.-Qrs., with the remaining four guns, marched back, after the battle of Ulundi, to Landman's Drift, where the Divis. was broken up. The whole battery was complimented by Gen. Newdigate on the services it had performed.

Orders were next received for the four guns to form part of the Column, consisting of one squadron K. D. Gs., four guns R.A., and two cos. 4th Regt., the whole, under command of Major Le Grice, which proceeded to Standerton in the Transvaal. That town was reached on the 21st Aug. On the 17th Sept. the battery proceeded to Heidelburg, where, on the 13th Oct., it received orders to march to Durban for embarkation for India. Passing through Standerton, it arrived at Maritzburg on the 26th Oct., having marched 320 miles in fourteen days. This march was the subject of a complimentary letter from the Deputy Adjt.-Gen., R.A., conveying H.R.H.'s. satisfaction at the credit done to the battery by the rapidity of its movements and the good condition of its horses on its arrival at its destination. On the 28th Oct. the battery embarked at Durban for India.

SERVICES OF OFFICERS OF THE N BATTERY, 6TH BRIGADE.

RANK.	NAME.	SERVICES.
Bt. Lieut.-Colonel.	Le Grice, F. T.	Commanded the battery throughout its various operations during the war, including the battle of Ulundi (mentioned in despatches). Commanded the Column which subsequently proceeded to the Transvaal.
Captain.	Crookenden, N. N.	Capt. Crookenden, Lieuts. Elliot, Trench, and Wodehouse, and Vet. Surg. Haggar served with the Field Forces from the date of the arrival of the battery till the conclusion of the war, being present at the battle of Ulundi; for his conduct during the engagement Lieut. Trench was mentioned in despatches. Capt. Crookenden and Lieut. Wodehouse served, on detachment, with Wood's Column from shortly after the battle of Ulundi until they rejoined the Hd.-Qrs.
Lieutenant.	Elliot, E. H.	
Lieutenant.	Trench, F. J. A.	
Lieutenant.	Wodehouse, J.	
Vet. Surgeon.	Haggar, W.	

O BATTERY, 6TH BRIGADE.

ON landing at Durban, from England, in April, 1879, the right half of Major Duncan's Battery proceeded to the Lower Tugela to form the Ammunition Column of Crealock's Divis. After arriving there, Major Duncan sent a detachment of the battery, under Lieut. Taylor, to Fort Chelmsford, to form a separate column; so that convoys proceeding backwards and forwards could be supplied with ammunition at that position, whilst reserve ammunition could be served at the Tugela to the troops advancing. On the forward movement being made by the Divis. to Port Durnford, the battery became again united.

Major Duncan and Lieut. Taylor took part in the advance of Clarke's Flying Column on Ulundi. After the capture of the King the battery returned to Natal.

SERVICES OF OFFICERS OF THE O BATTERY, 6TH BRIGADE.

Rank.	Name.	Services.
Bt. Lieut.-Colonel.	Duncan, A. W.	Served in command of the Ammunition Column formed out of O Battery, 6th Brigade, from the date of its arrival till the conclusion of the war. Commanded the R.A. which, with Clarke's Flying Column, advanced to Ulundi.
Captain.	Bally, J. F.	Capt. Bally, and Lieuts. Taylor, Anderson, and Douglas served in the Ammunition Column from the date of its arrival in Zululand till the conclusion of the war; Lieut. Taylor being in command of the detachment at Fort Chelmsford, and subsequently taking part in the advance of Clarke's Flying Column to Ulundi.
Lieutenant.	Taylor, W. H. F.	
Lieutenant.	Anderson, W. C.	
Lieutenant.	Douglas, J. S.	

No. 8 BATTERY, 7TH BRIGADE.

THIS battery served in the field in Zululand from the 2nd April, 1879, to the 2nd August. Though not actually engaged with the enemy, it went through many hardships on convoy and other duties.

The battery was stationed in April at Fort Pearson; in May, at Fort Tenedos; in June, at Fort Burke; in July, at Fort Crealock; and in August, at Camp Sacchini.

SERVICES OF OFFICERS OF No. 8 BATTERY, 7TH BRIGADE.

Rank.	Name.	Services.
Major.	Ellaby, H. L.	Major Ellaby served in command of the battery from the date of its arrival in South Africa till the conclusion of the war, Capt. Cooke, and Lieuts. Giles and De Lisle taking part in its various operations.
Captain.	Cooke, T. C.	
Lieutenant.	Giles, G. E.	
Lieutenant.	De Lisle, F. J.	

No. 10 BATTERY, 7TH BRIGADE.

CAPTS. MACLEAN and EVANS arrived at Durban on the 26th March, 1880, with half a battery of Garrison Artillery, three 7-pounder guns, and a co. of the 88th Connaught Rangers, forming a detachment sent from Mauritius on receipt of the news of the disaster at Isandhlwana.

Major Owen, who had been sent to Malta to represent the War Office on the important committee of inquiry on the bursting of a gun on board H.M.S. "Thunderer," arrived in Natal shortly afterwards, and, assuming command of the battery, proceeded to organize it as a Mounted Gatling Field Battery—the first of its kind in the British army. At the end of about a month a sufficiency of horses, mules, camp equipment, &c. was obtained to enable it to proceed up country, and, leaving Pietermaritzburg on the 5th May, it was able, by dint of rapid marching, to join Newdigate's Divis. before the latter left Landman's Drift. Joining the Flying Column at Mundhla Hill, Owen's Battery took part with that force, from the 26th May, in all its subsequent operations. After returning from the Upoko River to the position where Fort Newdigate was subsequently erected, the two Gatlings under Capt. Maclean, with Capt. Evans, remained temporarily on detachment at that post, the remainder of the battery going back with the column to Landman's Drift for supplies. The battery subsequently took part in the advance of the Flying Column into the enemy's country. On the 3rd July the Gatlings came into action to cover the retreat of the cavalry reconnaissance; and, on the 4th, took part in the battle of Ulundi, doing great execution. In his despatch, bearing date 5th July, 1879, Brig.-Gen. Wood writes: "The Gatling guns under Major Owen, R.A., and Lieut. Rundle, R.A., came into action a little in front of the square; combined with the fire of the infantry they effectually checked the daring attempt of the enemy to come to close quarters."

On the reorganization of the forces at the end of July, Owen's Battery was selected to form part of Clarke's Column, and subsequently took part in the operations of that force. On the breaking up of the Column the battery made a rapid march from St. Paul's to Durban, where guns, horses, and equipment were returned into store. At the latter end of October it embarked for Mauritius.

SERVICES OF OFFICERS OF No. 10 BATTERY, 7TH BRIGADE.

Rank.	Name.	Services.
Bt. Lieut.-Colonel.	Owen, J. F.	Served in command of his battery from the date of its formation till the conclusion of the war, including the battle of Ulundi. (Mentioned in despatches; Brevet of Lieut.-Col.)
Captain.	Maclean, A. H.	Capt. Maclean and Lieut. Rundle served in the battery from the date of its formation till the conclusion of the war, Capt. Maclean remaining on detachment at Fort Newdigate in command of the two Gatlings on the departure of the battery from that post.
Captain.	Evans, E. B.	Capt. Evans, who had taken an active part in the equipment of the battery, remained on detachment at Fort Newdigate with the two Gatlings, under Capt. Maclean, on the departure of the Hd.-Qrs. from that post. He was subsequently, in June, ordered to England in charge of an officer under arrest.
Lieutenant.	Rundle, H. M. L.	

No. 11 BATTERY, 7TH BRIGADE.

LIEUT.-COL. TREMLETT'S battery served with the Field Force through the whole of the war, a heavy share of arduous and important duty falling to its lot. The Hd.-Qrs. were with Wood's Column throughout its various operations, including the action at the Zunguin Nek, on the 24th Jan.; the battle of Kambula, on the 29th March; and the battle of Ulundi, on the 4th July—a detachment being also present at the action on the Zlobane on the 28th March, and two men of the battery at the battle of Ginghilovo on the 2nd April; while another division of the battery, under Lieut. Wilford Lloyd, served with Pearson's Column from the date of its formation till the relief of Etshowe—being present at the battle of Inyezane on the 22nd Jan., and throughout the subsequent blockade of the post; and afterwards taking part in the operations of Crealock's Divis. Major Russell, of the battery, was killed when in command of a rocket detachment at Isandhlwana on the 22nd July.

SERVICES OF OFFICERS OF No. 11 BATTERY, 7TH BRIGADE.

Rank.	Name.	Services.
Bt.Lieut.-Colonel.	Tremlett, E. G.	Commanded the R.A. of Wood's Column throughout the war, including the action on the Zunguin Nek, and the battles of Zlobane, Kambula, and Ulundi. (Repeatedly mentioned in despatches; Brevet of Lieut.-Col.)
Bt. Major.	Browne, H. R. Y.	Proceeded to South Africa, *vice* Major Russell, killed; joined the battery with a draft at Kambula Camp, and took part in Wood's advance on Ulundi. On the break-up of the Flying Column, returned with the battery to Durban. (Mentioned in despatches; Brevet of Major.)
Captain.	Bigge, A. J.	Served in the battery with Wood's Column. Was present at the action on the Zunguin Nek, the action on the Lower Zlobane, and the battle of Kambula. (Mentioned in despatches.)
Lieutenant.	Slade, F. G.	Served in the battery with Wood's Column throughout. Was present at the action on the Zunguin Nek, the battle of Kambula (mentioned in despatches), and the battle of Ulundi. After the conclusion of the war accompanied H.I.M. the Empress Eugénie in her journey to Zululand.
Lieutenant.	Lloyd, W. N.	Served in the battery throughout the war. Was in command of the R.A. of Pearson's Column, being present at the battle of Inyezane (mentioned in despatches) and the occupation of Etshowe (mentioned in despatches). Served throughout the subsequent advance of Crealock's Divis. (mentioned in despatches).

ROYAL ENGINEERS.

Rank.	Name.	Services.
Colonel.	F. C. Hassard, *C.B.*	On outbreak of Zulu war Col. Hassard proceeded to join Lord Chelmsford as C. R. E. in South Africa and Field, being second in command. Commanded the 2nd Divis. at Helpmakaar after the disaster at Isandhlwana. Proceeded to Cape Town by order, and remained there, in command, until conclusion of war.
Lieut.-Colonel.	Steward, E. H.	Commanded the Royal Engineers of the South African Field Force from 5th April, 1879, until it was broken up on the termination of the campaign, in succession to Col. Hassard, on the return of the latter to Cape Town.
Major.	Hamilton, A. C.	Proceeded to the Cape in command of the Telegraph troop. Was Director of Telegraphs and Signalling for the army throughout the campaign.
Bt. Lieut.-Colonel.	C. Warren, *C.M.G.*	Was Administrator of Griqualand West during the Zulu war. (Lieut.-Col. Warren had commanded the Diamond-field Horse in the previous Cape campaigns, and seen considerable service.)
Bt. Major.	Nixon, F. W.	When nearly all the troops were withdrawn from Cape Town for service in Natal and Zululand, in Dec., 1878, Major Nixon (who had commanded R. Es. with the Field Forces during the Gaika and Galeka campaigns, 1877-78) was left there as Commandant to take charge of the Depôt, and purchase and forward stores, horses, and mules.
Captain.	Hime, A. H.	Was Colonial Engineer in Natal. Accompanied Lieut.-Col. Steward in his tour of inspection. Commanded the Natal Pioneers which had been originally raised by Col. Durnford.
Captain.	Anstey, T. H.	Served with Newdigate's Divis. in the advance from Koppie Allein, and was present at battle of Ulundi. Subsequently made a triangulation survey of the route taken by the Divis. from Landman's Drift to Entonjaneni. On return to Maritzburg was ordered to survey in detail the battle-field of Isandhlwana and the ground adjacent thereto.
Bt. Major.	Jones, W. P.	Commanded the 5th co. throughout the war. Was *en route* up country when the battle of Isandhlwana took place. Subsequently occupied Helpmakaar. Took part in the advance on Ulundi (forming part of Wood's Advanced Guard) under Lord Chelmsford, and commanded the R. Es. at the battle.
Captain.	Courtney, D. C.	Served with Pearson's Column from Jan. to April, 1879. Present at battle of Inyezane, and throughout blockade of Etshowe. Succeeded to command of 2nd co. on death of Major Wynne, and served with it in the advance of 2nd Divis. on Ulundi; also with Baker Russell's Column to close of operations.

Rank.	Name.	Services.
Bt. Major.	J. R. M. Chard, *V.C.*	Proceeded to the Cape with the 5th co. Was detached with a few men at Rorke's Drift during the battle of Isandhlwana, and, as senior officer, commanded the troops in the gallant defence of that post. Accompanied the 5th co. in the advance on Ulundi. (*V.C.*, Brevet of Major.)
Lieutenant.	Hare, J.	Was in the Telegraph troop, and in charge of the southern line of telegraphs to St. Paul's, and subsequently to Ulundi.
Lieutenant.	MacGregor, J. C.	Proceeded to the Cape in the Telegraph troop. Had charge of the northern line of telegraphs and signalling up to Ulundi. Afterwards went to the Transvaal, and was C. R. E. at the attack and capture of Sekukuni's stronghold.
Lieutenant.	Watkins, T. W.	Was Adjt. to Lieut.-Col. Steward, C. R. E. Field Forces, and accompanied that officer in his tour of inspection of the Zulu frontier.
Lieutenant.	Cameron, J.	During the first phase of the Zulu war, Lieut. Cameron, who had served throughout the Gaika and Galeka campaign, was employed in Pondoland. During the second phase was attached to the base of operations and line of communications.
Lieutenant.	Rich, H. B.	Proceeded to the Cape in the Telegraph troop, and was employed on the southern line.
Lieutenant.	Main, T. R.	During the first phase of the Zulu war, Lieut. Main (who had served in the Gaika and Galeka campaign, and afterwards as Engineer officer with Glyn's Column in the Transkei), served with Pearson's Column, being present at the battle of Inyezane and throughout the subsequent occupation of Etshowe (mentioned in despatches). Served during the second phase with Newdigate's Divis. and the Flying Column until after the battle of Ulundi.
Lieutenant.	Sherrard, C. W.	Served in command of the 30th co. with Crealock's Divis. Joined Baker Russell's Column, and subsequently proceeded, with a detachment of the 30th co., with Clarke's Column to Ulundi. Returned, as C. R. E. of the Column, to Natal.
Lieutenant.	Porter, R. da C.	Proceeded to the Cape with the 5th co., and served with it throughout the campaign. Was present at the battle of Ulundi.
Lieutenant.	Baxter, J. C.	Was appointed Adjt. R. E. on 1st Jan., 1879, and accompanied the Hd.-Qr. staff. Was employed under Col. Hassard in making general preparations for the campaign. Arrived at Helpmakaar on 22nd Jan., and, after the disaster at Isandhlwana, assisted in the fortification of that position. Subsequently returned to Maritzburg, from whence, at the end of Feb., was invalided to Cape Town.
Lieutenant.	Mackean, K.	Proceeded to the Cape with the 30th co. Constructed the bridges over the Lower Tugela. Served with the co. in the southern columns throughout the campaign.

Rank.	Name.	Services.
Lieutenant.	Willock, H. B.	Landed in Natal with the 2nd co. on the 2nd Jan., 1879. Served with Pearson's Column during the first phase of the war, being present at the battle of Inyezane and throughout the subsequent occupation and blockade of Etshowe. Invalided home, 5th June. Mentioned in despatches.
Lieutenant.	Penrose, C.	Landed in Natal, 4th July, 1879. Served at Durban and Maritzburg as Divis. Officer R. E. and as Adjt. to the C. R. E. South African Field Force. Employed also in surveying in detail the battle-field of Isandhlwana and the ground adjacent thereto.
Lieutenant.	Haynes, C. E.	Proceeded to the Cape with the 2nd co. Was the officer who effected the communication with Pearson's force in Etshowe by means of heliostats. Accompanied 2nd co. in the march from the southern to the northern columns, and in the advance on Ulundi. Proceeded subsequently to the Transvaal.
Lieutenant.	Littledale, R. P.	Proceeded to the Cape with the 30th co., and served with it during the campaign. Proceeded subsequently to the Transvaal.
Lieutenant.	Commeline, C. E.	Proceeded to the Cape with the 5th co., and served with it throughout the campaign. Was present at the battle of Ulundi. Subsequently commanded a detachment which accompanied the force sent against Sekukuni. Was present at the capture of that chief's stronghold.
Lieutenant.	Bond, F. G.	Served on the lines of communication of the Hd.-Qr. Column in Zululand with the Telegraph troop, R.E., from the beginning of May until the conclusion of the war. Served subsequently in the Transvaal on the telegraph lines between Utrecht and Wakerstrom.
Lieutenant.	Brotherton, T. de la H.	Proceeded to the Cape with reinforcements; subsequently to Prætoria.
Veterinary Surg. (1st Class).	Walters, W. B.	Arrived at Durban, May 10th. Assumed charge as Senior Veterinary Surgeon at the base of operations, and established a sick horse depôt. Proceeded to the districts N. E. of the Cape Colony to purchase animals, and was absent during July and August. On return, resumed duties, assuming charge of the depôt, veterinary stores in addition.

2ND BATTALION 3RD REGIMENT (THE BUFFS).

DURING the summer of 1878 the Hd.-Qrs. and five cos. of this regt., which had been previously stationed at Pietermaritzburg, were scattered over a wide area at various strategically important positions in Natal. Towards the latter end of the year orders to concentrate at Thring's Post, twenty miles distant from the Tugela Mouth, were received; and early in Nov., the three remaining cos. of the regt. having arrived in Natal from Mauritius, the concentration was carried out. Shortly afterwards two cos. were sent to construct—near the mouth of the river and on the right bank, and commanding the drift—the earthwork which was subsequently known as Fort Pearson, a duty which they most successfully carried out.

On the 3rd Jan., 1879, the Hd.-Qrs. and remaining cos. struck camp, and, arriving on the 4th in the neighbourhood of the fort, took up a position near the Drift. The regt. now numbered over 800 men, and its fine appearance indicated its capacity—a capacity proved by subsequent events—to endure any amount of hardship which it might have to encounter.

From the 4th to the 12th Jan. the Buffs assisted the Naval Brigade in completing the arrangements made for the crossing of the Tugela by Pearson's Column, of which the regt. now formed part. On the 12th three cos. (under Capts. Forster, Alexander, and Maclear), under the command of Col. Parnell, crossed the river, and entrenched themselves on the rising ground on which Fort Tenedos was subsequently erected. The remainder of the column crossed on the following day; and on the 18th the advance towards Etshowe was continued. Two cos. of the Buffs, with Natal Pioneers, were sent forward, on the 20th, to the Amatakulu River, to prepare the drift; and on the following day other cos. of the regt., under Col. Parnell, marched to, and destroyed, the military kraal at Ginghilovo. In the advance of Pearson's force on the 22nd, the 1st wing of the column, of which six cos. of the regt. formed part, preceded the 2nd wing, which included the remaining cos., by an hour's march. In the engagement which ensued in the neighbourhood of the Inyezane River, two cos. of the regt., which were at the head of the col., bore the brunt of the first onslaught of the enemy, and the steady behaviour of the remainder contributed materially to the success of the day. The casualties sustained by the regt. in the battle were two men killed and five wounded.

On the 25th Jan. two cos. under Capts. Wyld and Maclear, together with a portion of the 99th Regt. under Major Coates, escorted a convoy of eighty waggons proceeding to the Tugela for supplies. Two cos. under Capts. Forster and Alexander, which had left Etshowe on the 24th, were met *en route*, escorting an up-convoy, and news of the disaster at Isandhlwana was received. The up-convoy—the last which Pearson's force was destined to receive—reached Etshowe late on the evening of the 26th, having had to abandon six waggons at the foot of the Kyoe ridge. On reaching the Tugela on the same day, the two cos. under Capts. Wyld and Maclear were ordered to form part of the garrison of Fort Tenedos.

The six cos. which were now at Etshowe formed part of the garrison of that post throughout the siege, and took part from time to time in the operations of the col. in the immediate neighbourhood of the fort. While superintending a party engaged in road-making, Lieut. Lewis was wounded in the head. Two popular officers of the regt., Capt. Williams and Lieut. Evelyn, and seven non.-com. officers and men, died during the blockade; and the names of no fewer than one officer and thirty-five non-com. officers and men were returned on the sick-list issued on the 1st April.

On the 28th March the Relief Column commenced its advance, the cos. under Capts. Wyld and Maclear forming part of the 1st Brigade. At the battle of Ginghilovo the cos. held the left front face of the laager, and, with the 99th, successfully repelled the enemy in the second phase of the attack. They remained to form a portion of the garrison of the laager during the relief of Etshowe by the main body of the col.; and subsequently marched back with the sick and wounded from Ginghilovo, rejoining the Hd.-Qrs. on their return to the frontier.

The Buffs formed part of the 1st Brigade of Crealock's Divis., and, from the date of the formation of that force, took part in the varied and harassing duties which fell to its lot. Throughout the succeeding months the men suffered considerably from sickness. In June the regt. took part in the advance of the Divis. to Port Durnford; and, after its arrival, remained stationed at various posts in the neighbourhood of that position till Ulundi was destroyed. In the last days of July orders were received for it to return to Natal. Reaching the Tugela on the 2nd Aug., it proceeded from thence to Pinetown, where it arrived on the 12th. At the latter end of Nov. it embarked at Durban for the Straits Settlement.

SERVICES OF THE OFFICERS OF THE 2ND BATTALION 3RD REGIMENT (THE BUFFS).

RANK.	NAME.	SERVICES.
Lieut.-Colonel.	H. Parnell, *C.B.*	Commanded the regt. throughout the war, including the battle of Inyezane, when his horse was shot under him (mentioned in despatches); the occupation of Etshowe (mentioned in despatches as "having rendered great service on all occasions by his tact and coolness"); and the advance to Port Durnford. (*C.B.* for services).
Major.	Graves, S.	Organized for the war the 2nd regt. N. N. C., consisting of two batts. Served with Pearson's Column in command of the regt. during the advance to Etshowe, taking part in the battle of Inyezane. (Mentioned in despatches.)
Major.	Halahan, H. T.	Proceeded to Natal whilst on passage home from India. Joined the regt. in Zululand, and served with it in the later operations of Crealock's Divis., including the advance to Port Durnford.
Major.	Hamilton, C. J.	Arrived in Natal too late to take part in the war. Joined the regt. at Pinetown on its return from Zululand.
Captain.	Forster, J. E.	Capts. Forster, Harrison, Alexander, Wyld, Maclear, Martin, and Backhouse served with the regt. throughout the war, and were present at the battle of Inyezane—the two former respectively as Acting Senior and Junior Majors. Both took a prominent part in the action, and, with Capts. Alexander and Martin, were present at Etshowe throughout the blockade. At the battle of Inyezane Capts. Wyld and Maclear commanded the cos. which repelled the attack of the Zulu left wing. Both officers, escorting a convoy, returned from Etshowe on the 25th Jan. to the Lower Tugela, where they formed part of the garrison of Fort Tenedos, in the construction of which their cos. took an active part. They subsequently held the advanced post of St. Andrew's Mission Station till the arrival of the reinforcements, when they took part in the advance of the Etshowe Relief Column, and, with Capt. Backhouse, who had also returned with the convoy in Jan., were present at the battle of Ginghilovo. Capt. Jackson, shortly after the battle of Inyezane, in which his co. was one of those most actively engaged, was invalided to England. Capt. Howarth proceeded to Natal in May, 1879, in charge of a draft, and, joining the regt. in Zululand, served with it in the later operations of Crealock's Divis., including the advance to Port Durnford.
Captain.	Harrison, H. D.	
Captain.	Alexander, G. A.	
Captain.	Wyld, W. H.	
Captain.	Maclear, H. W.	
Captain.	Jackson, A. C.	
Captain.	Howarth, W. C.	
Captain.	Martin, R. W. McG.	
Captain.	Backhouse, J. B.	
Lieutenant.	Moody, R. S. H.	Lieut. Moody accompanied the regt. as Adjt. to Thring's Post, from whence, having met with an accident, he was invalided home. Leaving England in April, he again rejoined Hd.-Qrs., and served with the regt. to the conclusion of the war. Lieut. Newnham-Davis served with the Mounted Infantry in the Hd.-Qrs. Columns, performing much important duty in
Lieutenant.	Newnham-Davis, N.	
Lieutenant.	Gordon, C. H.	

<table>
<tr><th>RANK.</th><th>NAME.</th><th>SERVICES.</th></tr>
<tr><td>Lieut. and Adjt.</td><td>Somerset, H. C.</td><td rowspan="11">reconnoitring. Lieuts. Gordon, Somerset, Lewis, Knight, Allen, Hughes, Middleton, Blackburn, Connellan, Knight-Bruce, and Vyvyan served with the regt. throughout the war, being present at the battle of Inyezane, and (with the exception of Lieut. Allen, who returned with the convoy to the Lower Tugela) at Etshowe throughout the blockade. Lieuts. Gordon and Lewis were with the colour party in the engagement, the former being in charge. Whilst subsequently covering a road-making party at Etshowe, the latter was severely wounded. Lieut. Somerset succeeded Lieut. Moody in Jan. as Adjt. Lieut. Knight acted as Orderly Officer to Col. Pearson throughout the war. (Mentioned in despatches.) Lieut. Allen, who had returned to the Lower Tugela in Jan., took part in the advance of the Relief Column, and was present at the battle of Ginghilovo. Lieut. Tylden-Pattenson, who, having proceeded to Natal in Feb., had marched to the Lower Tugela with the 60th Rifles, joined the detachment at Fort Tenedos, and, taking part in the advance of the Relief Column, was present at the battle of Ginghilovo.</td></tr>
<tr><td>Lieutenant.</td><td>Lewis, D. F.</td></tr>
<tr><td>Lieutenant.</td><td>Knight, H. R.</td></tr>
<tr><td>Lieutenant.</td><td>Allen, A. J. W.</td></tr>
<tr><td>Lieutenant.</td><td>Hughes, J.</td></tr>
<tr><td>Lieutenant.</td><td>Middleton, H. J. J.</td></tr>
<tr><td>Lieutenant.</td><td>Blackburn, H.</td></tr>
<tr><td>Lieutenant.</td><td>Connellan, C. L.</td></tr>
<tr><td>Lieutenant.</td><td>Knight-Bruce, J. C. L.</td></tr>
<tr><td>Lieutenant.</td><td>Vyvyan, C. B.</td></tr>
<tr><td>2nd Lieutenant.</td><td>Tylden-Pattenson, A. H.</td></tr>
<tr><td>Paymaster.</td><td>Gelston, A. W. H.</td><td>Capt. Gelston served with the Field Force throughout the war, and was with the regt. till its return from Etshowe.</td></tr>
<tr><td>Quartermaster.</td><td>Morgan, W. G.</td><td>Served with the regt. throughout the war, being present at the battle of Inyezane, and at Etshowe throughout the blockade. (Mentioned in despatches as having been "indefatigable in his exertions for the welfare of his regiment.")</td></tr>
</table>

2ND BATTALION, 4TH (KING'S OWN ROYAL) REGIMENT.

WHEN stationed at the North Camp, Aldershot, the batt. received orders, in the first week in Dec., 1878, to proceed to Natal on active service. It embarked in the transports "Dunrobin Castle" and "Teuton," on the 10th and 13th Dec. respectively, and arrived at Cape Town early in Jan. Three cos. under Major Elliott, with Capts. Knox and Leggett, and 2nd Lieuts. Bonomi and Ridley, were here landed from the "Teuton." The Hd.-Qrs., which had sailed in the "Dunrobin Castle," with two cos., landed at Durban, and were there subsequently joined by the three which proceeded on in the "Teuton." The batt. thus united marched to Pietermaritzburg, and from thence, on the receipt of the news of the disaster at Isandhlwana, to Helpmakaar. The three cos. left behind to garrison Cape Town received orders to join the Hd.-Qrs. They accordingly embarked, on the 26th Jan., 1879, in the "African," arrived at Durban on the 29th, and on the 2nd Feb. reached Maritzburg. There they remained until the arrival of the 21st Regt., when they proceeded to join the Hd.-Qrs., which had in the meantime moved from Helpmakaar to Utrecht and Greytown. After proceeding *viâ* Colenso, Ladysmith, and Newcastle to Utrecht, they were despatched to Balte's Spruit, Conference Hill, and Lüneberg. During this march Major Blake and Capt. Moore were surrounded by a Zulu impi (which, it is understood, was under orders to join the King), but were not attacked.

The cos. of the batt. were distributed in reserve over a wide area of country, including the Utrecht district, Potgreter's Farm, Lüneberg, Balte's Spruit, Conference Hill, &c. After the battle of Ulundi, the cos. were relieved by those of the 24th Regt., and proceeded to Lüneberg and Standerton in the Transvaal. On the 8th Sept., Col. Bray, with three cos. of the regt., assisted by the Frontier Light Horse and a detachment of Engineers, blew up the caves known as Umbellini's, in the neighbourhood of the

Intombi River. Manyanyoba, the independent chief who had long given great trouble, now surrendered, and the regt. received orders to return. On the road back the cos. which had been stationed at Newcastle, Ladysmith, and Dundee rejoined the regt., which, passing through Prætoria and Standerton, arrived at Pinetown on the 26th Jan., 1880. On the 8th Feb. the batt. embarked for Bombay, two cos. having been left at Greytown with the other forces which, under Major Twentyman, were destined for the defence of the frontier.

SERVICES OF OFFICERS OF THE 2ND BATTALION, 4TH (KING'S OWN ROYAL) REGIMENT.

Rank.	Name.	Services.
Colonel.	E. W. Bray, *C.B.*	Proceeded to Natal with the batt., and commanded it throughout the war. Commanded the expeditionary force which succeeded in destroying Umbellini's stronghold in the Intombi Valley.
Colonel.	Sykes, A. J.	(Retired.) Proceeded to Natal in command of the detachment in the transport "Teuton." Marched *viâ* Helpmakaar to Utrecht, and served with the batt. throughout the war.
Bt. Lieut.-Colonel.	Elliot, J. M'D.	(Retired.) Commanded the detachment landed at Cape Town in Jan., 1879. Proceeded thence, three weeks later, to Natal, and served with the batt. at Utrecht, Balte's Spruit, and Lüneberg. Was present at the destruction of Umbellini's stronghold.
Bt. Lieut.-Colonel.	Twentyman, A. C.	Commanded the forces at Greytown. Had his horse shot under him whilst inspecting the line of fortifications. Received Brevet of Lieut.-Col. in recognition of his services.
Major.	Blake, W. F.	Served with the batt. throughout the war. Proceeded to Helpmakaar, and from thence to Utrecht and Lüneberg. Whilst on the march was surrounded by a Zulu force which, however, failed to attack.
Major.	Middleton, O. R.	Served with the batt. throughout the campaign. Was Adjt. to Col. Bray at Utrecht.
Captain.	Knox, R. A.	Capts. Knox, Leggett, Lawrence, Sharp, Moore, Sutherland, Crofton, McCarthy, and Hutchinson served with the batt. throughout the war. Capts. Knox and Leggett were detained for a short time with the three cos. which were landed at Cape Town. The former subsequently commanded two cos. at Conference Hill, and afterwards at Standerton; the latter served at Balte's Spruit and Lüneberg, was present at the destruction of Umbellini's stronghold, and proceeded, subsequently, to Ladysmith and Standerton. Capt. Lawrence served at Helpmakaar and Potgreter's Farm; Capt. Sharp at Conference Hill, Standerton, and Prætoria; Capt. Moore at Lüneberg (he had previously assisted Col. Villiers in the Boundary Commission); Capt. Sutherland at Greytown; he was invalided home after meeting with an accident at Maritzburg, where he was Acting Garrison Adjt.; Capt. Crofton (then Adjt.), at Utrecht and Lüneberg; was present at the destruction of Umbellini's stronghold; Capt. McCarthy, in command of Mounted Infantry, was present at the battle of Kambula, after which he was invalided;
Captain.	Leggett, C. G.	
Captain.	Lawrence, H. B.	
Captain.	Sharp, J. R.	
Captain.	Moore, H.	
Captain.	Sutherland, H. B.	
Captain.	Crofton, M. E.	

Rank.	Name.	Services.
Captain.	McCarthy, R. H.	his place being taken by Capt. Hutchinson. That officer was present at the battle of Ulundi. His conspicuous gallantry in the field during a reconnaissance prior to the battle was brought to the notice of H.R.H. Commanding-in-Chief.
Captain.	Hutchinson, F. M. G.	
Lieutenant.	Ogilby, R. A.	Lieuts. Ogilby, Rowlandson, Shephard, Hay, Gawne, Elliott, Penrose, Matthews, Bonomi, Carter, and Ridley served with the batt. throughout the war—Lieut. Ogilby at Helpmakaar and Lüneberg; Lieut. Rowlandson at Utrecht and Lüneberg, was present at the destruction of Umbellini's stronghold; Lieut. Shephard at Helpmakaar; was subsequently invalided to Cape Town; Lieut. Hay at Utrecht; was subsequently invalided home; Lieut. Gawne at Greytown and Lüneberg; Lieut. Elliott at Helpmakaar, Greytown, and Lüneberg; Lieut. Penrose at Conference Hill; Lieut. Matthews at Utrecht and Lüneberg; Lieut. Bonomi (who, with Lieut. Ridley, had landed with the three cos. at Cape Town), at Balte's Spruit and Lüneberg; was present at the destruction of Umbellini's stronghold, and subsequently proceeded to Ladysmith and Standerton; Lieut. Carter at Greytown; Lieut. Ridley at Conference Hill, Standerton, and Prætoria. Lieuts. Dolphin and James joined the batt. at Greytown in Feb., 1879, and served with it until the conclusion of the war, the former at Maritzburg, and the latter at Utrecht and Lüneberg.
Lieutenant.	Rowlandson, J.	
Lieutenant.	Shephard, C. S.	
Lieutenant.	Hay, A. W.	
Lieutenant.	Gawne, J. M.	
Lieutenant.	Elliott, G. H. B.	
Lieutenant.	Penrose, E. R.	
Lieut. and Adjt.	Matthews, F. B.	
Lieutenant.	Bonomi, J. I.	
Lieutenant.	Carter, E. A. F.	
Lieutenant.	Ridley, A. B.	
2nd Lieutenant.	Dolphin, E.	
2nd Lieutenant.	James, W. L.	

1st BATTALION, 13th LIGHT INFANTRY.

PREVIOUS to the outbreak of the Zulu war the batt. was engaged in operating against Sekukuni on the Transvaal border, but on the war becoming imminent it was moved south, and formed part of Wood's Column, with which it remained throughout the whole of its operations. On the 2nd Jan., 1879, the Column left Utrecht, and reached the Blood River on the 4th, having left a detachment of two cos. 13th L. I. under Major Leet, at the fortified outpost of Balte's Spruit.

On the 6th the Column crossed into the enemy's country, the 13th L. I. leading. On the 18th the construction of a fort at Tinta's Drift on the White Umvolosi was commenced; D co., 13th L. I., and one co. 90th L. I. (under Major Moysey, R.E.) were left to garrison it, and the remainder of the batt. moved on towards Zunguin Nek.

The enemy was met with in force at that position on the 24th, and defeated with loss.

Taking the detachment at Tinta's Drift with it, the Column now fell back on Kambula, covering Utrecht, where it remained in camp for two months.

On the 27th March a patrol of mounted men and natives were sent out towards Zlobane, the Native Irregulars being under command of Major Leet. The gallantry displayed by this officer in the retreat after the encounter which ensued with the enemy, gained for him the Victoria Cross and Bt. Lieut.-Colonelcy.

At the battle of Kambula, on the 29th, the 13th gallantly checked the enemy at the right rear of the laager. The cattle laager was also held by the batt. throughout the engagement. Capts. Evans and Fowne's cos. were posted in Leet's redoubt, the fire from which made great havoc throughout the engagement. When the attack slackened, two cos. of the 13th, under Capts. Thurlow and Waddy, moving to the right front of the cattle laager, did great execution amongst the retreating Zulus, who were closely followed up and cut to pieces by the Mounted Corps. In the engagement Capts. Cox and Perssé were severely wounded, six men of the regt. were killed, and nineteen more were more or less severely wounded. The heroic conduct displayed on this occasion by Pte. Grovenor (who was killed) and Pte. Paye (who subsequently received the medal for distinguished conduct in the field) was singled out for special commendation in the batt. orders.

Lieut.-Col. Gilbert left the batt. on the 21st April, being invalided, and Major England assumed command.

No forward movement was made till the 5th May. During the interval supplies were got up in abundance, in which duty the 13th were much engaged. On that date, a move was made to the vicinity of the Zlobane, and from thence, subsequently, to Mundhla Hill.

On June 1st the batt. advanced to Umyanyanana, continuing a forward movement, with occasional halts. On the 23rd Ulundi became visible.

On 1st July the advancing Columns halted on the banks of the Umvolosi. In the battle of Ulundi, which ensued on the 4th, the 13th L. I. occupied the right of the square, within thirty yards of which numbers of the enemy's dead were subsequently found. In the engagement Lieut. Pardoe was mortally wounded, two men of the regt. were killed, and eleven were more or less severely wounded.

In the return to the frontier, St. Paul's Mission Station was reached on the 15th July. After a wet and trying march the batt. arrived at Durban, and embarked on board H.M.S. "Euphrates" for England, where it landed on the 18th Sept., after a total of $4\frac{9}{12}$ years' service in South Africa, and a total of $12\frac{3}{12}$ years abroad, including $4\frac{8}{12}$ years at Gibraltar, and $2\frac{9}{12}$ years in Malta.

Out of a total of twenty-eight years' service, this batt. passed only three years at home.

SERVICES OF OFFICERS OF THE 1ST BATTALION, 13TH LIGHT INFANTRY.

Rank.	Name.	Services.
Lieut.-Colonel.	P. E. V. Gilbert, *C.B.*	Served in command of the regt. with Wood's Column in the first phase of the war, taking part in the engagements at Zunguin and Kambula. (Mentioned in despatches; *C.B.*)
Bt. Lieut.-Colonel.	England, E. L.	Served in the regt. throughout the war, taking part in the engagements at Zunguin and Kambula. In command of the batt. at Ulundi. (Mentioned in despatches; Brevet of Lieut.-Col.)
Bt. Lieut.-Colonel.	W. K. Leet, *V.C.*	Served with Wood's Column throughout the war. Was present at the engagement at Zunguin. Was selected by Gen. Wood to command the natives attached to the force, styled "Wood's Irregulars." Commanded the corps in the storming of the stronghold in the Intombi Valley and the assault of the Zlobane, on which occasion his horse was shot under him, and his led horse also shot. Commanded the redoubt at Kambula. (Repeatedly mentioned in despatches; Brevet of Lieut.-Col. and Victoria Cross.)
Bt. Major.	Allfrey, I. S.	Served in Natal during the Zulu war.
Captain.	James, J. F.	(Since dead.) Served with the batt. throughout the campaign as Field Officer. Was second senior officer at the battle of Ulundi. (Capt. James died on the 24th Feb., 1880, his health having been completely broken by hardships endured during the campaign.)
Bt. Major.	Cox, W.	Served with the batt. throughout the first phase of the war. Was present at the action at Kambula, in which he was severely wounded. (Brevet of Major.)

Rank.	Name.	Services.
Bt. Major.	Perssé, D. T.	Major Perssé, Capts. Kinloch, Evans, Thurlow, Waddy, Fownes, and Gallwey served with the batt. throughout the war, and were present at the engagements at Zunguin Nek, Kambula, and Ulundi. In the latter engagement Major Perssé, who subsequently received his brevet rank, was severely wounded. Capt. Kinloch acted as Field Officer during the later phases of the war. Capt. Otway was present at the battle of Ulundi. Capt. Bradshaw (who had acted as Adjt. to the batt. throughout the Sekukuni campaign of 1878) served as Assist.-Director of Transport in Wood's Column; was present at the engagement at Zunguin Nek; and was mentioned in despatches. Capt. Gallwey served as Adjt. to the batt. throughout the war.
Captain.	Kinloch, G. H. A.	
Captain.	Evans, W. H.	
Captain.	Thurlow, W. H. H.	
Captain.	Waddy, J. M. E.	
Captain.	Otway, R. C.	
Captain.	Bradshaw, F. B.	
Captain.	Fownes, E. J.	
Captain.	Gallwey, E. J.	
Lieutenant.	Justice, F. J.	Lieuts. Clark, Poynton, Levinge, Williams, Pollock, Payne, and West served with the batt. throughout the war, and were present at the engagements at Zunguin Nek, Kambula, and Ulundi. Lieut. Justice was present at the battle of Ulundi. Lieuts. Townsend and Lovett were present at the engagements at Zunguin Nek and Kambula. Lieut. Walsh (who had served in the Mounted Infantry in the Sekukuni campaign of 1878) commanded a troop of Mounted Infantry throughout the war. He was present at the re-occupation of the camp at Isandhlwana by the Hd.-Qr. Column; and at the actions at the Zlobane, Kambula, and Ulundi. Lieut. Wilbraham was present at the action at Kambula. Lieuts. Allen and Hillas were present at the battle of Ulundi. Lieuts. O'Donnell and Snow served in Natal during the war.
Lieutenant.	Clark, E. W.	
Lieutenant.	Townsend, R. A. H.	
Lieutenant.	Poynton, E. M.	
Lieutenant.	Walsh, H. A.	
Lieutenant.	Levinge, R.	
Lieutenant.	Wilbraham, A. G.	
Lieutenant.	Williams, R. B.	
Lieutenant.	Pollock, A. W. A.	
Lieutenant.	Payne, R. L.	
Lieutenant.	Allen, J. C.	
2nd Lieutenant.	Lovett, H. W.	
2nd Lieutenant.	West, J. W. H.	
2nd Lieutenant.	Hillas, R. W. G.	
2nd Lieutenant.	O'Donnell, A. C.	
2nd Lieutenant.	Snow, T. D'O.	

2ND BATTALION, 21ST ROYAL SCOTS FUSILIERS.

THIS batt. was stationed at the Curragh Camp when, on the 12th Feb., 1879, a sudden order was received directing it out to Natal. The officers on leave and men on furlough were at once telegraphed to to rejoin. About three hundred men from other regts. in Ireland volunteered and were sent to the battalion to make it up to the strength for active service. On the 22nd Feb. it embarked at Queenstown in the hired transport "City of Paris." Whilst entering St. Simon's Bay the vessel struck on the Roman Rock, and met with such damage as to necessitate the transfer of the troops to H.M.S. "Tamar." The batt. (Hd.-Qrs. and eight cos.) disembarked at Durban on the 23rd March, and marched *viâ* Pietermaritzburg (where it left two cos. on detachment at Fort Napier) and Ladysmith to Dundee. It was there detailed to Newdigate's Divis., then in course of formation; and in the subsequent movements of that force the batt. did much arduous and important work. The Divis. left Dundee on the 2nd May. On the 8th three cos. of the 21st, under Bt. Lieut.-Col. Hazlerigg, were sent on to the Doornberg, a hill some eight miles distant from Landman's Drift, for the purpose of cutting wood for the Divis., and there constructed Fort Ayr; on the 17th the Hd.-Qrs. and remaining three cos. proceeded to the same district, and the whole regt. was employed for twelve days on the same duty. On the 30th the batt. marched to Koppie Allein on the Blood River, where the K. D. Gs. and 17th Lancers were already encamped; the next day it crossed into Zulu territory. On the Divis. quitting the encampment on the Upoko River, two cos. of the regt. were left in Fort Newdigate, where they remained until the conclusion of the war. On the 20th June two cos. were left in Fort Marshall, with Col. Collingwood in command of the garrison.

At the battle of Ulundi the regt. formed a portion of the right of the hollow square, and, with the 58th, bore the brunt of the first desperate onslaught of the enemy, large numbers of whom got to within thirty yards of the line before the galling and destructive fire which was poured into them could stay their advance. In the engagement Bt. Lieut.-Col. Winsloe was severely wounded in the chest. On the break up of the Divis. the batt. proceeded to the Transvaal.

SERVICES OF OFFICERS OF THE 2ND BATTALION, 21ST ROYAL SCOTS FUSILIERS.

RANK.	NAME.	SERVICES.
Colonel.	Collingwood, W. P.	(Late 21st Regt.) Commanded the batt. throughout its operations in the war. Commanded the garrison at Fort Marshall on the departure of the 2nd Divis.
Bt. Lieut.-Colonel.	Hazlerigg, A. G.	Served with the batt. during the war. Commanded the three cos. despatched to the Doornberg. Constructed Fort Ayr. Was in command of the batt. at the battle of Ulundi.
Bt. Lieut.-Colonel.	Winsloe, R. W. C.	Served with the batt. during the war. Present at the battle of Ulundi (severely wounded). (Mentioned in despatches.) Brevet of Lieut.-Col.
Bt. Major.	Bainbridge, E. T.	Major Bainbridge, Capts. Thorburn, Robinson, Browne, Willoughby, Gordon, Auckinleck, Falls, Spurgin, and Tew served in the batt. during the war; Capts. Willoughby, Falls, and Tew remaining in garrison at Fort Napier, Pietermaritzburg; Capt. Thorburn at Fort Newdigate; Major Bainbridge, Capts. Browne and Spurgin at Fort Marshall; Capts. Robinson, Gordon, and Auckinleck being present at the battle of Ulundi.
Captain.	Thorburn, W.	
Captain.	Robinson, C. B.	
Captain.	Browne, E. C.	
Captain.	Willoughby, R. T.	
Captain.	Gordon, J. M.	
Captain.	Auckinleck, D.	
Captain.	Falls, A. L.	
Captain.	Spurgin, J. H.	
Lieutenant.	Dunn, A. C.	Lieuts. Dunn, Lambart, Justice, Duckett, Alexander, Chichester, Lindsell, Browne, Young, and Hardinge served during the war. Lieuts. Collings, Stannell, Fiennes, Thorneycroft, and Lean, joined the batt. early in April at Maritzburg, the three latter remained on detachment at Fort Napier until the conclusion of the campaign; Lieuts. Dunn and Collings at Fort Newdigate; Lieuts. Justice, Duckett, and Chichester at Fort Marshall; Lieuts. Lambart, Browne, Young, Hardinge, and Stannell were present at the battle of Ulundi, the two latter carrying the colours. Lieuts. Alexander (who held the appointment of Regimental Transport Officer throughout the campaign) and Lindsell were employed on transport duty during the advance of the 2nd Divis.
Lieutenant.	Lambart, F. R. H.	
Lieutenant.	Justice, A. S.	
Lieutenant.	Duckett, W. M.	
Lieutenant.	Alexander, H. R.	
Lieutenant.	Collings, A. W.	
Lieutenant.	Chichester, S. F.	
Lieutenant.	Lindsell, C. F.	
Lieutenant.	Browne, P. W.	
Lieutenant.	Young, W. A.	
2nd Lieutenant.	Hardinge, Hon. A. S.	
2nd Lieutenant.	Twisleton-Wykeham Fiennes, G. C.	
2nd Lieutenant.	Stannell, H. S. McC.	
2nd Lieutenant.	Thorneycroft, A. W.	
2nd Lieutenant.	Lean, K. E.	
Paymaster.	Tew, N.	Capt. Tew served during the war, remaining on detachment at Fort Napier with the two cos. until its conclusion.
Quartermaster.	Clifford, J.	Served with the batt. during the war. Was present at the battle of Ulundi.

1st BATTALION, 24th (2nd WARWICKSHIRE) REGIMENT.

AT the latter end of Sept., 1878, two cos. of the batt., which was at that time stationed at the Cape of Good Hope, left King William's Town for Natal under Lieut.-Col. Pulleine, and subsequently were quartered at Pietermaritzburg and Durban respectively. A month later, in view of the impending hostilities with the Zulus, the Hd.-Qrs. and five more cos., under Col. Glyn, C.B., arrived in Natal, and proceeded, *viâ* Maritzburg and Greytown (where one co. was left on detachment), to Helpmakaar, which they reached on 12th Dec. Col. Glyn then assumed command of the 3rd Column (of which the regt. formed part) of the army of invasion, at that time in course of organization; and in the first days of Dec. the Hd.-Qrs. and four cos. advanced to Rorke's Drift, where Lieut.-Col. Pulleine joined the regt., and assumed command of it.

On the morning following the crossing of the Buffalo by Glyn's Column (12th Jan.) the regt. was engaged, attacking and capturing Sirayo's stronghold in the Bashee Valley, and dispersing the enemy in every direction. The Column then advanced to Isandhlwana. On the 21st the 1st squadron Mounted Infantry, including 20 men 1-24th Regt., under Lieut. Browne, were engaged with and defeated the enemy. On the 22nd Capt. Rainforth's co. received orders to march to Rorke's Drift, and another co., under Major Upcher, also marched for that post to join the Hd.-Qrs. About 4 p.m. news was brought to Major Upcher that the camp at Isandhlwana had been taken, and that the Zulus were advancing on Rorke's Drift. An immediate advance of the two cos. was made on Rorke's Drift, but on receiving intelligence from a staff officer and from fugitives (which afterwards proved to be false) that the post had fallen into the hands of the enemy, Major Spalding, D.A.A.G., who had assumed command of the party, ordered a retrograde movement on Helpmakaar, which was reached, without encountering the enemy, at 11.30 p.m. In the meantime the appalling disaster at Isandhlwana had occurred; in it the batt. lost 16 officers and 405 non-comm. officers and men.

On the 23rd Major Upcher assumed command of the regt. Early in March drafts (520 non-com. officers and men) for the batt., from various regts., embarked from England under the command of Col. Davies, of the Gren. Gds. The transport in which they sailed was wrecked off Dyer's Island, but the troops were safely landed, and, proceeding *viâ* Durban and Maritzburg, eventually reached Dundee in the first days of May. On the 9th May the two cos., under Major Upcher, arrived at Dundee from Helpmakaar, where they had been stationed from the 22nd Jan. On the 11th Major Dunbar assumed command of the regt. On the 13th the Hd.-Qrs. and seven cos. left Dundee, and marched to Landman's Drift, where it was brigaded, under Col. Glyn, with the 94th Regt. Newdigate's Divis.—of which, under the new constitution of the forces, the regt. formed part—advanced to Koppie Allein on the 28th, and, crossing the Blood River a few days later, advanced on Ulundi. On the 30th June two cos., under Major Upcher, were detached from the batt. to hold Entonjaneni. The Hd.-Qrs. and remainder advanced with ten days' rations and no tents to Umsirubani. The White Umvolosi was reached on the 31st, and two days later the Divis. was joined by the Flying Column. Throughout the 3rd July a co., under Lieut. Heaton, was engaged in protecting the water parties. The whole of the Mounted Irregulars of Wood's Column, including the Mounted Infantry under Lieut. Browne, advanced across the river, where they encountered vast numbers of the enemy, and retreated on to the camp. On the 4th, four cos. of the regt. remained in laager, while the remainder of the combined Columns, under Lord Chelmsford, advanced across the river, and encountered, and utterly routed, the enemy. The Divis. was shortly afterwards broken up, and the regt., under Col. Glyn, embarked at Durban for England.

SERVICES OF OFFICERS OF THE 1st BATTALION, 24th (2nd WARWICKSHIRE) REGIMENT.

Rank.	Name.	Services.
Colonel.	W. P. Glyn, *C.B.*	Commanded the 3rd Column of the army of invasion from 16th Dec., 1878, to 26th May, 1879. Present at the attack on Sirayo's stronghold, and at the operations at Matyana's stronghold. Commanded the Infantry Brigade, 2nd Divis., in Zululand, including the battle of Ulundi until the Divis. was broken up. (Mentioned in despatches.)

Rank.	Name.	Services.
Captain.	Brander, W. M.	Served with the batt. throughout the war. Was present at the battle of Ulundi.
Bt. Lieut.-Colonel.	Harrison, H. A.	Served in command of H co. at St. John's River throughout the war.
Captain.	G. Paton, *C.M.G.*	On outbreak of the war Capt. Paton was ordered to remain in the Cape Colony, to assist in winding up affairs connected with the late Kaffir war. Rejoined the batt. at Dundee on the 11th May, and served with it until the 28th, when he was ordered to proceed to the Transvaal, to serve on the staff of H. E. Col. Lanyon. In July, 1879, was ordered to proceed in command of 300 Mounted Volunteers to the Zulu Swazie border, to make a demonstration in that part of the country with a view to prevent Cetchwayo retreating to join Sekukuni.
Bt. Major.	Upcher, R.	Served with the batt. throughout the war (after having, in Sept., 1878, acted as Commandant of Durban). Commanded regt. from 23rd Jan. to 11th May. Commanded in laager at Entonjaneni during battle of Ulundi.
Bt. Major.	Much, W. T.	Served with the batt. until the 3rd March, when he was invalided home.
Captain.	Rainforth, T.	Commanded the co. which, on the 6th Dec., was left on detachment at Greytown, and which, advancing on Rorke's Drift, was directed to fall back on Helpmakaar. Took part in the subsequent operations of the batt., and was present at the battle of Ulundi.
Captain.	Morshead, A. A.	Served with the batt. throughout the war. Was in laager at Entonjaneni during the battle of Ulundi.
Captain.	Halliday, F. T. (2-24th.)	Went out with reinforcements for the regt. in March. Employed on staff duties at Durban. Was subsequently promoted to Captain in 2nd Batt.
Lieutenant.	E. S. Browne, *V.C.*	Lieut. Browne commanded the 1st squadron Mounted Infantry. Was present at the battles of Kambula and Ulundi. Received the Victoria Cross for conspicuous bravery in saving the life of a trooper in the attack made by the enemy on the Kambula camp. Lieuts. Heaton and Clements served with the batt. throughout the war, and were present at the battle of Ulundi; Lieuts. Spring and Roche served under Lieut.-Col. Harrison on detachment at St. John's River throughout the war; Lieut. Palmes proceeded with the batt. to Ladysmith, and was there invalided; Lieut. Lloyd, under Capt. Rainforth, at Greytown and Helpmakaar, and was present at the battle of Ulundi; Lieuts. Connolly, Moore, Williams, Godfrey, Yorstoun, and Campbell served with the batt. throughout the latter phase of the war, taking part in the march to Ulundi.
Lieutenant.	Heaton, W.	
Lieutenant.	Clements, R. A. P.	
Lieutenant.	Spring, W. E. D.	
Lieutenant.	Roche, Hon. N. de R. B.	
Lieutenant.	Palmes, G. C.	
Lieutenant.	Connolly, J. H.	
Lieutenant.	Moore, G. K.	
Lieutenant.	Lloyd, W. W.	
2nd Lieutenant.	Williams, J. D. M.	
2nd Lieutenant.	Godfrey, W. C.	
2nd Lieutenant.	Carthew-Yorstoun, M. E. (67th Regt.)	
2nd Lieutenant.	Campbell, R.	

2ND BATTALION, 24TH (2ND WARWICKSHIRE) REGIMENT.

ON the 21st July, 1878, the batt., whose term of active service had come to a conclusion only four weeks previously, with the cessation of hostilities against the Kaffirs, received orders at King William's Town for immediate embarkation for Natal. The 2-24th was the first regt. which landed in the Colony after a war with the Zulus became imminent, and it was welcomed by the people of Durban with many and deep expressions of relief.

Leaving one co. at Durban, the remaining seven marched to Pietermaritzburg, where they arrived on the 6th August. For three months the regt. was there kept persistently at drill, and all possible preparations for the campaign, which day by day appeared more imminent, were completed. Half the batt. lived in tents, the other half occupying the Kaffir huts and barracks inside Fort Napier. At length, early in Nov., orders to march to Greytown were received, and by successive cos. the regt. was concentrated there by the middle of the month. At the end of Dec., it advanced by half batts. to Helpmakaar. On the 7th Jan., 1879, it marched to Rorke's Drift, and on the 11th it crossed into Zululand with the remainder of the ill-fated 3rd Column. Lieut. Bromhead and one co. were left behind at Rorke's Drift to defend the post and line of communications. How gallantly they performed this duty is written elsewhere.

After the terrible disaster at Isandhlwana on the 22nd—in which the batt. lost five officers and 173 men, being every soul left by it in camp that day—all the eight cos. remained in laager at Rorke's Drift, where they were at first engaged in fortifying the old Mission Station, and afterwards in erecting a larger and stronger fort (Fort Melvill) on the bank of the river, with accommodation for a garrison of some 300. At first the men suffered considerable hardship from the want of proper clothing, shelter, and food; and several died. As the rainy season passed by, however, the spirits and health of the men improved, and all, having been for many months shut up within sight of the rock where such numbers of their comrades had fallen, became buoyant with the hope of an active life again. The expectations formed were not, however, destined to be fulfilled; the batt., deeply to its regret, was not permitted to join in the advance, and the cos. were scattered along the border at Rorke's Drift, Dundee, Landman's Drift, and Koppie Allein, to protect the line of communications. It henceforward took no active part in the campaign. Later on, two cos., under Major Bromhead and Capt. Harvey, proceeded to Ulundi with Sir Garnet Wolseley as his personal escort, and on their return were engaged under Lieut.-Col. Black in completing the burial of the dead at Isandhlwana, and in removing all traces of the battle. These two cos. returned *viâ* Helpmakaar and Greytown to Pietermaritzburg, where they joined the remaining six cos.—these having marched down country from Utrecht, where they had first assembled in the month of September.

The batt. remained at Pinetown under canvas from Nov. to Jan., 1880, when it embarked for Gibraltar.

SERVICES OF THE OFFICERS OF THE 2ND BATTALION, 24TH (2ND WARWICKSHIRE) REGIMENT.

RANK.	NAME.	SERVICES.
Lieut.-Colonel.	H. J. Degacher, *C.B.*	Commanded the batt. throughout the campaign; and the Dundee District during the advance on Ulundi.
Bt. Lieut.-Col.	Dunbar, W. M.	Served with the 2nd Batt. from the date of arrival in South Africa until (on 11th May, 1879) he obtained temporary command of the 1st Batt., after its reformation. Commanded 1st Batt. during its advance with Newdigate's Divis., and at the battle of Ulundi. (Brevet of Lieut.-Col.)
Bt. Lieut.-Col.	W. Black, *C.B.*	Served with 2nd Batt. until the 3rd Column crossed the Buffalo on 11th Jan., 1879; was then appointed D.A.Q.M.G. to Lord Chelmsford, with special charge of roads. Afterwards organized and conducted several reconnaissances from Rorke's Drift to Isandhlwana battle-field, for which he received the thanks of the officer commanding. Subse-

Rank.	Name.	Services.
		quently commanded a regt. of Native Contingent which operated in N.W. Zululand during the advance on Ulundi. (Brevet of Lieut.-Col., *C.B.*)
Bt. Lieut.-Col.	Tongue, J. M. G.	(1-24th.) Served with 2nd Batt. until he obtained his majority in Jan., 1879. Subsequently served with 1st Batt. throughout. Was present at the battle of Ulundi.
Bt. Lieut.-Col.	Chamberlain, W. R. B.	(Retired.) In consequence of injuries received while bush-fighting in the Kaffir war, Major Chamberlain was unable to go to the front with the 2nd Batt., and remained as Commandant of Fort Napier at Pietermaritzburg during the campaign.
Major.	Church, H. B.	(Retired.) Joined the 2nd Batt. from the depôt on the 13th Jan., 1879, and served with it throughout.
Bt. Major.	Bromhead, C. J.	Joined the batt. at Rorke's Drift in March, 1879. Commanded detachments at Dundee, Landman's Drift, and Koppie Allein. Commanded Sir Garnet Wolseley's personal escort at Ulundi.
Captain.	Symons, W. P.	Served with the 2nd Batt. until June, 1879, when sent by Major-Gen. Clifford to purchase horses for Government in the old Cape Colony.
Bt. Lieut.-Col.	F. Carrington, *C.M.G.*	Lieut.-Col. Carrington, who had performed distinguished service in the Kaffir war of 1877-78, and had acted as Commandant of the Transvaal Volunteer Forces throughout the first Sekukuni campaign, commanded the Advanced Guard and the Left attack at the final storming of the stronghold in Nov., 1879. (Mentioned in despatches; Brevet of Lieut.-Col., *C.M.G.*)
Captain.	Moffatt, H. B.	(1-24th.) Served with the batt. until invalided at Ladysmith.
Captain.	Harvey, J. J.	Served with the batt. throughout the campaign. Employed on Sir G. Wolseley's personal escort at Ulundi.
Captain.	Williams, H. M.	Served with the batt. throughout the campaign.
Captain.	Bennett, L. H.	(90th L. I.) Joined at Rorke's Drift in April, 1879. Afterwards promoted Capt. 1st Batt. Took part in the advance of Newdigate's Divis. Was present at the battle of Ulundi. Since exchanged.
Captain.	Sugden, W.	(1-24th.) Served in Crealock's Divis., with the Mounted Infantry. Was second in command of 2nd Squadron Mounted Infantry at the battle of Ginghilovo.
Bt. Major.	G. Bromhead, *V.C.*	Served with the batt. throughout the campaign. Commanded B co. in memorable and gallant defence of Rorke's Drift. (*V.C.*, and Brevet of Major.)
Captain.	Banister, G. S.	Served with the batt. throughout the campaign. Commanded Station of Dundee on line of communications.

Rank.	Name.	Services.
Lieutenant.	Mainwaring, H. G.	Lieuts. Mainwaring, Logan, Trower, and Weallens served with the regt. throughout the campaign; Lieut. Logan acting as Qr.-Mr. to the batt. from Jan. to May, and afterwards, until the end of Sept., as Adjt. to Lieut.-Col. Black; Lieut. Trower as Adjt. to the batt. *vice* Lieut. Dyer, killed at Isandhlwana. Lieut. Dobrée served with the batt. till the end of April. Lieut. Phipps was transferred to 1st Batt. after the battle of Isandhlwana, and subsequently acted as Orderly Officer to Col. Glyn during the advance of the 2nd Divis.; was present at the battle of Ulundi (severely wounded). Lieut. Curll served with the batt. throughout the campaign, and was employed on Sir G. Wolseley's personal escort at Ulundi. Lieut. Dolben proceeded to South Africa, but was invalided to England before joining the batt. Lieut. Lloyd joined the batt. at Rorke's Drift in March; accompanied Lieut.-Col. Black as a volunteer to Isandhlwana, and served with the batt. till the conclusion of the war. Lieuts. O'Donnell, Birch, Worlledge, Armitage, Hare, D'Aguilar, and Scott-Kerr joined the batt. in June, and served with it to the conclusion of the war.
Lieutenant.	Logan, L. M. K.	
Lieut. and Adjt.	Trower, C. V.	
Lieutenant.	Weallens, W. (1-24th.)	
Lieutenant.	Dobrée, L. G. L. (Retired.)	
Lieutenant.	Phipps, A. B.	
Lieutenant.	Curll, C. E.	
Lieutenant.	Dolben, H.	
Lieutenant.	Lloyd, J. D. A. T.	
Lieutenant.	O'Donnell, H.	
Lieutenant.	Birch, A. W.	
Lieutenant.	Worlledge, A. C.	
2nd Lieutenant.	Armitage, P. T.	
2nd Lieutenant.	Hare, T. L.	
Lieutenant.	D'Aguilar, L. G. H. (Grenadier Guards.)	
Lieutenant.	Scott-Kerr, R. (Grenadier Guards.)	
Paymaster.	J. Mahony, *C.M.G.*	Major Mahony, who had performed distinguished service in the Kaffir campaign of 1877-78, served with the batt. throughout the war. Was decorated *C.M.G.*

57TH (WEST MIDDLESEX) REGIMENT.

THE regt. was stationed at Ceylon when, in Feb. 1879, it received orders to proceed with all haste to Natal. It embarked, accordingly, on the 22nd of the month, in H.M.S. "Tamar," and, disembarking at Port Durban on the 10th and 11th March, arrived at the town on the 12th; a week later it marched to the frontier to join the Column destined for the relief of Etshowe, which, under the personal command of Lord Chelmsford, was then in course of formation on the Lower Tugela. The regt. reached Fort Pearson on the 26th March, and was there detailed to the 1st Brigade of the Column. The advance into the enemy's country was commenced on the 29th. At the battle of Ginghilovo, which ensued on the morning of the 2nd April, the regt. held the right flank face of the laager, and assisted in repelling the first desperate onslaught of the enemy. It was specially mentioned in Lord Chelmsford's despatch describing the battle as being distinguished for its steadiness under fire. On the 3rd the Column marched into Etshowe, and relieved Col. Pearson's force.

The regt. subsequently formed part of the 2nd Brigade of Crealock's Divis., being stationed for a considerable period at Fort Chelmsford, in the construction of which it had rendered material assistance. During this time it was employed, alternately with the 60th, in escorting convoys from the Amatikulu River to the Fort. On the 9th June it was joined at Fort Tenedos by Capt. Morewood with a draft of 117 men. Shortly afterwards the regt. advanced to Fort Durnford, burning krantzes, the chief of which was Ondine, and disarming the coast tribes. Subsequently to the arrival of Sir Garnet Wolseley it formed part of Clarke's Column in the second advance and occupation of Ulundi, where it remained for three weeks, and was employed in the pursuit and capture of the King. It then returned to Natal *viâ* Entumeni and Middle Drift, assisting in the subjugation of the border tribes in the neighbourhood of the Lower Tugela. Passing through Greytown, Pietermaritzburg, and Pinetown, it arrived, at the latter end of October, at Durban, from whence it embarked, on the 1st Nov., in the "City of Venice," for England.

SERVICES OF THE OFFICERS OF THE 57TH (WEST MIDDLESEX) REGIMENT.

Rank.	Name.	Services.
Colonel.	C. M. Clarke, *C. B.*	(Late 57th.) Commanded the regt. throughout, including the battle of Ginghilovo, and the relief of Etshowe. Commanded 2nd Brigade 1st Divis. South African Field Force. Commanded Column which marched to Ulundi and back *viâ* Middle Drift.
Lieut.-Colonel.	Tredennick, J. R. K.	Commanded the regt. from the middle of April till the conclusion of the war, including operations of Clarke's Column.
Major.	Bicknell, H. D.	Served with the regt. during the war. Was present at the battle of Ginghilovo and the relief of Etshowe.
Captain.	Matthews, C. J.	Capts. Matthews, Hinxman, and Weigall served with the regt. during the war, being present at the battle of Ginghilovo, the relief of Etshowe, the advance of Genl. Crealock to Port Durnford, and the subsequent operations of Clarke's Column. At the battle of Ginghilovo Capt. Hinxman was severely wounded. Capt. Collins acted as Staff Officer at Durban; he was afterwards invalided home. Capt. Morewood, in command of a draft of 117 men, joined the regt. in June, and took part in the advance of the 1st Divis. to Port Durnford, and the subsequent operations of Clarke's Column, acting as Field Officer throughout his service. Capt. Hughes-Hallett served with the regt. throughout the later phases of the war. Capt. Dewar served during the war, being present at the battle of Ginghilovo and the relief of Etshowe, and afterwards commanding at Fort Tenedos.
Captain.	Collins, C.	
Captain.	Morewood, H. F.	
Captain.	Hughes-Hallett, H. T.	
Captain.	Hinxman, H. C.	
Captain.	Weigall, A. A. D.	
Captain.	Dewar, G.	
Lieut. and Adjt.	Garstin, A. A.	Lieuts. Garstin, Hill, White, Graham, Bellingham, Bellers, Longe, Sharpe, Scott-Moncrieff, James, and Bodé served with the regt. during the war, being present at the battle of Ginghilovo, the relief of Etshowe, the advance of Crealock's Divis. to Port Durnford, and the subsequent operations of Clarke's Column. Lieut. Blake served with the regt. in the later phases of the war, and was Garrison-Adjt. at Fort Pearson. Lieut. Lyde joined the regt. in June with the draft under Capt. Morewood, and served with it in the later phases of the war. Lieuts. Warden and Towers-Clark were present at the battle of Ginghilovo and the relief of Etshowe; the latter subsequently acted as Orderly Officer to Col. Clarke in the second advance. Lieuts. Jones, Munro, and Litton joined the Hd.-Qrs. on the 13th April, and served with them till the conclusion of the war.
Lieutenant.	Hill, A. W.	
Lieutenant.	White, J. G.	
Lieutenant.	Blake, N. J. R.	
Lieutenant.	Graham, R. W.	
Lieutenant.	Lyde, M. T.	
Lieutenant.	Bellingham, S. E.	
Lieutenant.	Warden, C. W.	
Lieutenant.	Bellers, E. V.	
Lieutenant.	Towers-Clark, A.	
Lieutenant.	Longe, R. D.	
Lieutenant.	Sharpe, E. J.	
Lieutenant.	Scott-Moncrieff, W.	
2nd Lieutenant.	James, H.	
2nd Lieutenant.	Bodé, L. W.	
2nd Lieutenant.	Jones, G. G. J. S.	
2nd Lieutenant.	Munro, G. T.	
2nd Lieutenant.	Litton, T. E. F.	
Quartermaster.	Wood, T.	Served with the regt. during the war, being present at the battle of Ginghilovo, the relief of Etshowe, the advance of the 1st Divis. to Port Durnford, and the subsequent operations of Clarke's Column.

58TH (RUTLANDSHIRE) REGIMENT.

THE regt. was stationed at Grand Shaft Barracks, Dover, when, on the 11th Feb., 1879, it received orders to hold itself in readiness to proceed on active service in South Africa. On the 26th it embarked at Portsmouth in the hired transport "Russia," H.R.H. the F. M. Commanding-in-Chief having inspected it previously to its going on board. Disembarking at Durban on the 4th April, the regt., leaving one co. *en route*, proceeded *viâ* Pietermaritzburg and Ladysmith to Landman's Drift, where it arrived on the 2nd May. Here it remained until the 27th, when it proceeded with the N 5 Battery R.A. to Koppie Allein. At this place a fort was constructed by the men of the regt., subsequently named Fort Whitehead. The regt. now formed part of the 1st Brigade, Newdigate's Divis., and took part in the advance of that force into the enemy's country. On the 8th June it took part in the reconnaissance made by the 1st Brigade, with the cavalry and artillery, in the neighbourhood of the Upoko River. On the 24th it reached the position where Fort Evelyn was constructed by two of its cos. which were left to garrison it. Shortly after the Divis. had halted on the 3rd July, within a mile of the White Umvolosi, a water picquet of the 58th was fired upon by Zulus concealed behind rocks, and one man of the regiment was wounded. A desultory fire, which was returned by the picquet, was kept up for about three hours. At the battle of Ulundi, on the 4th, four cos. of the regt. were engaged, their fire being noticeably well directed. In the engagement Lance-Corp. Tomkinson, of the regt., was killed; Major Bond, Lieut. Liebenrood, and eleven non-commissioned officers and men were more or less severely wounded. In the Regimental Orders, bearing date 4th July, Col. Whitehead congratulated the officers, non-commissioned officers, and men, on the coolness exhibited by them when under fire; and Gen. Newdigate thanked the regt. for its gallant behaviour during the action.

After Ulundi was fired the Divis. returned to Natal. On the 6th Aug. it was joined by Clarke's Column, and on the following day it was overtaken by Sir Garnet Wolseley. On the 9th the regt. commenced building Fort Victoria, which it subsequently garrisoned. One co. marched, on the 15th, to Fort Marshall, to relieve the 21st Fusiliers. On the 26th the Hd.-Qrs. and two cos. left for Landman's Drift, leaving one co. at the fort; and on the 1st Sept. they crossed the Blood River and re-entered British territory.

SERVICES OF THE OFFICERS OF THE 58TH (RUTLANDSHIRE) REGIMENT.

RANK.	NAME.	SERVICES.
Colonel.	R. C. Whitehead, C.B.	Commanded the regt. during the war, including the battle of Ulundi. (Mentioned in despatches.)
Bt. Colonel.	Bond, W. D.	Col. Bond, Major Hingeston, Lieut.-Col. Hesse, and Major Anderson served with the regt. during the war, and were present at the battle of Ulundi; in that engagement Col. Bond was severely wounded. Major Foster took part with the regt. in the advance of Newdigate's Divis. on Ulundi; commanded the two cos. which built Fort Evelyn, and the garrison of the Fort from June to the conclusion of the war. Major Bowling served with the regt. during the war.
Major.	Hingeston, W. H.	
Lieut.-Colonel.	Hesse, J. V.	
Major.	Foster.	
Bt. Major.	Anderson.	
Bt. Major.	Bowling, C.	
Captain.	Saunders, H. M.	Capt. Saunders remained on detachment at Durban, in command of a co., from the date of departure of the regt. from that town, in April, till the conclusion of the war. Capts. St. John, Morris, Lovegrove, Nuthall, and Liebenrood served with the regt. during the war, and were present at the battle of Ulundi. Capt. St. John commanded the co. which remained at Victoria on the departure of the Hd.-Qrs. in Aug. Capt. Howley embarked from
Captain.	St. John, O. B.	
Captain.	Howley, P. A.	

Rank.	Name.	Services.
Captain.	Morris, A. W.	Portsmouth with a draft in May, and served with the regt. from the date of his arrival till the conclusion of the war. Capt. Morris relieved with a co. the 21st Fusiliers at Fort Marshall in Aug. Capt. Churchill remained on detachment at Ladysmith in command of a co. from the date of departure of the regt. from that town in April till the conclusion of the war. Capt. Hornby took part with the regt. in the advance of Newdigate's Divis. on Ulundi; remained on detachment at Fort Evelyn from the date of its construction in June until the conclusion of the war. Capt. Nuthall served on a detachment of K. D. Gs. which, under Major Stabb, completed the cordon between Fort Victoria and Quamagwasa, drawn to prevent the King from effecting his escape. Capt. Liebenrood commanded the water picquet which, on the 3rd July, was fired fired upon by the enemy.
Captain.	Churchill, M.	
Captain.	Hornby, C. L.	
Captain.	Lovegrove, E.	
Captain.	Nuthall, H. M.	
Captain.	Liebenrood, G. E.	
Lieutenant.	Power, W. Le P.	Lieut. Power remained on detachment at Durban from the date of departure of the regt. from that town in April till the conclusion of the war. Lieuts. Dolphin, Sandys, Compton, Fawcett, Collinson, Morgan, and Bolton served with the regt. during the war, and were present at the battle of Ulundi. Lieut. Collinson was also present with the water picquet which was fired on by the enemy on the 3rd July, and remained at Fort Marshall with Capt. Morris's co. from Aug. Lieuts. McMahon and O'Donel took part with the regt. in the advance of Newdigate's Divis. on Ulundi; and remained on detachment at Fort Evelyn from the date of its construction in June until the conclusion of the war. Lieut. Smyth remained on detachment at Durban from the date of departure of the regt. from that town in April till the conclusion of the war. Lieuts. Hill and Jopp, who joined the regt. at Ladysmith, remained there on detachment from the date of the departure of the regt. from that town in April till the conclusion of the war.
Lieutenant.	Dolphin, H.	
Lieut. and Adjt.	Sandys, E. Del.	
Lieutenant.	McMahon, L.	
Lieutenant.	Smyth, G. T. V. B.	
Lieutenant.	Jopp, S. J. M.	
Lieutenant.	Compton, T. E.	
Lieutenant.	O'Donel, C. M.	
2nd Lieutenant.	Fawcett, W. F.	
2nd Lieutenant.	Collinson, J.	
2nd Lieutenant.	Morgan, H.	
2nd Lieutenant.	Bolton, A. C.	
2nd Lieutenant.	Hill, A. R.	
Paymaster and Quartermaster.	Minchin, J. W.	Paymaster Minchin remained on detachment at Pietermaritzburg from the date of the departure of the regt. from that town in April till the conclusion of the war.
Quartermaster.	Lenton, C.	Quartermaster Lenton served with the regt. during the war, and was present at the battle of Ulundi.

3RD BATTALION, 60TH RIFLES.

WHEN stationed at Colchester the batt. received, on the 12th Feb., 1879, a telegram from the Horse Guards, ordering it on active service. A week later it embarked in the "Dublin Castle" (two cos., under Capt. Smith, remaining temporarily at Colchester), and arrived at Durban, Natal, on the 20th March. After remaining two days in camp it marched for the front, and reached Fort Pearson on the 27th, where it formed a depôt of sick and stores. Leaving a detachment in Natal under Major Ogilvy, the batt. crossed the Tugela on the 28th, and formed part of the Column organized for the relief of Etshowe. It took part, on the 2nd, in the battle of Ginghilovo, and in the subsequent relief of the garrison.

Col. Pemberton having been appointed to command the 2nd Brigade of the Column, the command of the batt. devolved on Capt. Tufnell.

On the 6th July the Column returned to Ginghilovo; and a post was there established consisting, in part, of the 60th Rifles. The garrison remained there till the 25th, during which time many officers and men were sick and invalided. Marching to the Inyezane River, the batt. was employed for the subsequent two months in building Fort Chelmsford, and in constant convoy duties towards the base at Fort Pearson. During this period it suffered much from sickness.

The batt. took part in the advance of Crealock's Divis., in the last days of June, to Port Durnford, which was reached on the 29th. On the 7th July Sir Garnet Wolseley arrived, and the Divis. was broken up. The batt. subsequently formed part of Clarke's Column. It arrived at Ulundi on the 11th Aug., and encamped. On the 22nd six cos., with a few mounted men and Native Contingent, marched to the Black Umvolosi, as a support to the detachments of cavalry and Mounted Irregulars sent to scour the country in search of Cetchwayo. It bivouacked there for ten days. On the 30th Major Marter arrived with the captured King. Two cos., as escort and guard, accompanied him to Ulundi, and the remainder of the batt. followed next day. Thus united, it returned to Natal *viâ* the Middle Drift, recrossing the Tugela on the 18th Sept., and reaching Pietermaritzburg on the 3rd Oct.

SERVICES OF OFFICERS OF THE 3RD BATTALION, 60TH RIFLES.

RANK.	NAME.	SERVICES.
Colonel.	W. L. Pemberton, *C.B.*	(Late 60th Rifles.) Commanded the batt. until the formation of the Etshowe Relief Column, when he was appointed to the command of the 1st Brigade. Commanded the brigade at the battle of Ginghilovo. Was ordered home on medical certificate at latter end of April. Proceeded to England in charge of the body of the Prince Imperial.
Major.	Ogilvy, W. L. K.	Remained in command, on detachment, at Fort Pearson, from the date of departure of the batt. from that post to the conclusion of the war.
Bt. Colonel.	Tufnell, A.	(Late 60th.) Served with the batt. during the campaign, succeeding to the command of it on the appointment of Col. Pemberton to that of the 1st Brigade of the Relief Column, and commanding it at the battle of Ginghilovo.
Captain.	Morris, A.	Capt. Morris remained on detachment at Fort Pearson from 27th Feb. till May, when he joined the Hd.-Qrs. at Fort Chelmsford. Took part, in June, in the advance of Crealock's Divis. on Port Durnford, from whence he was invalided to England. Capts. Cramer, O'Brien, and Hutton served with the regt. during the campaign, including the advance to, and relief of, Etshowe (present at the battle of Ginghilovo), the advance of Crealock's Divis. to Port Durnford, and the second advance on Ulundi; Capts. Cramer and O'Brien performed the duties of Major from date of assumption of command of batt. by Col. Tufnell; the former commanded the two cos. which acted as escort and guard to the King from the Black Umvolosi to Ulundi; Capt. Hutton served as A.D.C. to Gen. Crealock. Capts. Robinson, Smith, Thurlow, and Thorne joined the batt. at Fort Chelmsford in May,
Captain.	Cramer, C. P.	
Captain.	O'Brien, A. V.	
Captain.	Robinson, R. C.	
Captain.	Bircham, A. H.	
Captain.	Smith, C. H.	
Captain.	Thurlow, E. H.	
Captain.	Turnour, Hon. K.	

Rank.	Name.	Services.
Captain.	Hutton, E. T. H.	and served with it throughout the remainder of the campaign, being present in the advance of Crealock's Divis. to Port Durnford, and the second advance on Ulundi. Capts. Bircham, Turnour, and Mitchell served with the batt. in the advance to, and relief of, Etshowe, being present at the battle of Ginghilovo; were invalided home from Fort Chelmsford.
Captain.	Mitchell, C.	
Captain.	Thorne, C. R. B.	
Lieutenant.	Fetherstonhaugh, R. S. R.	Lieuts. Fetherstonhaugh, Miles, Nevill, Myers, O'Connell, Lysley, and Pigott joined the batt. at Fort Chelmsford in May, and served with it during the remainder of the war, including the advance of Crealock's Divis. to Port Durnford, and the second advance on Ulundi. Lieuts. Astell, Allfrey, Wilkinson, and Baker served with the batt. during the advance to, and relief of, Etshowe (present at the battle of Ginghilovo); they were invalided home from Fort Chelmsford. Lieuts. Gunning and Crawley served with the batt. during the war, taking part in the advance to, and relief of, Etshowe (present at the battle of Ginghilovo), the advance of Crealock's Divis. to Port Durnford, and the second advance on Ulundi. Lieut. Ryder remained on detachment at Fort Pearson from date of departure of batt. till the conclusion of the war.
Lieutenant.	Astell, G.	
Lieutenant.	Allfrey, H. (1-60th.)	
Lieut. and Adjt.	Wilkinson, E. O. H.	
Lieutenant.	Gunning, R. H.	
Lieutenant.	Miles, A. E.	
Lieutenant.	Nevill, H. J. (1-60th.)	
Lieutenant.	Crawley, A. P.	
Lieutenant.	Ryder, D. G. R.	
2nd Lieutenant.	Baker, G. C. B.	
2nd Lieutenant.	Myers, W. J.	
2nd Lieutenant.	O'Connell, M.	
2nd Lieutenant.	Lysley, W. Du V.	
2nd Lieutenant.	Pigott, C. B.	
Paymaster.	Haynes, E. C.	Capt. Haynes remained on detachment at Fort Pearson from the date of departure of the batt. from that post till the conclusion of the war.
Quartermaster.	Ireland, J.	Served with the batt. during the war, taking part in the advance to, and relief of, Etshowe (present at the battle of Ginghilovo), the advance of Crealock's Divis. to Port Durnford, and the second advance on Ulundi.

80th REGIMENT (STAFFORDSHIRE VOLUNTEERS).

AT the latter end of 1878 this regt., which had performed distinguished service in the first Sekukuni campaign, was scattered over a wide extent of territory in the Transvaal and Natal. In view of the impending hostilities with the Zulus, detachments were ordered to proceed, about this time, to the frontier; and at the beginning of Jan., 1879, five cos. of the regt., under Lieut.-Col. Tucker, formed part of the No. 5 Column of the army of invasion, which, under Col. Hugh Rowlands, was then concentrated at Derby—a sixth co. of the regt. being stationed at Prætoria.

On the 14th Feb. Lieut.-Col. Tucker, following Col. Rowlands and the Hd.-Qrs., marched with the five cos. and the remainder of the Column to Lüneberg, which was reached on the 19th.

Towards the end of the month the No. 5 Column was broken up: the mounted troops joined Wood's Column at Kambula; Col. Rowlands and Staff were directed to proceed with all speed to Prætoria, to strengthen the garrison (the one co. of the 80th), in view of the threatened advance of 5,000 Boers who were encamped near the city; and the five cos., under Lieut.-Col. Tucker, were left to occupy Fort Clery and the laager at Lüneberg.

On the 5th March Capt. Prior proceeded with a mounted patrol from Lüneberg in the direction of the Upper Pongolo, and hearing that Zulus were taking horses from the valley, went in pursuit. Eighteen horses were recovered, the Zulus being put to flight and one of their number slain.

As it had been found impossible on the departure of the Transvaal Column from Derby to carry away the heavy accumulation of stores at that position, convoys of waggons, escorted by two cos. of the

80th, with a proportion of mounted men, were despatched in succession for this purpose from Lüneberg. After the withdrawal of the mounted troops and the native contingent, the two cos. only were available for this duty. In the first days of March the two cos., under Capt. Moriarty, were accordingly sent to conduct a convoy over that portion of the road which passes between the mountain fastnesses then occupied on the one side by the Zulu chief Manyoba and on the other by Umbelini. As is related elsewhere, this escort became, unhappily, divided by the Intombi River, and was surprised before daybreak on the 12th March by a force of 5,000 of the enemy. In the desperate encounter which ensued, Capt. Moriarty, Civil Surgeon Cobbin, Conductor Whittington, and 61 non.-com. officers and men of the regt. were slain; the remainder of the party, 45 in number, managing with the utmost difficulty to make their escape to Lüneberg.

On being relieved by a detachment of the 24-th Regt. in April, the force under Lieut.-Col. Tucker, now reduced to four cos., joined Wood's Column at Kambula, and was, for a time, principally engaged in assisting in bringing in the large quantity of supplies being their accumulated. On the 5th May the regt. took part in the forward movement of the Column to the vicinity of the Zlobane, and, subsequently, in the advance of the Column in conjunction with Newdigate's Divis. into the heart of the enemy's country. At the battle of Ulundi five men of the regt. were more or less severely wounded.

On the renewal of hostilities with Sekukuni, two cos. of the regt. formed part of Major Bushman's force (the right attack) which advanced against the chief's stronghold, acting conjointly with the main body of the troops under Sir Garnet Wolseley. Crowning the heights in the rear of Sekukuni's town, this force successfully opposed the retreat of the Kaffirs, and materially assisted in their subsequent complete defeat.

On the cessation of hostilities the various scattered cos. joined the Hd.-Qrs. Thus united, the regt. marched through Natal to Durban, from which port it embarked, at the latter end of February, for England.

SERVICES OF THE OFFICERS OF THE 80TH REGIMENT.

Rank.	Name.	Services.
Lieut.-Colonel.	C. Tucker, *C.B.*	Commanded the regt. whilst forming part of Rowland's Column on the Swazi border, and, subsequently, the troops at Lüneberg. Commanded the regt. whilst forming part of Wood's Column, during the march through Zululand and at the battle of Ulundi. (*C.B.*)
Bt. Lieut.-Colonel.	Tyler, C. J. R.	(Retired.) Commanded a detachment of the regt. in the Transvaal during the war.
Major.	Creagh, C. A. F.	Served during the war, first in command of three cos. on the Transvaal frontier, and afterwards as Commandant of the Leydenburg district. Served subsequently in the operations against Sekukuni till invalided.
Major.	Bradshaw, J. L.	Proceeded to Natal in May, 1879, in command of a draft of 143 men for the regt.
Captain.	Howard, W.	Capts. Howard, Roworth, and Saunders served on detachment in the Transvaal during the Zulu war, Capt. Roworth being temporarily in command of three cos. in the Leydenburg District. Capts. Anderson, Johnson, Sherrard, and Potts served with the regt. throughout its operations with Rowland's and Wood's Columns, including the second advance into Zululand and the battle of Ulundi. Capt. Prior served during the war, first in command of a troop of Frontier Light Horse, and subsequently with the regt. in its later operations with Wood's Column, including the battle of Ulundi. Capt. Cole proceeded to Natal in May, 1879, with the draft under Major Bradshaw.
Captain.	Roworth, C. E. W.	
Captain.	Saunders, A.	
Captain.	Anderson, W. T.	
Bt. Major.	Prior, J. E. H.	
Captain.	Johnson, H. J.	
Captain.	Sherrard, J. O.	
Captain.	Cole, C. C.	
Captain.	Potts, L. C.	

Rank.	Name.	Services.
Lieutenant.	Chamberlain, T. J.	Lieuts. Chamberlain, Hast, Lindop, Daubeney, and Ussher served with the regt. throughout its operations with Rowland's and Wood's Columns, including the second advance into Zululand and the battle of Ulundi. Lieut. Harward served with the regt. throughout its operations with Rowland's Column, and in its earlier operations with Wood's Column. Lieuts. Cameron, Horsburgh, Moore, Savage, Griffin, Lyons, Raitt, Marshall, and Williams served on detachment in the Transvaal during the Zulu war; Lieut. Moore as District Adjt. of the Colony, and Lieut. Lyons, temporarily, as District Adjt. at Leydenburg. Lieuts. Horsburgh, Lyons, and Marshall subsequently served throughout the operations against Sekukuni, being present at the capture and destruction of the stronghold.
Lieutenant.	Cameron, S. W.	
Lieutenant.	Hast, A. W.	
Lieutenant.	Horsburgh, A. B.	
Lieutenant.	Moore, W.	
Lieutenant.	Savage, H. C.	
Lieutenant.	Harward, H. H. (Late 88th.)	
Lieut. and Adjt.	Griffin, T. E.	
Lieutenant.	Lindop, A. H.	
Lieutenant.	Lyons, F. W.	
Lieutenant.	Raitt, H. A.	
Lieutenant.	Daubeney, E. K.	
Lieutenant.	Ussher, B. W. R.	
Lieutenant.	Marshall, F. M.	
Lieutenant.	Williams, G. A.	

88TH REGIMENT (CONNAUGHT RANGERS).

ON the conclusion of the Kaffir war of 1877-78, the Hd.-Qrs. of the regt. returned from the eastern frontier to their old station—Cape Town; one co. (F) still remaining at St. Helena, and three others (B, E, and H) being sent, under Col. Owen, to relieve the Buffs at Mauritius. The difficulty of concentration, in consequence of this dispersion, ultimately prevented the regt. being employed at the commencement of hostilities with the Zulus.

In Oct., 1878, on the departure of the forces for Natal, the Cape Town cos. were recalled to King William's Town to garrison the frontier, and remained there till subsequently to the outbreak of the war. Immediately after the occurrence of the disaster at Isandhlwana, in Jan., 1879, orders were received to move at once with all available men to Natal. Four cos. being, unfortunately, on detachment in inacccessible stations, viz., St. Helena and Mauritius, it was not considered advisable to move a half batt. at once to the front; consequently the Hd.-Qrs. and one co., under Col. Lambert, *C.B.*, proceeded to Pietermaritzburg, and three cos., under Col. Hopton, marched to Fort Tenedos, Lower Tugela, where they remained in reserve until after the relief of Etshowe.

About this time Capt. Bradshaw, of H.M.S. "Shah," touched at St. Helena, and, acting on his own responsibility, embarked the garrison of the island (which included one co. of the regt., under command of Capt. Baldwin), and transported it to Natal.

News of the great disaster reached Mauritius only on the 1st March. On the 12th, one co. (B) of the Rangers and half a battery of Artillery—all that could be spared from the garrison of the place—embarked under command of Capt. Bowen, with Lieuts. Moore and Webb, for the seat of war, and landed at Durban on the 26th instant.

At the beginning of May the regt., with the exception of the two cos. still remaining at Mauritius, concentrated at the Lower Tugela, and, with the Buffs and the 99th, formed the 1st Brigade of Crealock's Divis. The duties of the troops at the Tugela were of a very arduous description, consisting in the main of escorting convoys and loading provision waggons for the expected advance. Considerable sickness prevailed during this time amongst the troops of the Divis., but the men of the 88th being hardier and more inured to the climate than those of the newly-arrived regts., suffered very slightly, losing from disease but one officer and four men. So marked was this superiority in stamina that, though numbering only six cos., the regt. mustered more men on parade than any other in the Divis.

The regt. took part in the advance made by the Divis. in June, moving successively to Fort Crealock, Fort Chelmsford, and Fort Napoleon. At the last-named post two cos. were detached, and advanced with the main body of the Divis. to Port Durnford. About this time Sir Garnet Wolseley arrived upon the scene, and shortly after the battle of Ulundi reorganized the distribution of the forces. The 88th received orders to march from Fort Chelmsford to Etshowe, by a new route, to meet a portion of Lord Chelmsford's force then retiring on Natal *viâ* St. Paul's, and supply it with provisions—a duty which it successfully accomplished. From this time till the conclusion of peace the regt. was broken up into detachments, and stationed at Etshowe, Fort Chelmsford, and Fort Crealock. About the beginning of August it was ordered to return to Natal, and Pine Town was reached before the end of the month. Proceeding thence to Cape Town, the regt. embarked, on the 1st Oct., for India.

SERVICES OF THE OFFICERS OF THE 88TH REGIMENT (CONNAUGHT RANGERS).

Rank.	Name.	Services.
Lieut.-Colonel.	W. Lambert, *C.B.*	Was in command of the regt. throughout the war, including the march up country subsequently to the concentration of the six cos. at the Lower Tugela.
Bt. Lieut.-Colonel.	Hopton, E.	Materially assisted, after arriving in Natal, in the organization of the transport for the war. Commanded the first wing of the regt. which advanced into Zululand.
Bt. Lieut.-Colonel.	Owen, A. A.	Commanded a draft batt. of 1,300 men, composed of volunteers from home regiments, in Natal during the latter part of the war. Was subsequently attached to Major-Gen. Clifford's Staff on special duty as President of the Board adjusting war claims.
Captain.	Bowen, H. G.	Capts. Bowen, Penton, Baldwin, Brind, De Hochepied-Larpent, Jeffreys, Curran, and Gardner served with the regt. throughout its various operations during the war. Bt. Lieut.-Col. Dalrymple held an appointment on Lord Chelmsford's personal Staff; was Brigade-Major to Glyn's Column; and was present at the battle of Ulundi. (Mentioned in despatches; Brevet of Lieut.-Col.) Capt. Acklom served in Natal during the war.
Bt. Lieut.-Colonel.	Dalrymple, W. L.	
Captain.	Penton, C. T. W.	
Captain.	Baldwin, F. C.	
Captain.	Brind, E. A.	
Captain.	Acklom, S.	
Captain.	De Hochepied-Larpent, Sir G. A.	
Captain.	Jeffreys, P. D.	
Captain.	Curran, J. P.	
Captain.	Gardner, S. H.	
Lieutenant.	Mann, H. B.	Lieuts. Mann, Kell, Wood, and Freckleton served in Natal during the operations of the regt. in the Zulu war; Lieut. Kell holding a Staff appointment at Durban. Lieuts. Moore, Hammond, Webb, Wyncoll, Elton, Haldane, and Rickards served with the regt. throughout its various operations in the war; Lieut. Hammond being Adjt. Lieuts. Acton and Barton served with regt. in the war during its earlier operations.
Lieutenant.	Kell, W. C. F. (38th Regt.)	
Lieutenant.	Wood, A. H.	
Lieutenant.	Moore, M. G.	
Lieut. and Adjt.	Hammond, D. T.	
Lieutenant.	Webb, D. J. N.	
Lieutenant.	Wyncoll, C. E.	
Lieutenant.	Elton, A. G. G.	
Lieutenant.	Acton, J. L. C.	
Lieutenant.	Freckleton, G. W.	
2nd Lieutenant.	Barton, N. A. D.	
2nd Lieutenant.	Haldane, E. H. V.	
2nd Lieutenant.	Rickards, F. S. H.	
Quartermaster.	Cousins, S.	Quartermasters Cousins and Morrison served in the war with the regt. throughout.
Quartermaster.	Morrison, C.	

90TH LIGHT INFANTRY.

AT the latter end of 1878 the 90th Light Infantry was concentrated at Utrecht—the Hd.-Qrs. cos. having marched across country shortly after the conclusion of the Old Colony war, in which they had taken a prominent part, and joined the remaining three cos. which, under Major Rogers, *V.C.*, had proceeded thither some months previously.

On the 1st Jan., 1879, the regt., together with the 1st Batt. 13th Light Infantry, four guns Royal Artillery, the Frontier Light Horse, and some Native Irregulars—the whole under Col. Evelyn Wood, *V.C.*, *C.B.*, forming No. 4 column of the army of invasion—marched from Utrecht, and on the 6th crossed the Blood River into Zululand, and encamped at Bemba's Kop. On the 21st the 90th Light Infantry, with some Dutch Volunteers and Wood's Irregulars, advanced against, and drove before them, a large body of the enemy on the Zunguin heights. On this occasion Capt. Wilson's co. of the 90th, having to escort some waggons back to camp, returned immediately that duty was performed, having marched thirty-six miles in twenty-four hours. A second attack was made on the enemy's position on the 24th, when the 90th advanced in line against 4,000 Zulus, who turned and fled. In both attacks the enemy suffered severely from the well-directed fire of the Regt.

The news of the disaster at Isandhlwana having been received, Col. Wood fell back, in the last days of Jan., to the Umvolosi River for the purpose of covering Utrecht; and an entrenched camp was formed at the base of the Kambula Hill. There the Column remained for a period of three months. On the 28th March, whilst the attack was being made on the Zlobane Mountain, the 90th was left to protect the camp—Lieut. Lysons and eight men of the regt. proceeding, however, to the scene of action with Col. Wood as his personal escort. During the action Lieut. Lysons and Pte. Fowler distinguished themselves by their conspicuous gallantry. In the battle of Kambula, which was fought on the 29th, the 90th took a prominent part. Laye's co. was stationed in Major Leet's redoubt, and materially contributed to the success of the day. At a critical juncture two cos. of the regt., gallantly led by Major Hackett, advanced against the cattle laager, which had been taken by the enemy. During the engagement many acts of individual gallantry were performed by both officers and men. The casualties of the regiment were one officer and 11 non-com. officers and men killed, and two officers and 22 non-com. officers and men wounded.

A portion of the 90th, under Lieut. Rawlins, formed part of the mounted force under Major Barrow which operated so successfully at the battle of Ginghilovo on the 2nd April.

The regt. next took part in the advance of Wood's Column (now styled the "Flying Column") with Newdigate's Divis. into the enemy's country. On the 7th June it formed part of the force which, under Br.-Gen. Wood, left Landman's Drift as an escort for 800 waggons proceeding to Koppie Allein for supplies. On the 17th the march of the Flying Column and the Divis. was continued. At the battle of Ulundi which ensued on the 4th July, 11 men of the regt. were more or less severely wounded.

Immediately after the defeat of the enemy, the return march was commenced. On the 15th July the Flying Column reached St. Paul's Mission Station. The regt. remained at that post till the last days of September, when it marched *viâ* Pine Town to Durban. On the 20th Oct. it embarked in H.M.S. "Serapis" for India.

SERVICES OF OFFICERS OF THE 90TH LIGHT INFANTRY.

RANK.	NAME.	SERVICES.
Bt. Colonel.	R. M. Rogers, *V.C.*	Commanded the regt. throughout the war, including the engagement on the Zunguin Nek, 24th Jan., the battle of Kambula, and the battle of Ulundi. (Mentioned in despatches; Bt. of Lieut.-Col. and Col.)
Bt. Lieut.-Colonel.	Cherry, A.	Served with the regt. throughout the war. Present at the battle of Ulundi. (Bt. of Lieut.-Col.)
Major.	Ward, R. I.	Served with the regt. throughout the war.

Rank.	Name.	Services.
Bt. Lieut.-Colonel.	Hackett, R. H.	Served with the regt. during the war till March, 1879. Present at the engagement on the Zunguin Nek, and at the battle of Kambula in which, whilst leading two cos., he was most dangerously wounded, permanently losing the sight of both eyes. (Mentioned in despatches; Bt. of Lieut.-Col.)
Bt. Major.	Hamilton, W. S.	Served with the regt. throughout the war, including the engagement on the Zunguin Nek, the battle of Kambula, and the battle of Ulundi. (Bt. of Major.)
Captain.	Wilson, W. F.	Capts. Wilson, Lawrence, Maude, Hutchinson, and Heathcote served with the regt. throughout the war, being present at the engagement on the Zunguin Nek, the battle of Kambula, and the battle of Ulundi. Capt. Lethbridge served with the regt. till April, and was present at the two former engagements. Bt.-Major Laye served with the regt. throughout, being present at the engagement on the Zunguin Nek, the battle of Kambula (mentioned in despatches), and the battle of Ulundi (Bt. of Major). Capt. Rawlins served throughout the war in command of the mounted men of the regt.; was present at the battles of Inyezane and Ginghilovo; the investment and relief of Etshowe; the recovery of the Isandhlwana guns; the capture of Cetchwayo; and, from first to last, was actively employed in scouring the enemy's country. (Repeatedly mentioned in despatches; promoted to the local rank of Captain for services.)
Captain.	Lawrence, R.	
Captain.	Lethbridge, E.	
Bt. Major.	Laye, J. H.	
Captain.	Maude, A. B.	
Captain.	Hutchinson, G. W.	
Captain.	Rawlins, H. de C.	
Captain.	Heathcote, G. R.	
Lt. and Adjt.	Lomax, S. H.	Lieut. Lomax served as Adjt. to the Regt. throughout the war, including the engagement in the Zunguin Nek, the battle of Kambula, and the battle of Ulundi. Lieuts. Smith and Sheehan served with the regt. till April, and were present at the engagement on the Zunguin Nek and the battle of Kambula. At the latter engagement Lieut. Smith was severely wounded in the right arm. (Mentioned in despatches.) Lieut. Campbell was present at the battle of Ulundi. Lieuts. Gordon, Strong, Hotham, Hopkins, Lysons, White, and Ross served with the regt. throughout the war—Lieuts. Gordon, Strong, Hotham, Lysons, White, and Ross being present at the engagement on the Zunguin Nek, the battle of Kambula, and the battle of Ulundi; Lieut. Lysons acting as Orderly Officer to Br.-General Wood (mentioned in despatches), and Lieut. Hopkins being present at the battles of Kambula and Ulundi. Lieut. Fell served with the regt. till April, and was present at the action on the Zunguin Nek and the battle of Kambula.
Lieutenant.	Smith, F.	
Lieutenant.	Campbell, H. M.	
Lieutenant.	Sheehan, P. E. C.	
Lieutenant.	Gordon, A.	
Lieutenant.	Strong, S. P.	
Lieutenant.	Hotham, H. E.	
Lieutenant.	Hopkins, C. H. I.	
Lieutenant.	Lysons, H.	
Lieutenant.	White, A. O.	
Lieutenant.	Fell, R. B.	
Lieutenant.	Ross, J.	
Paymaster.	Taylor, F.	Paymaster Taylor and Quartermaster Newman served with the regt. throughout the war, being present at the engagement on the Zunguin Nek, the battle of Kambula, and the battle of Ulundi.
Quartermaster.	Newman, J.	

91st HIGHLANDERS.

THIS regt. was stationed at Aldershot when a sudden order was received on the 12th Feb., 1879, for it to proceed to Natal. It was made up to active service strength by receiving 400 volunteers from various regts., and embarked at Southampton in the ss. "Prætoria." The transport sailed on the 20th Feb., arrived at Cape Town on the 12th March, and at Port Natal on the 16th. The regt. landed on the following day; on the 19th it marched for the Tugela, and on the 20th encamped in Zulu territory on the left bank of the river.

The regt. formed the advanced guard of the Etshowe Relief Column, which, under the personal command of Lord Chelmsford, commenced its advance into the enemy's country on the 29th. At the battle of Ginghilovo on the 2nd April, the regt. held the rear face of the laager, and sustained the brunt of the second desperate assault which was made on it by the enemy. In the engagement one man of the 91st was killed, and eight others were more or less severely wounded. Detaching two cos. at Ginghilovo, the regt. formed the rear guard of the Column in its advance to Etshowe. The fort was abandoned on the 5th April, and on the 7th the Relieving Column again laagered at Ginghilovo.

From this time to the 15th June the regt. was employed on convoy duty. It then took part in the advance of Crealock's Divis. to Port Durnford, which was reached on the 28th June. On the 5th July a Column, of which the 91st formed part, advanced to the Umlatoosi, but returned to Port Durnford on the following day. On the 24th another advance was made to the Umlatoosi, where the regt. built Fort Argyll. There it remained until the 14th Sept., sending detachments to Port Durnford, Half-way House, and Fort Napoleon. On the 14th commenced the return march to Natal. On its arrival at Durban the regt. embarked in the "City of Venice" for Cape Town, leaving three cos. to proceed, subsequently, to Mauritius.

During half the time it was employed on active service the regt. was without tents; and during the remainder of the time it had sufficient for merely a portion of its strength.

SERVICES OF THE OFFICERS OF THE 91st HIGHLANDERS.

Rank.	Name.	Services.
Lieut.-Colonel.	A. C. Bruce, *C.B.*	Commanded the regt. during the war, including the battle of Ginghilovo and the relief of Etshowe. Commanded Forts Crealock and Argyll. Was in command of the 2nd Brigade during the illness of Col. Clarke.
Bt. Lieut.-Colonel.	Gurney, W. P.	(Since deceased.) The late Lieut.-Col. Gurney, who died at Mauritius, served with the regt. throughout the war, being present at the battle of Ginghilovo and the relief of Etshowe, and subsequently commanding convoys.
Captain.	Stevenson, G. U.	Capts. Stevenson, O'Sullivan, Boulderson, Craufurd, and MacDonald, served with the regt. during the war, being present at the battle of Ginghilovo, and the advance of Crealock's Divis. to Port Durnford; Capts. Boulderson and Craufurd were also present at the relief of Etshowe; the latter subsequently commanded convoys. Capts. Rogers and Prevost served with the regt. during the earlier phase of the war (being present at the battle of Ginghilovo and the relief of Etshowe) until they were invalided home in July. Capts. Mills and Fallowfield served with the regt. in the earlier phase of the war, being present at the battle of Ginghilovo and the relief of Etshowe; they were invalided to Durban in April and May, but rejoined the Hd.-Qrs. in July. Capt. Chater was employed on Gen. Crealock's staff; he was invalided home when the Divis. was broken up.
Captain.	Rogers, J. T.	
Captain.	Mills, W. S.	
Captain.	Chater, V.	
Captain.	O'Sullivan, G. L.	
Captain.	Boulderson, J.	
Captain.	Prevost, W.	
Captain.	Fallowfield, H. G.	
Captain.	Craufurd, W. R. H.	
Captain.	MacDonald, D. J. McG.	

Rank.	Name.	Services.
Lieut. and Adjt.	St. Clair, J. L. C.	Lieuts. St. Clair, Tottenham, Collings, and Johnston served with the regt. during the earlier phase of the war (being present at the battle of Ginghilovo and the relief of Etshowe) until they were invalided home in May. Lieut. Cookson served with the Mounted Infantry; was present at the battle of Ginghilovo; was invalided from April to July; and served in pursuit of the King after the battle of Ulundi. Lieuts. Robbins, Fowler, Goff, Fraser, and Richardson served with the regt. during the war, taking part in the advance to, and relief of, Etshowe (present at the battle of Ginghilovo), and in the advance of Crealock's Divis. to Port Durnford; Lieut. Fowler acted as Adjt. during the war; Lieuts. Fraser and Richardson carried the colours. Lieuts. Dickson, Wyllie, and Lane-Fox joined the regt., with draft, on the 23rd April, and served with it to the conclusion of the war, taking part in the advance of Crealock's Divis. to Port Durnford. Lieut. Wilson joined the regt., with draft, in Aug., and served with it till the conclusion of the war.
Lieutenant.	Tottenham, A. E. H.	
Lieutenant.	Cookson, F.	
Lieutenant.	Robbins, G. B.	
Lieutenant.	Fowler, D. G. M.	
Lieutenant.	Goff, G. L. J.	
Lieutenant.	Collings, G. D.	
Lieutenant.	Johnston, H. F. C.	
2nd Lieutenant.	Fraser, T.	
2nd Lieutenant.	Richardson, C. J.	
2nd Lieutenant.	Dickson, D. J. A.	
2nd Lieutenant.	Wyllie, F.	
2nd Lieutenant.	Lane-Fox, W. A.	
2nd Lieutenant.	Wilson, A.	
Quartermaster.	Gillies, J.	Served with the regt. during the war, taking part in the advance to, and relief of, Etshowe (present at the battle of Ginghilovo), and the advance of Crealock's Divis. to Port Durnford.

94TH REGIMENT.

THIS regt. was stationed at Aldershot when a sudden order was received, on the 12th Feb., 1879, directing it out to Natal. All officers and men were recalled at once, and about 350 volunteers joined the batt. to make it up to its war strength. On the 26th Feb. it embarked in the SS. "China" from Southampton, and arrived at Durban on the 2nd April. Disembarking on the same day, the regt. went into camp. On the 8th it proceeded by rail to Botha's Hill, and from thence marched *viâ* Pietermaritzburg, Greytown (where it detached two cos. to relieve two of the 4th Regt.), "The Thorns," Tugela River, and Helpmakaar, to Dundee, where it arrived on the 26th April. It then formed part of Newdigate's Divis., at that time in course of organization. On the 29th April the regt. was ordered forward to form an advance post at Conference Hill. Reaching its destination on the 3rd May, the regt., under the direction of R.E. officers, built two forts, and also a large stone laager. Large quantities of stores soon began to arrive. For some considerable time the post was commanded by Gen. Malthus, the force under his command consisting of, in addition to the six cos. of the regt., a troop of Natal Horse, 200 Native Contingent, and some Engineers; later, Col. Davies, Grenadier Guards, took over the command. On the 30th May the regt. marched to Koppie Allein, where it met the remainder of the Divis.; it then took part in the advance of that force into the enemy's country. At the battle of Ulundi the 94th was the only regiment in Newdigate's Divis. that had six cos. present; in the engagement two of its men were killed, and one officer and 18 men were more or less severely wounded. The regt. retired to Entonjaneni on the 5th April; there it received an order to send two cos. to Quamagwasa. The remainder of the Divis. shortly afterwards returned to the Upoko, where it was broken up, the 94th receiving orders to hold itself in readiness to join the infantry of the Flying Column under Col. Baker Russell, destined to assist in disarming the Zulus. The two cos. having rejoined from Quamagwasa, the regt. marched to Enklongana, where forts were built, and, in time, the inhabitants of the surrounding neighbourhood disarmed. The Column then marched to the Zlobane Mountain, on it being reported that a chief in its neighbourhood was likely to give trouble; all arms were at once given up, however, on the appearance of the regt. At the Zlobane, traces of the fatal engagement on the 28th March were found on the mountain side; and the remains of several who had fallen on that day were buried. The regt., which was here joined by the two cos. which had been left on detachment at Greytown, constructed a fort; it then marched into the Lüneberg Mountains, and from thence proceeded into the Sekukuni district to take part in the reduction of the chief's stronghold.

SERVICES OF THE OFFICERS OF THE 94TH REGIMENT.

RANK.	NAME.	SERVICES.
Lieut.-Colonel.	S. Malthus, *C.B.*	Commanded the regt. during the war. Was in command of the advance post at Landman's Drift. Present at the battle of Ulundi. (Mentioned in despatches; *C.B.*)
Bt. Lieut.-Colonel.	J. Murray, *C.B.*	Served with the regt. during the war. Was present at the battle of Ulundi. Commanded a portion of the attack against Sekukuni's stronghold. (Mentioned in despatches; *C.B.*)
Bt. Lieut.-Colonel.	Anstruther, P. R.	Served during the war. Was present at the battle of Ulundi. (Mentioned in despatches.) Commanded the two cos. on detachment at Quamagwasa. Was present at the taking of Sekukuni's town. (Mentioned in despatches; Brevet of Lieut.-Col.)
Bt. Major.	Browne, J.	Served with the regt. during both the Zulu and Sekukuni campaigns.
Captain.	Montague, W. E.	Capt. Montague served with the regt. until he was appointed Staff Officer to Col. Collingwood, commanding 2nd Brigade, Newdigate's Divis., in which capacity he served until the forces were reorganized. Served also in the Sekukuni campaign until invalided home in consequence of a severe fall from his horse. Capts. Campbell, Nairne, and E. S. Brook served with the regt. during the war, were present at the battle of Ulundi, and served also through the whole of the Sekukuni campaign. The late Capt. Bowlby, who was killed, on the 12th July, by a wounded leopard in the Transvaal, served with the regt. during the war. Capts. Froom and Poe served with the regt. until, early in April, they were left on detachment at Greytown (Capt. Froom commanding), where they remained until they rejoined the Hd.-Qrs. at the Zlobane; they subsequently took part in the Sekukuni campaign. Capt. L. G. Brooke was Adjt. of the regt. during the war; he was slightly wounded at the battle of Ulundi. (Mentioned in despatches.) Capt. Spooner served with the regt. during the war.
Captain.	Campbell, F. B.	
Captain.	Bowlby, G. R. S.	
Captain.	Froom, G.	
Captain.	Nairne, S. N. M'L.	
Captain.	Brook, E. S.	
Captain.	Poe, J. H.	
Captain.	Brooke, G. L.	
Captain.	Spooner, H. W. W. (Late 94th.)	
Lieutenant.	Campion, H. F. G.	Lieuts. Campion, McSwiney, Harrison, Harding, Massy, and Hume served with the regt. during both the Zulu and Sekukuni campaigns; Lieut. Harrison acting as Adjt. of the regt. during the latter; Lieuts. Massy and Hume carrying the colours at the battle of Ulundi. Lieut. O'Grady served during both campaigns; he was appointed to the Mounted Infantry, and was severely wounded during the taking of Sekukuni's town. Lieuts. Gordon and Nicol served with the regt. during
Lieutenant.	McSwiney, J.	
Lieut. and Adjt.	Harrison, H. A. C.	
Lieutenant.	O'Grady, J. de C. (Gren. Guards.)	
Lieutenant.	Gordon.	
Lieutenant.	Carroll, F. H.	
Lieutenant.	Harding, E. (Late 94th.)	
Lieutenant.	Maclean, A. W. D.	
Lieutenant.	Cowper, H.	

Rank.	Name.	Services.
2nd Lieutenant.	Campbell, A. D.	the war. Lieuts. Carroll, Maclean, and Cowper served during the war, proceeding, in April, on detachment, to Greytown; the former was invalided home from that post; the two latter joined the Hd.-Qrs. at the Zlobane, and subsequently served with the regt. throughout the Sekukuni campaign.
2nd Lieutenant.	Massy, G. L. E.	
2nd Lieutenant.	Hume, J. J. F.	
2nd Lieutenant.	Nicol, L. L. (4th Batt., Rifle Brigade.)	
Paymaster.	Elliott, J. M.	Capts. Elliott and Quartermaster Lacey served with the regt. during both the Zulu and Sekukuni campaigns.
Quartermaster.	Lacey, P.	

99TH (DUKE OF EDINBURGH'S) REGIMENT.

THIS regt. was quartered at Chatham when, about the end of Nov., 1878, orders were received for it to embark for active service at the Cape. Two cos. sailed on the 2nd Dec. in the s.s. "Walmer Castle," four cos. on the 5th, in the s.s. "American," and Hd.-Qrs. and two cos. on the 6th, in the s.s. "Asiatic."

The cos. from the "Walmer Castle" and "American" landed at Natal on the 3rd and 4th Jan., 1879, respectively, and proceeded up the coast, leaving Durban on the 6th Jan., and arriving at the Lower Tugela on the 11th, one co. having been left to garrison Durban, and another, *en route*, at Stanger. The Hd.-Qrs., leaving women and children at Cape Town, disembarked at Durban on the 10th Jan. On the 15th they reached the Tugela, and, leaving one co. to garrison Fort Tenedos, and three cos. to bring on a convoy, marched on the 19th. The convoy left on the 22nd, and arrived at Etshowe on the 28th (the day the Mounted Infantry and Native Contingent were sent back to the Tugela). The two cos. which advanced on the 19th joined Col. Pearson on the 20th, were present at the battle of Inyezane on the 22nd, and were sent back to the Tugela with a convoy of waggons, arriving there on the 27th. The Hd.-Qrs. and three cos. were in Etshowe during the investment until relieved on the 3rd April. The cos. from Durban and Stanger were eventually concentrated at the Lower Tugela, and, with the three cos. already there, formed part of the Relieving Column under Lord Chelmsford, and were present at the battle of Ginghilovo on the 2nd April. After the relief of Etshowe the regt. was stationed at the Lower Tugela, and, with the Buffs and Connaught Rangers, formed the 1st Brigade of Crealock's Divis. Convoy duty was the principal occupation of the regt. until the middle of June, when three cos. proceeded up country to garrison Fort Crealock. Hd.-Qrs. and four cos. occupied Fort Chelmsford from the 28th June till the 31st July, when they were relieved by the Rangers, and marched down country. Hd.-Qrs. and two cos. were subsequently stationed at Fort Napier, Pietermaritzburg, having arrived there on the 14th Aug.; two cos. at Greytown; one at Rorke's Drift; one at the Lower Tugela; one at Durban; and one at St. John's River. In Sept. orders were received for the regt. to proceed to Bermuda. It was concentrated at Pine Town at the end of Oct., and, on the 31st Dec., embarked in H.M.S. "Himalaya."

SERVICES OF OFFICERS OF THE 99TH (DUKE OF EDINBURGH'S) REGIMENT.

Rank.	Name.	Services.
Lieut.-Colonel.	W. H. D. R. Welman, *C.B.*	Commanded the regt. throughout the war. Was present at the action at the Inyezane, and throughout the occupation of Etshowe. (Mentioned in despatches; *C.B.*)
Bt. Lieut.-Colonel.	Ely, H. F. W.	Lieut.-Cols. Ely and Coates served with the regt. throughout the war; Lieut.-Col. Ely being present throughout the occupation of Etshowe; and Lieut.-Col. Coates at the action on the Inyezane.
Bt. Lieut.-Colonel.	Coates, C. (late 99th.)	

Rank.	Name.	Services.
Captain.	Moir, A. M'A.	Capts. Moir, Story, Wayman, Kennedy, Cotton, Hanson, Macklin, and Nevile served with the regt. throughout the war; Capts. Moir, Story, Kennedy, and Hanson being present at the battle of Ginghilovo, and Capts. Story and Kennedy also present at the action on the Inyezane; the former was subsequently employed on the lines of communication and at the base; Capts. Wayman, Cotton, Macklin, and Nevile being present throughout the occupation of Etshowe.
Captain.	Story, F. L.	
Captain.	Wayman, G. A.	
Captain.	Kennedy, C. H. S.	
Captain.	Cotton, R. B.	
Captain.	Hanson, J. M.	
Captain.	Macklin, G. R. W.	
Captain.	Nevile, C. C.	
Lieutenant.	Turner, A. W.	Lieuts. Turner, Alexander, Jones, Payne, Johnson, Guille, Young, Justice, Cockburn, Elderton, and Gavin served with the regt. throughout the war; Lieuts. Turner and Alexander being present at the battles of Inyezane and Ginghilovo; the former acting as Adjt. and the latter as Qr.-Mr. to the cos. under Lieut.-Col. Walker in the latter engagement; Lieuts. Jones, Payne, and Johnson being present throughout the occupation of Etshowe, and the latter also present at the action on the Inyezane; Lieuts. Guille, Young, Justice, Cockburn, Elderton, and Gavin being present at the battle of Ginghilovo. Lieut. Rowden served with the Mounted Infantry, and was present at the action on the Inyezane and throughout the occupation of Etshowe. Lieut. Welman joined the regt. at the Lower Tugela in April, and served with it during the remainder of the campaign.
Lieutenant.	Alexander, C. H.	
Lieutenant.	Rowden, H. W.	
Lieutenant.	Jones, W. D.	
Lieutenant.	Payne, A. V.	
Lieutenant.	Johnson, T. G.	
2nd Lieutenant.	Guille, J. S.	
2nd Lieutenant.	Young, C. F. G.	
2nd Lieutenant.	Justice, C. Le G.	
2nd Lieutenant.	Cockburn, F. P.	
2nd Lieutenant.	Elderton, A.	
2nd Lieutenant.	Gavin, M. W. (21st Hussars).	
2nd Lieutenant.	Welman, H. L. (88th Regt.)	
Quartermaster.	Bateman, J.	Served with the regt. throughout the war. Was present at the action on the Inyezane, and throughout the occupation of Etshowe.

COMMISSARIAT DEPARTMENT.

Rank.	Name.	Services.
Commy.-Gen.	Sir E. Strickland, *K.C.B.*	At the outbreak of the war was placed in charge of the Commissariat in the Natal Country, and intrusted with the organization of the Transport Service. This service worked with perfect success during the whole campaign. Established bases for the supplies requisite for the several columns of advance, and along the line of the Tugela. (*K.C.B.* for services.)
Depy. Commy.-Gen.	Palmer, C.	On his arrival at Pietermaritzburg in Feb., 1879, was placed in charge of the accounts and returns. Was afterwards, for a short time, in charge of the Department, but was subsequently attacked with paralysis, and invalided.
Depy. Commy.-Gen.	E. Morris, *C.B.*	Served during the war from April, 1879. Appointed D.C.G. of lines of communication and base. Subsequently Commy.-Gen. to the Northern Columns with Lord Chelmsford. Present during the march to Ulundi and operations there. Afterwards proceeded to Prætoria in charge of the Department in the Transvaal; and on the departure of Sir Edward Strickland to England, assumed charge in the South African command.
Depy. Commy.-Gen.	Long, J.	Prior to disembarkation at Durban in April, 1879, this officer received on board ship a serious injury, from which he never completely recovered. He proceeded, notwithstanding, to Pietermaritzburg, and served as Director of Supplies to the Forces.
Depy. Commy.-Gen.	Brownrigg, H. I.	Proceeded to Helpmakaar in Jan., 1879, in Commissariat and Transport charge on the N.E. frontier, and was engaged in replacing losses and restoring organization after the disaster at Isandhlwana and subsequent panic in Natal. Was Commy.-Gen. of Newdigate's Divis., and eventually took charge of the Northern Depôts and lines of communication of the Northern Columns. Returned to Pietermaritzburg in Nov. on account of ill-health. Eventually relieved D.C.G. Morris of the S. A. charge.
Assist. Commy.-Gen.	Healy, R. C.	Proceeded in Jan., 1879, to Fort Tenedos, and assumed Commissariat and Transport charge of the Southern Column. Was afterwards Director of Transport and President of Remount Committee at Hd.-Qrs. Subsequently served as Commy.-Gen. to Crealock's Divis., and established base of supply at Port Durnford. On the breaking up of the Divis. assumed charge of lines of communication and posts from Lower Tugela and Port Durnford to Ulundi. Superintended removal of stores and evacuation of Zululand on the southern line, and clearance of Ordnance Depôt on Lower Tugela.

Rank.	Name.	Services.
Assist. Commy.-Gen.	Phillips, G. H.	On the outbreak of hostilities proceeded in charge of Commissariat and Transport to the Transvaal, and served in that country throughout the Zulu and Sekukuni campaigns.
Commissary.	Furse, P. G. F.	Served in Natal during the whole of the war. Was Supply Accountant to all the forces engaged, in addition to having Commissariat charge at Pietermaritzburg, and the duty of provisioning the various bodies of troops on the march, and establishing and maintaining the depôts and posts from Botha's Hill to Ladysmith. Broke his leg while on duty, and was for some time incapacitated.
Commissary.	Le Mesurier, T. A.	Served during the war as Senior Account Officer in the Transvaal.
Commissary.	Elmes, J. W.	Was Transport Officer at Hd.-Qrs., where his duties embraced the provision of transport for all troops and convoys proceeding from and through the capital, all transport and equipment accounts, and the establishment of means of conveyance on all roads used by the troops, together with the provision and maintenance of Mule Trains and Public Riding Horses.
Commissary.	Walton, C. E.	On arrival in Natal in Feb., 1879, proceeded to Fort Pearson in charge of Commissariat and Transport of Coast Column. All arrangements connected with these services for the Relief Column were made by him. He accompanied the Column, and was present at the battle of Ginghilovo. Promoted. Subsequently joined Crealock's Divis., and was in Commissariat and Transport charge at Port Durnford, superintending establishment of depôt there, the despatch of convoys to the front, and finally the re-embarkation of stores and withdrawal. Superintended compilation and pre-audit of supply accounts of Coast Columns and posts. At the conclusion of these duties proceeded to the Transvaal.
Commissary.	E. Hughes, *C.M.G.*	Served throughout the war. Was in charge of Commissariat and Transport Services of Wood's Column. Was present at the battles of Kambula and Ulundi, acting as Orderly Officer to Gen. Wood in the latter engagement. On the reorganization of the forces, remained for a time in Commissariat charge of the troops at St. Paul's. On being relieved, proceeded to Hd.-Qrs. (*C.M.G.;* promoted.)
Depy. Commy.	Bridgman, W.	Served during the war as S.C.O. at Fort Tenedos, Lower Tugela, and subsequently at Newcastle, Natal.
Depy. Commy.	Warneford, W. J. T.	Served during the war as S.C.O. at Greytown, Natal.
Depy. Commy.	Granville, S. G.	Served during the war as S.C.O. at Durban, base of communications.
Depy. Commy.	Bridgman, F. H.	Was Commissary of Supplies at Pietermaritzburg, and subsequently S.C.O. on the Lower Tugela, until invalided.
Depy. Commy.	Coates, G.	Served under Commy. Hughes as Transport Officer to Wood's Column, and marched with it to Ulundi. Was afterwards S.C.O. at Utrecht.

Rank.	Name.	Services.
Depy. Commy.	Ramsey, G.	Performed Transport duties at Utrecht till death of Commissary Alderton, when he was appointed Adjt. of the Army Service Corps in South Africa.
Depy. Commy.	Noake, R. D.	Commanded No. 3 co. A. S. Corps, and was employed in organizing the mule transport at Durban and along the lower lines of communication.
Depy. Commy.	Young, J. S.	Was in charge of the landing arrangements for all troops and stores which were sent to Natal. Received the thanks of the Colonial Government for his services.
Depy. Commy.	Dunne, W. A.	Was present at the defence of Rorke's Drift. (Mentioned in despatches; promoted.) Took part in the advance of Newdigate's Divis., and was present at the battle of Ulundi.
Depy. Commy.	Richardson, W. D.	Served during the war as Secretary to Sir Edward Strickland. (Promoted.)
Assist. Commy.	Santi, C. H.	Commanded No. 8 co. A. S. Corps till invalided.
Assist. Commy.	Chermside, R. A.	Proceeded to Helpmakaar in Dec., 1878, as Commissariat Officer (temporary) to Glyn's Column. Formed the Rorke's Drift Depôt. Joined Wood's Column at the end of Jan., and acted as Ordnance Officer to it till end of March; then took over the duties of the Ordnance Officer at Utrecht, and continued to perform them till Aug., when invalided home.
Assist. Commy.	Smith, J.	Served under A.C. Gen. Healy as Transport Officer to Crealock's Divis. Commanded No. 5 co. A. S. Corps.
Assist. Commy.	Kevill-Davies, E. L. B.	Was Transport Officer to Pearson's Column, and was present at the battle of Inyezane and throughout the occupation of Etshowe. Returned, after the relief of that post, seriously ill, and was invalided.
Assist. Commy.	Wilson, J. G. Y.	Commanded No. 7 co., A. S. Corps, employed on the lines of communication.
Assist. Commy.	Lawrence, W. M.	Performed Transport duty at the Hd.-Qrs. at Pietermaritzburg during the war.
Assist. Commy.	Heygate, B.	Was Supply Officer to Pearson's Column, and was present at the battle of Inyezane and throughout the subsequent occupation of Etshowe. Was afterwards employed on the lower line of communications.
Assist. Commy. Assist. Commy.	Bampfield, W. J. B. Fagan, F. St. J.	Performed duty with Wood's Column, and on the northern lines of communication.
Assist. Commy.	Whitley, J.	Performed general Commissariat duty with Wood's Column.
Assist. Commy.	Stanley, G.	Performed general Commissariat duty with Crealock's Divis.
Assist. Commy.	Cousins, H. J.	Commanded No. 4 co. A. S. Corps, and was employed with mule transport on communications of Crealock's Divis.
Assist. Commy.	Winspear, W. H.	Took part in the advance of the Etshowe Relief Column, and was present at the battle of Ginghilovo. Subsequently served with Crealock's Divis.

Rank.	Name.	Services.
Assist. Commy.	Carter, E. T. S.	Commanded No. 6 co. A. S. Corps, and was employed with mule transport along the lower line of communications.
Assist. Commy.	Hope, L. A.	Was S.C.O. at Dundee, and was employed along line of communications to Newdigate's Divis.
Assist. Commy.	Boyd, J. A.	Served with Newdigate's Divis., and was present at the battle of Ulundi.
Sub-Asst. Commy.	E. L. Dalton, *V.C.*	Was present at the defence of Rorke's Drift, during which he was severely wounded. Was awarded the *V.C.* for conspicuous gallantry displayed on that occasion. Was afterwards S.C.O. at Fort Napier.
Sub-Asst. Commy. Sub-Asst. Commy.	Armstrong, J. Phillips, E.	Performed general Transport duty along the lines of communication.
Sub-Asst. Commy.	Howland, J.	Was S.C.O. at Balte's Spruit, the depôt of the Flying Column.
Sub-Asst. Commy.	Myers, G. L.	Was S.C.O. at Stanger, and served for some time with Crealock's Divis.
Sub-Asst. Commy.	De Lisle, F.	Served with No. 3 co. A. S. Corps on the Northern lines of communication.
Sub-Asst. Commy.	Collett, W.	Was Qr.-Mr. of the A. S. Corps at Pietermaritzburg.
Sub-Asst. Commy. Sub-Asst. Commy.	Battersby, F. Stead, J.	Performed general Transport duty along the lines of communication.
Sub-Asst. Commy.	Bolton, G.	Performed general Commissariat duty along the lines of communication.
Sub-Asst. Commy.	McCaffery, J.	Performed general Transport duty along the lines of communication.
Sub-Asst. Commy.	Ledsham, W.	Performed general Transport duty with Crealock's Divis.
Sub-Asst. Commy.	Grier, G. R.	Was S.C.O. at Ladysmith.
Sub-Asst. Commy.	McLoughlin, J.	Was S.C.O. at Helpmakaar, and subsequently at Landman's Drift.
Sub-Asst. Commy.	Barrell, W.	Was S.C.O. at Fort Pearson, Lower Tugela.
Sub-Asst. Commy. Sub-Asst Commy.	Nicholls, R. McVeigh, W. E.	Performed general Commissariat duty along the lines of communication.
Sub-Asst. Commy.	Joyce, H.	Performed general Commissariat duty along the northern lines of communication.
Sub-Asst. Commy.	Wishart, W.	Performed Supply duty with Pearson's Column. Was present at the battle of Inyezane, and throughout the occupation of Etshowe.

Conductors of Supplies G. S. Reilly, J. H. Tucker, F. H. Field, H. Hickie, E. Luck, L. Latten, A. C. Jewell, D. Miller, F. L. Cassell, J. Burrett, A. Brooks, H. Marshall, J. Sexton, G. Simon, S. Reid, R. Cleghorn, W. Parsons, D. O'Loughlin, G. Sidmouth, C. Watts, J. Fletcher, J. Arthur, C. Murdoch, H. S. Ward, E. S. Stott, H. E. Champion, J. Hatton, J. R. Wager, J. G. Jebb, H. Duncan, and R. Egerton performed various and arduous general duties over a wide extent of territory, and by their zeal and ability materially conduced to the successful carrying out of the plans of the Head of the Department.

ORDNANCE STORE DEPARTMENT.

ON the transfer of the Hd.-Qrs. of the forces in South Africa to Natal in view of impending hostilities, it became necessary to make provision of camp equipment, arms, ammunition, and transport stores, not only for all arms of the service, but also for the large number of irregulars which the Government contemplated raising in the Colony, and heavy demands were, in consequence, made upon the War Office. The Ordnance Store staff serving in the command consisted at this time of but five executive officers (Depy. Comms. Hillier and Moors; Assist. Comms. Phillimore, Mellis, and Wyon), in addition to the Commy.-Gen. (Wright) in charge, and was distributed at various stations in the Old Colony (Natal) and the Transvaal. Application was therefore made to the home authorities for additional strength. Two officers (Assist. Comms. De Ricci and Hobbs) arrived in Natal in Dec., 1878, and another (Assist. Commy. Wainwright) in Jan., 1879.

Military preparations being pushed rapidly forward, and delay having arisen in the transmission from England of the supplies indented for, the strain of work on the Department was, from the outset, of the most severe description. Twelve more officers were consequently applied for by Lord Chelmsford; and the resources of Natal and the Cape Colony were fallen back upon for the arms, accoutrements, clothing, harness, saddlery, tents, tools, waggons, and articles of every description of which the forces stood urgently in need. The work of purchasing, collecting, examining, receiving, and issuing these commodities fell upon the Department; and the passing of contractors' claims became, in itself, a labour of some magnitude. The duties devolving upon the Main Depôt—the standing Ordnance Store Reserve station at Pietermaritzburg, of which Depy. Commy. Moors had been in charge for some two years—and upon that at Durban, under Assist. Commy. De Ricci, were particularly trying, occupying, for a considerable period, both day and night in their discharge. Local clerical assistance was engaged, whenever practicable, to meet the pressing applications received from every station, but the supply proved to be, with few exceptions, of a most indifferent character.

With the progress of military events, the strain on the Department grew more and more severe, and inability to meet it became imminent. At this juncture, urgent requests that the demand for stores and additional strength might be met were telegraphed home. With the arrival of the reinforcements of troops in Feb., immense supplies of war material reached Natal. No Ordnance Store officers, however, with the exception of one (S.A. Commy. Spinks), commanding an insignificant detachment of the Army Service Corps, O.B., accompanied them. The consequence was that the small depôt at Durban (from which the landing-place was two miles distant) became quite unable to cope with the additional work entailed; and the disembarkation of the stores at the Point had to be abandoned by it as being beyond its powers. The "Regulations for the Supply of Military Stores to an Army in the Field"—rules drawn up with the utmost care—were thus, so far as concerned Lord Chelmsford's forces, absolutely valueless; and had it not been for the realization by the military of the difficulties of the Department, and the zeal displayed by the Ordnance Store Officers in relieving the more pressing wants, utter disorganization must have prevailed.

In March, six additional officers (Commy. March; Depy. Commy. Gordon; Assist. Comms. Campbell, Steevens, and Mulcahy; and S.A. Commy. Cox) arrived at Durban. The first-named was appropriated to the depôt there: he assumed the duties of S.O.S.O. in the District, and was in charge throughout the lines of communications to the Lower Tugela and to Crealock's advancing Divis. A responsible part of his duty was that of laying out heavy sums in the purchase of articles of equipment from the trading community, and of clearing the bills of lading of the numerous large vessels constantly arriving. One of the other five officers remained at the base; another was appointed to Crealock's Divis.; two more passed on to Utrecht; and one to Helpmakaar.

The supply of the forces in the field continuing to press severely on the strength of the Department, six more officers (Commy. Angell; Assist. Comms. Sadler, Heron, Barrett, and Appelbe; and S.A. Commy. Carlin) were despatched from England to the scene of operations, and arrived in Natal on the 1st June. Commy. Angell, being next in seniority to the officer in charge of the Department, was ordered to Dundee, it being in contemplation at the time to establish a new and important base depôt on a large scale at the camp at that position. On his arrival, he took up the duties of S.O.S.O. of the District—which included Utrecht and Newcastle; and was in charge throughout the lines of communication from the first-named depôt to the advancing Columns in Zululand—all officers of the Department in the District, as well as those with the Flying Column and Newdigate's Divis., communicating through him. Two of the other officers were appointed to the Dundee District; two more were retained at Durban; and the sixth proceeded to Pietermaritzburg.

In consequence of the urgent demands made for clerks, storeholders, artificers, and military labourers, and of the impossibility of providing them locally, Lord Chelmsford, acting on the application of the Head of the Ordnance Store Department, had telegraphed to the home authorities, early in May, for 100 additional men of the Ordnance Branch, Army Service Corps. B Company, under Depy. Commy. Cook, was now ordered out, and arrived at Durban towards the end of June. The Hd.-Qrs. of the contingent proceeded to Pietermaritzburg; and detachments were distributed along the lines at nearly every post where troops were stationed. The remarkable zeal and ability with which the non.-com. officers and men of the corps discharged their infinitely varied duties were highly appreciated by the Department, and deserve special notice.

At the end of the campaign the Department found itself in good working order, capable of doing any duty that might devolve upon it. Its organization was simple. It consisted of Hd.-Qrs. and Grand Depôt at Pietermaritzburg, with depôts along the two lines of communication into Zululand, one of which was also towards the Transvaal, and with a base depôt on each line, viz., at Dundee and at Durban—the latter being the nominal base of operations.

Not the lightest part of the duty which fell to the lot of the Department was the collection and disposal of the vast quantities of stores on the retirement of the troops from the advanced positions. Many of these now surplus supplies were condemned and sold; the bulk were passed on to the Transvaal lines or returned upon the Grand Depôt, or to Durban, or again on to the Point for re-shipment to England. The equipment, too, of every branch of the service had to be similarly dealt with by the Department on the conclusion of hostilities.

SERVICES OF THE OFFICERS OF THE ORDNANCE STORE DEPARTMENT.

RANK.	NAME.	SERVICES.
Deputy Commissary-General of Ordnance.	W. F. Wright, *C.B.*	Depy. Commy.-Gen. Wright, who was in charge of the O. S. Department throughout the Kaffir war of 1877-78, proceeded to Natal with Lord Chelmsford's Hd.-Qrs. on their transfer to that colony. Remained at Durban with the Heads of other Departments, and subsequently at Pietermaritzburg with the Inspector-Gen. of lines of communication and base, throughout the war. (Was promoted local Depy. Commy.-Gen. in Jan., 1879, which rank was confirmed on the conclusion of hostilities. *C.B.* for services.)
Assistant Commissary-General of Ordnance.	Angell, J. C.	Arrived at Durban, 1st June, 1879, and was ordered to take charge of the Utrecht and Dundee Districts with lines of communication forward to the advancing Columns, viz., to the Flying Column and Newdigate's Divis. Remained at the Dundee Camp till the close of the campaign, and after witnessing the withdrawal of all material of war from Zululand, and arranging the final disposition of the same, returned to Pietermaritzburg. (Recommended for A.C.G., which position he held.)
Assistant Commissary-General.	March, G. E.	Landed at Durban in March, and was placed in charge of the depôt there. Remained in charge till the conclusion of hostilities, and till most of the surplus stores were shipped for England or otherwise disposed of, when he proceeded to the Transvaal. (Recommended for A. C. G., which position he held.)

Rank.	Name.	Services.
Assistant Commissary-General of Ordnance.	Moors, H. G.	Was stationed at Pietermaritzburg, in charge of the Department, on the entry of the Forces into Natal. Remained at that post throughout the war. All the ordnance stores landed at Durban were passed through his accounts, and he thus retained charge of the Main Reserves until the conclusion of hostilities. (Was granted temporary rank of Commissary, which has since been confirmed.)
Deputy Commissary.	Gordon, W. C.	Arrived in Natal in March, and was at once appointed Commissary of Ordnance to the Coast Column. Was afterwards attached to Crealock's Divis. on the Lower Tugela line, where he remained until the troops retired. Was subsequently attached to Durban. (Recommended for rank of Commissary, which position he held.)
Deputy-Assistant Commissary-General of Ordnance.	Campbell, C. G. L.	On arriving at Durban in March, 1879, proceeded to Utrecht to take charge of the depôt there. Was afterwards attached to the Flying Column, and was present at the battle of Ulundi as Orderly Officer to Sir Evelyn Wood. (Mentioned in despatches; Depy. Commy. for services.)
Deputy-Assistant Commissary-General of Ordnance.	Steevens, J.	Landed at Durban in March, 1879, and proceeded to Helpmakaar to join Glyn's Column. On the removal of that force to Dundee, was appointed Commissary of Ordnance to Newdigate's Divis., with which he remained until after the battle of Ulundi. (Mentioned in orders; Depy. Commy. for services.)
Deputy-Assistant Commissary-General of Ordnance.	Cooke, W. B.	Commanded the Ordnance Branch of the Army Service Corps engaged in the campaign. Remained at Pietermaritzburg on staff of Commy.-Gen. Wright, and was granted local rank of Depy. Commy. while serving in South Africa.
Deputy-Assistant Commissary-General of Ordnance.	Markwick, E. E.	Was stationed at Durban from date of arrival at end of June till conclusion of hostilities. Subsequently proceeded to the Transvaal.
Deputy-Assistant Commissary-General of Ordnance.	Wyon, H. T.	Was in charge of the Department at Prætoria, Transvaal, during the first Sekukuni campaign. On the outbreak of the Zulu war, arranged field reserves of No. 5 Column operating on the northern border, and provided equipment, arms, and ammunition for all the irregular forces despatched from Prætoria. Was in charge of the Department during the second Sekukuni campaign, and formed advanced depôts in the field during the final successful attack. Held the local and temporary rank of Depy. Commy. from Aug., 1878, till the conclusion of hostilities in Dec., 1879.
Assistant Commissary.	De Ricci, R. S. M.	Was in charge at Durban during the critical period extending from Dec., 1878, to March, 1879, when he was relieved by Commy. March. He remained, however, at Durban till the conclusion of hostilities, when he was invalided home.

Rank.	Name.	Services.
Deputy-Assistant Commissary-General of Ordnance.	Hobbs, G. R.	On arriving in Natal in Dec., 1878, was appointed to Glyn's Column. Was stationed within a few miles of Rorke's Drift on the night of the 22nd Jan., 1879. On arriving at Helpmakaar a day or two afterwards was attacked with fever, and was eventually invalided home.
Assistant Commissary.	Wainwright, E. C.	Was placed in charge of the depôt at Fort Tenedos in Jan., 1879, immediately after arriving at the front, and was Commissary of Ordnance to Pearson's Column till the formation of the first Divis. Remained in charge at Fort Pearson till Sept., when he was invalided home, suffering from the effects of fever.
Assistant Commissary.	Sadler, A.	Immediately after arriving in Natal, on the 1st June, 1879, was placed in charge of Ordnance Stores at Dundee Camp, and remained there till the conclusion of the war. Subsequently proceeded to the Transvaal.
Assistant Commissary.	Heron, T.	Landed at Durban, 1st June, 1879, and proceeded at once to Landman's Drift, where he assumed charge of the depôt. Remained at that station till the conclusion of the war, when he proceeded to the Transvaal. Was attached to Baker Russell's Column in the second Sekukuni campaign, and was present at the storming and destruction of the chief's stronghold.
Assistant Commissary.	Barrett, H. W.	Was placed in charge of the depôt at Port Durnford in June, 1879, immediately after arriving in Natal. Was subsequently in charge of the depôt at St. Paul's Mission Station, from whence he was invalided home in Sept., suffering from fever.
Assistant Commissary.	Mulcahy, F. E.	Arrived in March, 1879, at Durban, and remained there for general duties till the conclusion of the war.
Assistant Commissary.	Appelbe, E. B.	Had charge of the depôt at Fort Chelmsford from the date of his arrival there, in June, 1879, till the evacuation of the post in Sept. Was subsequently stationed at the Pine Town Camp.
Quartermaster (S. A. Commissary).	Cox, W. S.	Was stationed at Utrecht from the date of his arrival there in March, 1879, till the conclusion of the war. Had charge of the Reserve Stores at that post and at Newcastle. Was subsequently transferred, with his depôt, to the latter station.
Quartermaster.	Spinks, G.	Went out with the reinforcements in Feb., 1879, in command of a detachment of Army Service Corps, O.B. Was stationed first at Durban and afterwards at Port Durnford. Subsequently joined the Hd.-Qrs. at Pietermaritzburg.
Quartermaster.	Johnson, W.	Arrived at Durban with B Company A.S.C., O.B., and did duty with it till the conclusion of the war.
Quartermaster.	Carlin, H.	Landed at Durban in June, 1879, and proceeded to Pietermaritzburg, where he remained for general duties till the conclusion of the war.

ARMY MEDICAL DEPARTMENT.

RANK.	NAME.	SERVICES.
Brigade Surgeon.	T. Tarrant, *M.D.*	Was appointed S. M. O. of Pearson's Column on its formation. After completing three field hospitals for the Column, established the Base Hospital at Herwen, and remained there till March, 1879. Was then appointed S. M. O. of the Relief Column, and, taking part in its advance, was present at the battle of Ginghilovo. Mentioned in despatches. Was afterwards S. M. O. of Crealock's Divis., remaining with it in that capacity till it was broken up. On returning from Zululand was appointed S. M. O. of the camp and convalescent station at Pine Town.
Surgeon-Major.	Ingham, W. J.	Was Senior Surgeon-Major in charge of the Field Hospital, Pietermaritzburg, Base of Operations Natal and Lower Tugela.
Surgeon-Major.	F. B. Scott, *M.B.*	Served on the personal Staff of Lord Chelmsford, and in medical charge of the Hd.-Qrs. Staff during the war. Was present at the battle of Ulundi. (Mentioned in despatches.)
Surgeon-Major.	Dudley, W. E.	Arrived at Durban in March, 1879, and was nominated to the medical charge of the 57th Regt. Was detained at Herwen Hospital to take charge during the absence of Surg.-Maj. Tarrant with the Relief Column. Received the sick from Etshowe and the wounded from Ginghilovo, remaining at Herwen until appointed M. O. of the Buffs. Subsequently acted as S. M. O. of all the forces on the Lower Tugela, and had charge of Fort Pearson Hospital. Was invalided home in July.
Surgeon-Major.	R. C. C. Hickson, *M.D.*	Was in medical charge at Cape Town in Nov., 1878. Volunteered, in May, 1879, for employment in the war, and proceeded *viâ* Durban to Newcastle to take charge of the depôt there. Was S. M. O. of the Utrecht District till the conclusion of the war.
Surgeon-Major.	Fitzmaurice, J.	Served in the first phase of the war with Pearson's Column. Was present at the battle of Inyezane, and was S. M. O. at Etshowe throughout the blockade. Afterwards had temporary charge of the Base Field Hospital on the Lower Tugela. Subsequently proceeded to Utrecht, and was in charge of the Base Field Hospital of the Flying Column at that station till the conclusion of the war.
Surgeon-Major.	J. A. Anderson, *M.D.*	Served during the war with the Flying Column. Was present at the battle of Ulundi in command of the bearer company of the Column, and in medical charge of the detachment of Artillery and Engineers. (Mentioned in despatches.)
Surgeon-Major.	W. C. Gasteen, *M.B.*	Served throughout the Zulu and Sekukuni campaigns as Secretary and Statistical Officer to the Surgeon-General of the Forces in the Field.

CIVILIAN SURGEONS.

NAME.	SERVICES.
Thrupp, J. G.	Was attached to the 1st Batt. 24th Regt., and was in charge of the Staff and Dept. during the first phase of the war. Was subsequently in charge of No. 1 Field Hospital of Glyn's Column.
G. E. Twiss, *M.D.*	Served first with Villier's force in the operations against Umbellini's brothers (being present at the encounter with the enemy at Emlahlanlelah), and subsequently with the K. D. G.'s and the Transvaal Field Force.

Dr. Apthorp, F. W.
Dr. Beresford, W. H.
Dr. Boomer, J. Mc W.
Dr. Brannington, H. C.
Dr. Bridwood, R. A.
Dr. Burton, J. R.
Dr. Busby, A. R.
Dr. Cheyne, W. R.
Dr. Clubbe, C. P. B.
Dr. Cobbin, W. J.
Dr. Duncan, A. S.
Dr. Garland, G. H.
Dr. Giles, B. F.
Dr. Giles, G. M.
Dr. Gill, J.
Dr. Gordon, S. F.
Dr. Greer, T.
Dr. Gubbins, C. O. F.
Dr. Hare, E. H.
Dr. Hartley, W. D.
Dr. Hayes, T. E. D.
Dr. Heath, J. L.
Dr. Hebb, R. G.
Dr. Hope, T. M.
Dr. Illingworth, C. R.
Dr. Jennings, E.
Dr. Johnston, R. C.
Dr. Jolly, R. W.
Dr. Leslie, A.
Dr. Leslie, R. B.
Dr. Lewis, C. B.
Dr. Linden, H. C.
Dr. McCrea, J. F.
Dr. Macdonald, W. C. C.
Dr. Mansell, E. R.
Dr. Moir, J. H.
Dr. Mulligan, E. J.
Dr. O'Neill, J. G.
Dr. Reynolds, L. M.
Dr. Roberts, F. J.
Dr. Roe, C.
Dr. Ryley, J. R.
Dr. Wilson, E. M.
Dr. Woods, A. A.
Dr. Wood, R. E.

The above-named officers of the Medical Department and Civilian Surgeons served in the war over a very wide extent of territory, performing much arduous and important duty with the troops in the field, on the lines of communication, and at the bases. The services of those whose names only are recorded have not reached the compilers of this work in time for insertion in this, its first, edition.

ARMY HOSPITAL CORPS.

Rank.	Name.	Services.
Lieut. of Orderlies. (Hon. Capt.)	Sylvester, H. J.	Served throughout the war as District Officer of Orderlies; as Actg. Adjt. and Qr.-Mr. A. H. C. had charge of all Medical Stores in S. Africa, and was Direct Accountant to M. O. for hospital camp equipment used in the campaign. (Promoted Hon. Captain for services.)
Lieut. of Orderlies. (Hon. Capt.)	Gorman, L.	Embarked with the S. African expeditionary force in Feb., 1879, and served on the line of communication till the conclusion of the war, and throughout the Sekukuni campaign. (Mentioned in despatches; honorary rank of Captain.)
Lieut. of Orderlies.	McGreal, F.	Embarked for Natal in November, 1878, and served with the Field Force and on the lines of communication throughout the war.
Lieut. of Orderlies.	Johnson, H.	Embarked with the S. African expeditionary force in Feb., 1879, and served with the Field Force and on the lines of communication during the war.
Lieut. of Orderlies.	Pike, W.	Embarked for Natal in Feb., 1879 in command of a detachment A. H. C. Proceeded to join Newdigate's Divis. At Landman's Drift, taking over the equipment and stores of the Base Hospital at Ladysmith, and establishing a Field Hospital at Dundee *en route.* On reaching Hd.-Qrs. formed two movable field hospitals for infantry and cavalry, and sent a third to Conference Hill. Took part, in charge of four field hospitals, in the advance of the Divis. into Zululand. Was present at the battle of Ulundi (horse killed at the commencement of the action). On the break-up of the Divis. was strongly recommended by the S. M. O. for promotion. Supplied movable field hospitals to Baker Russell's Column.
Lieut. of Orderlies.	McIntyre, D.	Landed at Durban in April, and was ordered to join Crealock's Divis. Subsequently joined the Flying Column at Utrecht, and was posted at the Base Field Hospital till the whole of the troops and stores were cleared out of Zululand. At the latter end of Oct. joined the Base Field Hospital of the Transvaal Field Force at Newcastle, and remained there till the break-up of the establishment.
Lieut. of Orderlies.	Cox, C. A.	Proceeded to Natal in Nov., 1878, and served with the Field Force and on the lines of communication throughout the war.
Lieut. of Orderlies.	Marshall, J. D.	Proceeded to Natal with detachments in Feb., 1879, and served with the Field Force and on the lines of communication till the conclusion of the war. Lieut. Horn subsequently served with the Field Force in the operations against Sekukuni.
Lieut. of Orderlies.	Horn, J.	

Rank.	Name.
Surgeon-General.	J. A. Woolfryes, *M.D.*, *C.B.*, *C.M.G.*
Depy. Surg.-Gen.	J. L. Holloway, *C.B.*
Surgeon-Major.	A. Semple, *M.D.*
Surgeon-Major.	W. Skeen, *M.D.*
Surgeon-Major.	R. W. Jackson, *C.B.*
Surgeon-Major.	A. C. Robertson, *M.D.*
Surgeon-Major.	J. G. Leask, *M.B.*
Surgeon-Major.	B. C. Kerr, *M.D.*
Surgeon-Major.	D. F. de Hodgson, *M.D.*
Surgeon-Major.	Hunt, J. H.
Surgeon-Major.	Giraud, C. H.
Surgeon-Major.	Wallace, J.
Surgeon-Major.	Stafford, P. W.
Surgeon-Major.	Boulton, E. J.
Surgeon-Major.	J. D. Edge, *M.D.*
Surgeon-Major.	Lamb, H.
Surgeon-Major.	C. S. Wills, *C.B.*
Surgeon-Major.	R. W. Hare, *M.B.*
Surgeon-Major.	G. Ashton, *M.B.*
Surgeon-Major.	C. M'D. Cuffe, *C.B.*
Surgeon-Major.	Smith, W. P.
Surgeon-Major.	Elgee, W.
Surgeon-Major.	D. A. Leslie, *M.D.*
Surgeon-Major.	Babington, T.
Surgeon-Major.	Stock, J. N.
Surgeon-Major.	J. Hector, *M.B.*
Surgeon-Major.	Robinson, A. B.
Surgeon-Major.	Ward, E.
Surgeon-Major.	D. Renton, *M.D.*
Surgeon-Major.	Mally, R. N.
Surgeon-Major.	W. Johnson, *M.D.*
Surgeon-Major.	H. Comerford, *M.D.*
Surgeon-Major.	W. A. Jennings, *M.D.*
Surgeon-Major.	Burnett, W. F.
Surgeon-Major.	J. H. Reynolds, *M.B.*, *V.C.*

Rank.	Name.
Surgeon-Major.	Murphy, R.
Surgeon-Major.	E. Townsend, *M.D.*
Surgeon-Major.	J. O'Reilly, *M.B.*
Surgeon-Major.	Parkinson, R. C.
Surgeon-Major.	S. T. Cotter, *M.D.*
Surgeon-Major.	Heather, D. C. W.
Surgeon-Major.	H. Jagoe, *M.B.*
Surgeon-Major.	J. Fraser, *M.D.*
Surgeon-Major.	J. H. Ussher, *M.B.*
Surgeon-Major.	W. Geoghegan, *M.B.*
Surgeon-Major.	Brown, A. L.
Surgeon-Major.	Jennings, C. B.
Surg.-Major (h. p.)	Alcock, N.
Surg.-Major (h. p.)	J. Carlaw, *M.D.*
Surgeon.	Ryan, G.
Surgeon.	A H. Stokes, *M.B.*
Surgeon.	Saunders, W. E.
Surgeon.	J. B. Wilson, *M.D.*
Surgeon.	Leake, G. D. N.
Surgeon.	J. W. O'M. Martin, *M.B.*
Surgeon.	Ward, E. C. R.
Surgeon.	R. V. Ash, *M.B.*
Surgeon.	Connolly, B. B.
Surgeon.	R. Drury, *M.D.*
Surgeon.	C. J. L. Busche, *M.B.*
Surgeon.	H. H. Stokes, *M.B.*
Surgeon.	J. King, *M.D.*
Surgeon.	M'Gann, J.
Surgeon.	Landon, A. J.
Surgeon.	Ritchie, J. L.
Surgeon.	Wallis, K. S.
Surgeon.	Lloyd, O. E. P.
Surgeon.	Harding, A.
Surgeon.	Falvey, J. J.
Surgeon.	Dowman, J. F.
Surgeon.	Cross, H. R. O.

THE NAVAL BRIGADE.

H.M.S. "ACTIVE."

Rank.	Name.	Time on Shore. From	To	Services.
Acting Captain.	Campbell, H. J. F.	20 Nov., '78.	23 July, '79.	Landed in command of "Active's" Naval Brigade; superintended the transport of troops, &c. of No. 1 Column, under Col. Pearson, across the Tugela River; was present at the action of Inyezane; formed part of garrison of Etshowe during the holding of that post; given acting rank of Capt. of "Active" and command of Naval Brigade, consisting of crews of "Active," "Shah," "Boadicea," and "Tenedos," and forming part of Crealock's Divis.; superintended the landing of stores at Port Durnford. (Mentioned in despatches, naval and military; promoted; *C.B.*)
Commnder.	Kingscote, A.	8 Feb., '79.	17 Mar., '79	Commanded the Brigade of the "Tenedos" during the Zulu war; Senior Officer commanding on the Lower Tugela, assisting at the transport of troops, &c. across the river, and at the building of Forts Tenedos and Pearson; formed part of advance guard of the Etshowe Relief Column, and had charge of two guns at the battle of Ginghilovo. (Mentioned in despatches; promoted.)
Commnder. (Gunnery).	Craigie, R. W.	20 Nov., '79.	20 July, '79.	Commanded Fort Cunningham; again served with the Naval Brigade in Zululand as Adjt.; present at the action of Inyezane; formed part of the garrison of Etshowe with Pearson's Column; afterwards joined Crealock's Divis. and advanced to Port Durnford. (Mentioned in despatches; promoted.)
Lieutenant.	Hamilton, W. des V.	20 Nov., '78.	20 July, '79.	Was present at the action of Inyezane, 22nd Jan., 1879; formed part of garrison of Etshowe with Pearson's Column; afterwards joined Crealock's Divis. and advanced to Port Durnford. (Mentioned in despatches.)
Lieutenant.	Milne, A. B.	20 Nov., '78.	20 July, '79.	Was attached as A.D.C. to Lord Chelmsford's Staff; present at capture of Sirayo's stronghold, and with No. 3 Column when retiring on Isandhlwana and Rorke's Drift; present with the Etshowe Relief Column at the battle of Ginghilovo, and relief of Etshowe; accompanied Hd.-Qr. Column during June and July; present at the battle of Ulundi (wounded). (Mentioned in naval and military despatches.)

Rank.	Name.	Time on Shore. From	Time on Shore. To	Services.
Lieutenant.	Startin, James.	8 Feb., '79.	17 Mar., '79.	Was present on the River Tugela; formed part of garrison of Fort Tenedos during Feb. and March; was with the advance guard of the Etshowe Relief Column; present at the battle of Ginghilovo. (Mentioned in despatches; promoted.)
Lieutenant.	Fraser, T. G.	20 Nov., '78.	20 July, '79.	Was present at the action of Inyezane; formed part of the garrison of Etshowe with Pearson's Column; afterwards joined Crealock's Divis. and advanced to Port Durnford. (Mentioned in despatches; promoted.)
Lieutenant.	Heugh, J. G.	22 Dec., '78.	20 July, '79.	Was present at the action of Inyezane; afterwards joined Crealock's Divis. and advanced to Port Durnford. (Mentioned in despatches; promoted.)
Fleet-Surg.	Norbury, H. F.	20 Nov., '78.	20 July, '79.	Was in medical charge of the Naval Brigade of "Active" during the war; was principal Medical Officer of Pearson's Column (being present at the battle of Inyezane, 22nd Jan., 1879), and of the garrison of Etshowe (several times mentioned in despatches); afterwards joined Crealock's Divis. as Principal Medical Officer of the entire Naval Brigade, and advanced to Port Durnford. (Twice mentioned in despatches; promoted; *C.B.*, 27th Nov., 1879; Sir G. Blane's Gold Medal, 1879.)
Fleet-Surg.	Longfield, W. D.	8 Feb., '79.	17 Mar., '79.	Was Senior Medical Officer at Lower Tugela, Feb. and March; was with the Etshowe Relief Column; at the battle of Ginghilovo was dangerously wounded in left shoulder. (Mentioned in despatches; promoted; Sir G. Blane's Gold Medal, 1879.)
Surgeon.	Thompson, W.	20 Nov., '78.	20 July, '79.	Was present at the action of Inyezane; formed part of garrison of Etshowe with Pearson's Column; afterwards joined Crealock's Divis. and advanced to Port Durnford. (Mentioned in despatches.)
Chief Boatswain.	Cotter, J.	20 Nov., '78.	20 July, '79.	Had charge of rockets at the action of Inyezane; formed part of garrison with Pearson's Column in Etshowe; afterwards joined Crealock's Divis., and advanced to Port Durnford. (Mentioned in despatches; promoted.)

H.M.S. "BOADICEA."

Rank.	Name.	Time on Shore. From	Time on Shore. To	Services.
Captain.	Richards, T.W.	19 Mar., '79.	11 June, '79.	Was Commodore on the West Coast of Africa during the Zulu war, from March, 1879. Accompanied the Etshowe Relief Column; was present at the battle of Ginghilovo. (*C.B.*)
Commnder.	Romilly, F.	24 April, '79.	6 Aug., '79.	Landed in command of "Boadicea's" Naval Brigade, and advanced to Port Durnford. (Mentioned in despatches.)
Commnder.	Kingscote, A.	18 Mar., '79.	9 May, '79.	(*See* H.M.S. "Active.")
Senior Lieutenant (Gunner).	Carr, F. R.	19 Mar., '79.	30 June, '79.	Commanded "Boadicea's" Naval Brigade in Zululand; formed part of rear-guard of Etshowe Relief Column; had charge of rocket battery at the battle of Ginghilovo and at relief of Etshowe. (Mentioned in despatches.)
Lieutenant.	Smythies, P. K.	13 May, '79.	6 Aug., '79.	Served during the war in the brigade forming part of Crealock's Divis.
Lieutenant.	Hobkirk, E. C.	19 Mar., '79.	10 June, '79.	Accompanied the Etshowe Relief Column; present at the battle of Ginghilovo; accompanied the Brigade to Port Durnford.
Lieutenant.	Benett, J. B.	19 Mar., '79.	9 June, '79.	
Lieutenant.	Preedy, H.	20 Mar., '79.	6 Aug., '79.	Accompanied the Etshowe Relief Column as A.D.C. to Commodore Richards; was present at the battle of Ginghilovo and relief of Etshowe; accompanied Brigade to Port Durnford.
Sub-Lieut.	Startin, J.	18 Mar., '79.	9 May, '79.	Served during the war in the Brigade forming part of Crealock's Divis.
Lieutenant.	Lyon, H.	19 Mar., '79.	6 Aug., '79.	Accompanied the Etshowe Relief Column; present at the battle of Ginghilovo; and accompanied the Brigade to Port Durnford.
Acting Sub-Lieut.	Cotesworth, H.	20 Mar., '79.	21 July, '79.	Was Naval A.D.C. to Gen. Crealock, and accompanied the Divis. to Port Durnford.
Acting Sub-Lieut.	Warrender, G. J. S.	19 Mar., '79.	27 May, 79.	Accompanied the Etshowe Relief Column; were present at the battle of Ginghilovo, and accompanied the Brigade to Port Durnford.
Midshipmn.	Hewett, W. W.	19 Mar., '79.	6 Aug., '79.	
Midshipmn.	Crookshank, A. F.	19 Mar., '79.	3 May, '79.	
Midshipmn.	Colville, Hon. S. C.	19 Mar., '79.	6 Aug., '79.	
Fleet Surg.	Longfield, W. D.	18 Mar., '79.	10 July, '79.	(See H.M.S. "Active.")
Staff. Surg.	Grant, R.	16 April, '79.	16 Aug., '79.	Accompanied the Naval Brigade to Port Durnford. (Mentioned in despatches.)
Surgeon.	Pollard, E. R. H.	19 Mar., '79.	6 Aug., '79.	Accompanied the Brigade to Port Durnford.
Surgeon.	Vasey, S. W.	28 April, '79.	6 Aug., '79.	
Secretary.	Carlisle, J.	17 Mar., '79.	11 June, '79.	Was Secretary to the Commodore on the West Coast of Africa during Zulu war. (Mentioned in despatches.)

H.M.S. "SHAH."

Rank.	Name.	Time on Shore. From	To	Services.
Captain.	Richards, F.W.	12 June,'79.	24 July, '79.	(See H.M.S. "Boadicea.")
Captain.	Bradshaw, R.	11 Mar.,'79.	16 Mar.,'79.	While on passage home from the Pacific, on hearing at St. Helena of the disaster at Isandhlwana, immediately sailed for the Cape with all the available troops. His decisive action on this occasion received the approval of Parliament and the Admiralty, and gave occasion for an address of thanks from the Town Council of Natal. (*C.B.*)
Commnder.	Brackenbury, J.	8 Mar., '79.	21 July, '79.	Commanded the "Shah's" Naval Brigade during the war. Formed part of the advance guard of the Etshowe Relief Column; had charge of Gatling guns at the battle of Ginghilovo; afterwards joined Crealock's Divis. and advanced to Port Durnford. (Mentioned in despatches. *C.M.G.*)
Commander (retired).	Drummond, M. H.	8 Mar., '79.	11 June, '79.	Formed part of the advance guard of the Etshowe Relief Column; had charge of a Gatling and 9-pounder gun at the battle of Ginghilovo; afterwards joined Crealock's Divis. and advanced to Port Durnford.
Lieut. (Gunnery).	Lindsay, C.	8 Mar., '79.	21 July, '79.	Was Senior Lieutenant of "Shah's" contingent landed in March; accompanied Etshowe Relief Column; present at the battle of Ginghilovo; afterwards joined Crealock's Divis. and advanced to Port Durnford. (Mentioned in despatches.)
Lieutenant.	Henderson, G. P.	8 Mar., '79.	21 July, '79.	Accompanied Etshowe Relief Column; present at battle of Ginghilovo; afterwards joined Crealock's Divis. and advanced to Port Durnford.
Lieutenant.	Abbott, T. F.	8 Mar. '79.	21 July, '79.	Transported the Etshowe Relief Column across the Tugela River; afterwards joined Crealock's Divis. and advanced to Port Durnford. (Mentioned in despatches.)
Lieutenant.	Hely-Hutchinson, Hon. P.M.	8 Mar., '79.	21 July, '79.	Accompanied the Etshowe Relief Column; present at the battle of Ginghilovo; afterwards joined Crealock's Divis. and advanced to Port Durnford. (Mentioned in despatches; promoted.)
Sub.-Lieut.	Hamilton, F. S.	8 Mar., '79.	29 May, '79.	
Sub.-Lieut.	Smith-Dorrien, A. H.	8 Mar., '79.	21 July, '79.	
Staff. Surg.	Shields, J.	8 Mar., '79.	21 July, '79.	Accompanied the Etshowe Relief Column, and were present at the battle of Ginghilovo. (Mentioned in despatches.)
Surgeon.	Sibbald, T. M.	8 Mar., '79.	21 July, '79.	
Surgeon.	Connell, J. J.	8 Mar., '79.	16 July, '79.	
Secretary.	Carlisle, J.	12 June, '79.	24 July, '79.	(See H.M.S. "Boadicea.")
Clerk.	Chapple, J. H.	8 Mar., '79.	21 July, '79.	Accompanied the Etshowe Relief Column, and were present at the battle of Ginghilovo.
Gunner.	O'Neil, D. [G.	8 Mar., '79.	21 July, '79.	
Gunner.	Cook, J.	8 Mar., '79.	27 May, '79.	
Boatswain.	Bumpus, J.	27 April, '79.	22 July, '79.	Served during the war in the Brigade forming part of Crealock's Divis.
Boatswain.	Hammett, T.	8 Mar., '79.	21 July, '79.	Accompanied the Etshowe Relief Column; present at the battle of Ginghilovo.

H.M.S. "TENEDOS."

Rank.	Name.	Time on Shore. From	To	Services.
Senr. Lieut. (Gunnery.)	Kingscote, A.	1 Jan., '79.	7 Feb., '79.	(*See* H.M.S. "Active.")
Sub.-Lieut.	Startin, J.	1 Jan., '79.	7 Feb., '79.	(*See* H.M.S. "Active.")
Staff Surg.	Longfield, W. D.	1 Jan., '79.	7 Feb., '79.	(*See* H.M.S. "Active.")

ROYAL MARINE ARTILLERY.

Rank.	Name.	Time on Shore. From	To	Services.
Captain.	Burrowes, A. L. S.	8 Mar., '79.	21 July, '79.	Accompanied the Etshowe Relief Column; present at the battle of Ginghilovo and relief of Etshowe; afterwards accompanied Crealock's Divis. (Mentioned in despatches.)

ROYAL MARINE LIGHT INFANTRY.

Rank.	Name.	Time on Shore. From	To	Services.
Major.	Phillips, J.	8 Mar., '79.	20 July, '79.	Commanded the Marines landed for service during the Zulu war; accompanied the Etshowe Relief Column; present at the battle of Ginghilovo and relief of Etshowe; afterwards accompanied Crealock's Divis. (Mentioned in despatches; brevet of Major.)
Captain.	Dowding, T.W.	20 Nov., '79.	20 July, '79.	Commanded the Royal Marines at the action of Inyezane; formed part of the garrison of Etshowe; afterwards joined Crealock's Divis. and advanced to Port Durnford (mentioned in despatches). "Admiralty, November 18th, 1879.—Royal Marine Forces.—The Lords Commissioners of the Admiralty have been pleased to promote Lieutenant T. W. Dowding, Royal Marine Light Infantry, to the rank of Captain, under the provisions of Section 6 of Her Majesty's Order in Council of January 15th, 1878, in special recognition of the services performed by him during the recent campaign in South Africa."—*Naval Gazette.*
Lieutenant.	Robyns, J. W.	18 Mar., '79.	6 Aug., '79.	Accompanied the Etshowe Relief Column; present at the battle of Ginghilovo, and relief of Etshowe; afterwards accompanied Crealock's Divis.

INDEX.

			PAGE
MAP OF ZULULAND		*facing*	1
INTRODUCTION			1
SKETCH MAP OF ISANDHLWANA		*facing*	11
PORTRAITS AND BIOGRAPHICAL NOTICES :—			
THE PRINCE IMPERIAL			35
CAPTAIN W. G. LAWRELL	4TH, *Hussars*		45
CAPTAIN THE HON. E. V. WYATT-EDGELL	17TH, *Lancers*		49
LIEUTENANT F. J. COKAYNE FRITH	„ „		53
MAJOR STUART SMITH	*Royal Artillery*		57
MAJOR F. B. RUSSELL	„ „		61
LIEUTENANT F. NICOLSON	„ „		65
COLONEL A. W. DURNFORD	*Royal Engineers*		69
MAJOR W. R. C. WYNNE	„ „		75
LIEUTENANT F. H. MACDOWEL	„ „		81
CAPTAIN THE HON. R. G. E. CAMPBELL	*Coldstream Guards*		85
CAPTAIN R. J. BARTON	„ „		89
CAPTAIN THE HON. H. R. GOUGH			93
CAPTAIN H. J. M. WILLIAMS	3RD, *The Buffs*		97
LIEUTENANT C. E. MASON	„ „		101
2ND LIEUTENANT G. R. J. EVELYN	„ „		105
LIEUTENANT G. A. PARDOE	13TH, *Light Infantry*		109
LIEUTENANT J. H. SCOTT DOUGLAS	21ST, *Scots Fusiliers*		113
LIEUTENANT-COLONEL H. B. PULLEINE	24TH, *2nd Warwickshire*		117
CAPTAIN W. DEGACHER	„ „ „		121
CAPTAIN W. E. MOSTYN	„ „ „		125
CAPTAIN G. V. WARDELL	„ „ „		129
CAPTAIN R. YOUNGHUSBAND	„ „ „		133
LIEUTENANT T. MELVILL	„ „ „		137
LIEUTENANT F. P. PORTEOUS	„ „ „		143
LIEUTENANT C. D'A. POPE	„ „ „		147
LIEUTENANT C. W. CAVAYE	„ „ „		151
LIEUTENANT E. O. ANSTEY	„ „ „		155
LIEUTENANT N. J. A. COGHILL	„ „ „		159
LIEUTENANT J. P. DALY	„ „ „		165
LIEUTENANT G. F. J. HODSON	„ „ „		169
LIEUTENANT J. C. ATKINSON	„ „ „		173
LIEUTENANT H. J. DYER	„ „ „		177
LIEUTENANT F. GODWIN-AUSTEN	„ „ „		181
SUB-LIEUTENANT T. L. G. GRIFFITH	„ „ „		185
2ND LIEUTENANT E. H. DYSON	„ „ „		189
LIEUTENANT R. W. FRANKLIN	„ „ „		193
STAFF PAYMASTER AND HON. MAJOR F. F. WHITE	„ „ „		197
QUARTER-MASTER E. BLOOMFIELD	„ „ „		201

		PAGE
Quarter-Master J. Pullen	24th, *2nd Warwickshire*	205
Lieutenant C. C. Williams	58th, *Rutlandshire*	209
Lieutenant-Colonel F. V. Northey	60th, *Rifles*	213
Lieutenant H. L. Farmer	" "	217
2nd Lieutenant A. C. B. Mynors	" "	221
Captain M. Stourton	63rd, *West Suffolk*	225
Captain D. B. Moriarty	80th, *Staffordshire*	229
Lieutenant J. Thirkill	88th, *Connaught Rangers*	233
Captain G. Sandham	90th, *Light Infantry*	237
Lieutenant A. Tyndall Bright	" " "	241
Lieutenant G. C. J. Johnson	99th, *Duke of Edinburgh's*	247
Lieutenant A. S. F. Davison	" " "	251
2nd Lieutenant W. I. D'Arcy	" " "	255
Lieutenant H. J. Hardy	Rifle Brigade	259
The Hon. S. W. P. Vereker		263
Assistant-Commissary J. Alderton	Commiss. and Transp. Dept.	267
Deputy-Commissary S. T. Phillimore	Ordnance Store Dept.	271
Assistant-Paymaster J. Hardwick	Army Pay Dept.	275
Surgeon-Major P. Shepherd	Medical Dept.	279
Lieutenant of Orderlies A. W. Hall	" "	283
Lieutenant of Orderlies J. A. Gissing	" "	287
Lieutenant of Orderlies J. Troy	" "	291
Midshipman L. C. Coker	Royal Navy	295

Records of Service:—

	PAGE
Officers who were Employed on Special Service	297
King's Dragoon Guards	317
17th Lancers	320
Royal Artillery	322
Royal Engineers	328
2nd Battalion, 3rd Foot	331
2nd " 4th "	333
1st " 13th "	335
2nd " 21st "	337
1st " 24th "	339
2nd " 24th "	341
57th "	343
58th "	345
3rd Battalion 60th "	346
80th "	348
88th "	350
90th "	352
91st "	354
94th "	355
99th "	357
Commissariat Department	359
Ordnance Store Department	363
Medical Department	367
Civilian Surgeons	368
Army Hospital Corps	369
Naval Brigade	371

-10a-